COMBAT READY?

Number 129: Williams-Ford Texas A&M University Military History Series

COMBAT READY?

THE EIGHTH U.S. ARMY ON
THE EVE OF THE KOREAN WAR

Thomas E. Hanson

Texas A&M University Press
College Station

Copyright © 2010 by Thomas E. Hanson
Manufactured in the United States of America
All rights reserved
First edition

This paper meets the requirements of ANSI/NISO Z39.48-1992 (Permanence of Paper).
Binding materials have been chosen for durability.

Library of Congress Cataloging-in-Publication Data
Hanson, Thomas E., 1965–
Combat ready? : the Eighth U.S. Army on the eve of the Korean War /
Thomas E. Hanson. — 1st ed.
p. cm. — (Williams-Ford Texas A&M University military history series ; no. 129)
Includes bibliographical references and index.
ISBN-13: 978-1-60344-167-4 (cloth : alk. paper)
ISBN-10: 1-60344-167-0 (cloth : alk. paper)
1. Korean War, 1950-1953—Regimental histories—United States.
2. United States. Army. Army, 8th—History.   3. Operational readiness (Military science)
I. Title.   II. Series: Williams-Ford Texas A&M University military history series ; no. 129.
DS919.H364   2010
951.904'242—dc22
2009050623

To my father, Lee A. Hanson
Second Lieutenant, U.S. Army
Korea, 1953
and to
Dick Mickelson
Infantryman, Patriot, Friend

CONTENTS

List of Illustrations	ix
Foreword, by Gen. James C. Yarbrough	xi
Preface	xv
Acknowledgments	xvii
1. Introduction	1
2. Postwar or Prewar Army?	13
3. The Bumpy Road from Rhetoric to Readiness	29
4. The 27th Infantry Regiment, 25th Infantry Division	45
5. The 31st Infantry Regiment, 7th Infantry Division	56
6. The 19th Infantry Regiment, 24th Infantry Division	75
7. The 8th Cavalry Regiment (Infantry), 1st Cavalry Division (Infantry)	91
8. Conclusions	109
Notes	119
Bibliography	141
Index	153

LIST OF ILLUSTRATIONS

A gallery of figures and photographs follows page 90.

Standard U.S. Army infantry regiment organization, post-1948
Standard U.S. Army infantry battalion organization, post-1948
Standard U.S. Army infantry rifle company organization, post-1948
Secretary of Defense Louis A. Johnson
General of the Army Omar N. Bradley and Gen. J. Lawton Collins
Pres. Harry S. Truman
General Collins aboard an M8 scout car
Lt. Gen. Walton Walker
Military policemen at the gates of the emperor's palace, Tokyo
Members of the 25th Armored Reconnaissance Company in training
Troops of the 1st Cavalry Division assist Japanese police in strike control
Maj. Gen. Louis A. Craig talks with Pvt. Sidney McCoy
Students at Shinodayama Maneuver Area use a field radio
Linemen from Company B, 394th Signal Operations Battalion
Pfc. Matthew F. Bazzano operates a radio
Aerial view of Maizuru Maneuver Area
Members of the 95th Light Tank Company training at Chigasaki, Japan
Lieutenant Jackson, Heavy Mortar Company, 35th Infantry Regiment
Members of the Heavy Mortar Company, 35th Infantry Regiment
25th Infantry Division and 1st Cavalry Division hit the shore
Unidentified Eighth Army soldier awaits instruction
1948 Far East Command Small Arms Tournament
Members of the 65th Engineer Combat Battalion engage targets
Soldier of the 31st Infantry Regiment in an inclined prone firing position
A Polar Bears soldier fires from behind a tree trunk
A soldier of the 31st Infantry fires through a simulated window
A rifleman uses a mound of dirt as he engages targets
Aerial view of the cantonment area of Camp Fuji
Bazooka team training
A two-man 60-mm mortar crew from the 19th Infantry

Two Wolfhounds soldiers man an M1919A6 light machine gun
Two 24th Infantry Division soldiers fire a water-cooled machine gun
Men of Company B, 27th Infantry, attack a line position
Wolfhounds infantrymen maneuver against the "aggressor" force
Forward observers Lt. E. K. Andreasen and Pfc. Bobby L. Mayton
Members of 82nd Field Artillery Battalion, observe and adjust fire
A rebuilt truck engine being installed at the Fuchu Ordnance Center
Vehicles and equipment await refurbishment
Japanese workers repair jeeps at the Nissan Automobile Factory
Members of the 1st Cavalry Division maintain their equipment
Morning physical training
Men of Company H, 31st Infantry Regiment, celebrate the arrival of 1950
The "gunboggan"

MAPS
Task Force Smith at Osan	3
Division of Occupation Zones of Responsibility	19

FOREWORD

Organized or not, most Korean War veterans simply want respect. When it comes right down to it, the outcome of a geopolitical conflict is no measure of the men who fought it. The Americans who served in Korea fought as valiantly as any before or since, and they deserve to be remembered for it. Korea vets are now in their 60s. Nevertheless, their entitlement to national respect is as valid today as ever. The GI's performance in Korea outmatches the behavior of those who fought in our wars of certainty and victory. This is something to be recorded with respect and humility.

—Eric Sevareid, November 1997

Battlefield success is the ultimate validation of any army's training and readiness program. Viewed only at the macro level, one could argue that Eighth Army was not ready for combat in the summer of 1950. Oppressive heat, unforgiving terrain, and an implacable foe combined to deal Eighth Army's soldiers a defeat of enormous psychological dimensions as first the pitifully weak South Korean Army—"the best damn army in Asia" as described by its American advisors—and then the U.S. 24th and 25th Infantry Divisions were pushed down the Korean peninsula and cornered at a muddy port village named Pusan. To outside observers on both sides of the Iron Curtain it appeared that North Korea's Soviet-sponsored Korean Peoples' Army would indeed reunite the nation in time to celebrate the fifth anniversary of Japan's defeat in World War II. Taken at face value, the defeats incurred by American units in nine weeks of hard combat give credence to descriptions of Eighth Army as "Boy Scouts with guns" lacking any understanding of basic tactics as well as any training in their execution.

As is so often the case, face value offers only a one-dimensional view, a distorted reflection of reality. The Eighth Army on Occupation duty in Japan on the night of June 24, 1950, could be described as unready, but not using the metrics that most historians and soldiers have used since that night. The American soldiers sent to Korea in the summer of 1950 suffered from gaps in their professional preparation, from missing and broken equipment, and from unevenly trained leaders at every level of command. Nevertheless, they expected to defeat the Communist enemy. Their confidence resulted from many factors, not least of which was an appreciation of the skill and cohesion developed over the course of the previous twelve months—a year of progressive, focused, and iterative collective training based on the lessons of combat in World War II. No one was more surprised than they when the North Koreans not only didn't turn and run, but instead fought with courage and skill that required Herculean efforts to overcome. But because these American troops did not instantly stop the Red forces, their performance became an indictment of the Eighth Army, and the U.S. Army as a whole, in the years after 1950. This judgment is based on a misguided and simplistic interpretation of events. The men of Task Force Smith and tens of thousands like them in the understrength infantry regiments of Eighth Army achieved a signal strategic victory by preventing the communists from completing their conquest of South Korea. This could not have been done had the men of the 7th, 24th, and 25th Infantry Divisions and the 1st Cavalry Division not possessed a significant degree of familiarity with U.S. doctrine and tactics, a proficiency that could only have been gained through execution of a planned and progressive training program. Without doubt there were shortfalls in training, ammunition, vehicles and spare parts, weapons, and even clothing. But unlike American soldiers of previous wars, the men of 1950 found themselves hastily projected into what was later termed a "come-as-you-are" war. Denied the luxury of a months-long mobilization and training period such as their fathers and older brothers experienced in 1917 and 1941, the soldiers of Eighth Army fought with the tools at hand, and won. It bears repeating: they won. The landings at Inchon confirmed the destruction of Kim Il-sung's army of conquest. It had already been crippled, battering itself to death against the men of Eighth Army dug in on the hills above the Naktong River.

As the army implements the latest version of its capstone training manual, *Training for Full Spectrum Operations*, it is worth remembering that training in 1949, as today, required a balance between training management and execution. Training management includes setting conditions for success by minimizing external "distracters" that hinder execution. In 1949 the number and type of distracters affecting Eighth Army grew smaller but did not disappear. Today, the press of operational requirements often requires a telescoping of training experiences; the same was true in 1949 as commanders juggled their occupation requirements and their training requirements. It goes without saying that no army ever perfectly balances management and execution to achieve indefinite readiness. This book shows that Eighth Army's leadership built an acknowledgment of this fact into the training program. Lieutenant General Walker and his principal subordinates knew from experience that training proficiency is a journey, not an end-state. They accepted cyclical peaks and valleys of potential effectiveness in combat as the price of doing business. The logic of this argument remains compelling into the 21st century and is reflected by the adoption of the Army Force Generation cycle. We may judge the men and officers of the Eighth Army according to our standards and find them wanting, or we can measure their performance using the standards by which they viewed themselves. Doing the former may make us feel smug and superior but unjustifiably smears the reputation of our fathers and grandfathers. Doing the latter gives them their due while acknowledging that training methods have improved greatly since 1949.

Acknowledgment of the Eighth Army's accomplishments in 1949 and early 1950 should facilitate a shift in the debate away from the lack of preparedness of "occupation troops" and back onto a discussion of policy decisions made by numerous Truman Administration officials and senior Army officers in the wake of World War II. These decisions required a much larger military than President Truman was willing to support, despite the sworn testimony of no less a figure than Army Chief of Staff Omar Bradley. In another time and under other circumstances, one of Bradley's successors warned of the dangers of embracing "a twelve-division strategy with a ten-division Army." He could have just as easily been speaking to the Truman Administration. Recognizing the significant constraints under which the Eighth Army operated in 1949 and 1950 will finally allow scholars and soldiers to discard what Douglas MacArthur called the "pernicious myth" of professional, physical, and moral ineffectiveness that has heretofore prevented an honest discussion of Eighth Army's capabilities and limitations on the eve of war in 1950.

JAMES C. YARBROUGH
Brigadier General, U.S. Army
Commander, Joint Readiness
Training Center
Fort Polk, Louisiana
March 2010

PREFACE

To those who know me well, the passion I devoted to this work was no surprise. My career as an infantryman, both enlisted and officer, leads me to believe that there is a special place in heaven reserved for members of the profession of arms who are called to do their country's bidding under the most extreme conditions imaginable. I grew up knowing little more than that my father had served in Korea. A stoic, self-effacing man who eschews the limelight, my father didn't begin to share his experiences in Korea with my siblings or me until well after I had joined the army. In the same way, many of the men I interviewed while researching this book or met as acquaintances at the local VFW and American Legion halls avoided direct discussion of Korea. They are not ashamed of their service or their participation. On the contrary, when one finally coaxes them to speak, they become indistinguishable from veterans of any period. They stand taller, speak louder, and punctuate their remarks with pointed fingers that leave no doubt that they do not accept the many labels thrown at them by commentators over several decades.

This book allows them to speak their minds, answer their critics, and claim the respect and gratitude due them by their countrymen for having accepted the truth of the words carved on the Korean War Veterans Memorial on the National Mall: "Freedom is not free."

ACKNOWLEDGMENTS

I am indebted to a host of family, friends, mentors, colleagues, veterans, and archivists, all of whom contributed significantly to this project. In the interest of brevity I can thank by name only a few, though my burden to many is immense.

By far I owe the greatest debt to my faculty advisors at The Ohio State University. Prof. Allan Millett helped me refine the project after an innocuous conversation about competing interpretations of U.S. Army and Marine Corps combat effectiveness in 1950. His guidance, suggestions, and long-distance mentorship throughout the life of this project ensured it would reach fruition. Professors John Guilmartin and Alan Beyerchen cheerfully endured hours of painstaking review of several drafts, and Dr. Beyerchen's willing digressions from our "official" lunch topics to cover various points of argument proved to be some of the most intellectually rewarding events of my life. Their comments and suggestions have made this an infinitely better product than I could have rendered without their support.

I must also recognize the moral and intellectual support given me by my colleagues and superiors at the U.S. Military Academy, especially Brig. Gen. (Ret.) Robert Doughty, Col. Matthew Moten, Prof. Jenny Kiesling, and Lt. Cols. Tom Rider, Bryan Gibby, and Rick Black as well as the cadets in the fall of 2003 who enrolled in History 386: Korea and Vietnam. Their encouragement and our many spirited discussions helped me refine my argument in several places.

A host of archivists at several repositories ensured that I found the requisite documentary evidence upon which to base my thesis. The staff of the National Archives and Records Administration at College Park, Maryland; the U.S. Army Military History Institute; the Truman Library; and the U.S. Military Academy Library provided outstanding support during my several visits. Despite the fact that I descended upon them annually with a dizzying variety of requests, they managed to find almost every document and photo I sought. Without their assistance this project would have been impossible.

The many veterans and family members with whom I spoke brought this project to life and gave it purpose. All veterans are proud of their personal involvement in the military, whether the overall experience was pleasant or not.

The men of the Eighth Army with whom I spoke remained defiantly proud of their outfits despite decades of boilerplate referring to them as everything from slackers to cowards. If my work accomplishes nothing except to give those men the satisfaction of knowing that their contributions are recognized and appreciated, then I will have begun to repay the debt I owe them for taking the time to talk to me.

Mary Lenn Dixon and the staff of the Texas A&M University Press have demonstrated the patience of Job throughout my many delays in delivering required items, delays for which I alone am to blame. Their acceptance of an unexpected eighteen-month extension resulting from a tour in Iraq and their timely reminders sustained me and focused my efforts.

Finally and most importantly I must thank those closest to me. My wife Karen served as my editor and my timekeeper during the last crucial months; she is the real reason I finished this project. I owe my children Regina, John, and Aimee an ineradicable debt for their patience, their understanding, and their love over the course of the last several years. My father Lee and our comrades at VFW 5919 in Excelsior, Minnesota, motivated and sustained me while I served in Iraq so I could return and finish this project. The soldiers, sergeants, and officers with whom I've served taught me daily that excellence in service to others is the highest of man's endeavors, and I have striven to live up to their example and pass that virtue on to others.

With all the help and support I have received, I have rendered as accurate and complete a record of the achievements of the Eighth U.S. Army as is physically possible. Knowing that any work of history must remain imperfect, I accept full responsibility for any errors that remain.

1

Introduction

ON a rainy morning in early July 1950, American soldiers went to war for the second time in a decade. Four hundred-two men of Lt. Col. Charles B. Smith's 1st Battalion, 21st Infantry Regiment, fought a delaying action against the communist Korean People's Army (KPA) near Osan in South Korea. Beginning with its June 25, 1950, invasion, the KPA had repeatedly crushed all Republic of Korea (ROK) Army units in its path. American political and military leaders were stunned by the speed and audacity of the communist assault. Pres. Harry S. Truman on June 30 authorized General of the Army Douglas MacArthur to employ U.S. ground troops in Korea to restore the *status quo ante*. MacArthur, the commander-in-chief, Far East Command (FECOM), believed that without direct American intervention the North Koreans would quickly overrun the weakly armed, numerically smaller ROK Army. Like most Americans, however, he also felt that a demonstration by a small American ground force as "an arrogant display of strength" would suffice to halt the KPA and save South Korea from communist domination. As a result, on July 5, 1950, the soldiers of Task Force Smith became the physical embodiment of what MacArthur later described as a desire "to fool the enemy into a belief that I had greater resources at my disposal than I did."[1]

The officers and men of Task Force Smith began their fight at 0816, pitting their six 105-mm howitzers against thirty-three Soviet-built T-34 medium tanks. As the tanks closed on the infantry position, soldiers armed with 57-mm recoilless rifles and 2.36-inch rocket launchers joined the fight. The combined fires disabled just two tanks; the others passed through the American position and continued south toward Pyongtaek. Two hours later the main body of the KPA 4th Division (about four thousand infantry escorted by three more tanks) came within range of the defending Americans. After fighting until mid-afternoon, Colonel Smith ordered a withdrawal. Low on ammunition, unable to communicate with supporting artillery or mortars, and pressed closely by enemy infantry, Smith's unit disintegrated, and the withdrawal became a rout. American casualties totaled 148 enlisted men and five officers killed, wounded, or missing, including several who were apparently executed after being captured. Approximately 125 North Koreans died or suffered wounds; none were captured.[2]

The next day at Pyongtaek, the 1st Battalion, 34th Infantry Regiment withdrew in the face of attacks by the same KPA 4th Division. Both 1st and 3rd Battalions of the 34th Infantry Regiment subsequently failed to hold the town of Chonan. The remainder of the 21st Infantry Regiment fought a series of delaying actions from July 8 to July 12, 1950, between Chonui and Chochiwan but ultimately failed to halt the North Koreans' progress. On the night of July 15–16, KPA units pushed across the Kum River in the 19th Infantry Regiment's sector, forcing the entire 24th Infantry Division to withdraw toward Taejon. Frustrated by repeated American "bug-outs," on July 29 Lt. Gen. Walton H. Walker, commanding general, Eighth U.S. Army, issued his famous "stand or die" order. Even so, Walker's forces required another six weeks to stabilize their defenses sufficiently to allow MacArthur to conduct his decisive turning movement at Inchon on September 15.[3]

Historians and soldiers have not been kind to either MacArthur or the soldiers whom he placed in harm's way in the summer of 1950. The circumstances of MacArthur's relief in April 1951 have colored all subsequent interpretations of his actions during the Korean War. Post-1975 revolutions in training methods have led professional soldiers to condemn the army of 1950 for tolerating a crisis of "institutional environment and values." Such arguments fail to account for many mitigating factors, however, and merely add to the insults heaped on the men of the Eighth Army. Instead of lauding the significant operational advantages gained by Task Force Smith's delaying action, standard interpretations portray that unit as the epitome of unreadiness. Indeed, as early as July 24, 1950, the editors of *Life* blamed the soldiers of the Eighth Army generally for failing to emulate the example of their World War II forebears, beginning a historiographic trend that continues to this day.[4]

This study seeks to redress the imbalance that exists between fact and interpretation. For too long historians and soldiers have roundly criticized Task Force Smith's performance, extrapolated from its fate a set of assumptions about what constitutes readiness, and then used those assumptions to condemn the entire Eighth Army. The reality is much more complex. A proper examination

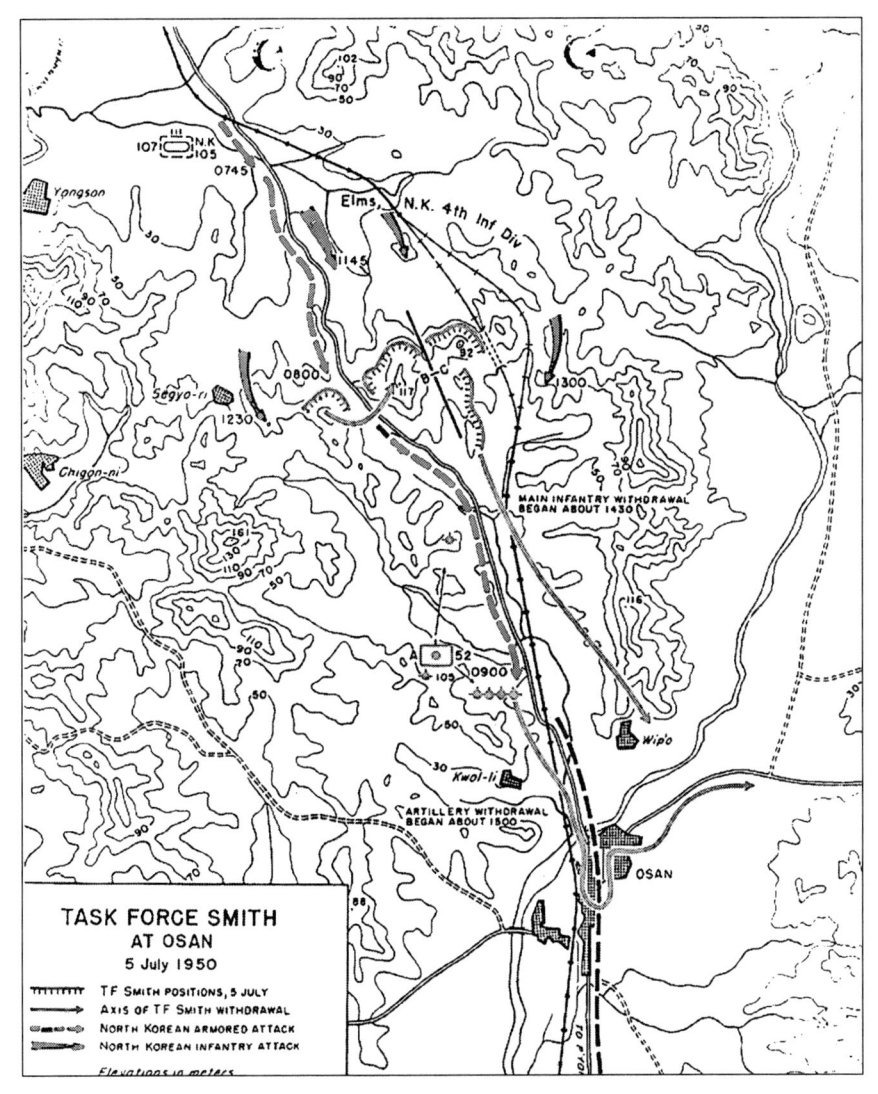

Task Force Smith at Osan, July 7 1950. (U.S. Army Center of Military History)

of the historical record reveals wide disparities in the readiness and combat effectiveness of the subordinate units of America's first forward-deployed Cold War field force. To gain a comprehensive understanding one must consider contemporary doctrine and expectations, the documented state of training in the Eighth Army, and the testimony of officers, noncommissioned officers, and soldiers who actually served in Japan in 1949 and early 1950. No longer should the reputation of the Eighth Army rest on the one-legged stool of hindsight critiques based on doctrine and performance measures developed two decades after the Korean War. Certainly the U.S. Army of 1950 labored under significant constraints that proved difficult to overcome in the immediate aftermath of the North Korean invasion. Contrary to the prevailing view, however, enough units in 1950 possessed sufficient tactical skill to salvage a precarious operational and strategic situation. This work will demonstrate how units achieved that readiness by means of case studies of four infantry regiments, one from each of the four infantry divisions that constituted the Eighth Army in 1950. It synthesizes contemporary training doctrine, training records generated by maneuver units, unit histories, reports of inspections by outside agencies, contemporary self-assessments, and the observations of veterans who served in Japan in the fifteen months before the outbreak of the Korean War. It challenges the long-standing reputation of the Eighth Army as flabby, dispirited, and weak. The uneven records of each of these regiments in combat in Korea during the first weeks of war reflect the uneven progress toward combat effectiveness that each of the four Occupation divisions made. Nevertheless, enough evidence exists to conclude that successful infantry regiments in Korea in the summer of 1950 owed their success not to luck but to hard training, and that the Eighth Army's prewar training program represented not just a rhetorical shift but a fundamental reordering of priorities within the Far East Command.

Assigning Blame in the Aftermath of Failure

What evidence allowed a negative interpretation to dominate most accounts of the army's performance in the summer of 1950? The diagnosis of senior officers in the Far East suggested a lack of will and stamina on the part of the American soldiers thrown so hastily into combat from their supposedly comfortable life in Japan. More than three decades after the fact, Lt. Gen. W. W. Dick, in July 1950 the acting commander of the 25th Division's artillery, believed that "rather than soft, we were weak—peacetime weak" in the years after World War II—meaning mentally and philosophically, perhaps, rather than physically. Articles in popular magazines by World War II veterans ridiculed much of the "New Army" reliance on psychology and keeping soldiers informed, a practice derided by veterans for supposedly producing weaker and more effete soldiers than good, old-fashioned "chickenshit."[5]

Few correspondents in Korea echoed the positive remarks of Compton Pakenham in *Newsweek*, who found the men of the 24th Infantry Division "astonished" at the strength of the KPA but wrote that "they knew they had dealt out more than they had taken" in their initial fights. Most other journalists copied the tone of war correspondents Carl Mydans and Frank Gibney, whose long experience in the Pacific war should have given them greater perspective. One of Mydans's earliest reports quotes an exhausted Lt. Col. Harold B. "Red" Ayres, commanding 1st Battalion, 34th Infantry Regiment, who asked about reinforcements near Pyongtaek: "We were just wondering if there was any more American army coming in here and we were kind of hoping that if it came it would come soon enough for us to see it." Gibney's sensationalistic coverage of the destruction of the 34th Infantry Regiment set the tone for much of the press coverage of events in Korea that summer.[6]

As a result, the American public, its government, and its military leaders began the process of assigning blame for tactical reverses even before the strategic situation had been sorted out. It did not take long for a scapegoat to emerge. Specifically, the fault lay with the soldiers and their leaders at the regimental level and below, the "high-priced soldiers" whom Americans "expected always to be in top physical shape, to fight hard, to remain in their assigned positions and never to run from the enemy." The American Legion, dominated by veterans of World War II, joined in denigration of the men of 1950. Indeed, they could hardly do otherwise: "The U.S. had won so significantly in Europe and the Pacific, and lost so disgracefully" in the opening weeks of the Korean War, that to treat Korean War veterans with anything warmer than indifference somehow demeaned the accomplishments of the World War II veterans. Implicit in this criticism lay the argument that the fault must lie with the officers and men of the field army, since many of the same officers who had orchestrated the victories in World War II still led the army five years later.[7]

Many of these same leaders subscribed to this explanation whether they had been on the ground in those first critical weeks or not. Lt. Gen. Matthew B. Ridgway, who became Eighth Army commander upon General Walker's death in December 1950, magnified his own significant contributions to U.N. success in Korea by declaring his belief that the Eighth Army under Walker was "professionally, physically, and spiritually unqualified for combat." The highly decorated Col. John T. Corley believed the emphasis placed by army recruiters in the late 1940s on postservice G.I. Bill benefits ruined soldiers. In his view, "service in the Army itself should only promise privation." Army basic training should constitute not an intermediate phase but "a hardening process whereby an American makes the transition from soft civilian to hard soldier, to the meager conditions under which he must exist when he fights an enemy who lives on a shoestring." Civilian journalist Eugene Kinkead followed Corley and Ridgway's lead. His book *In Every War but One*, a pseudopsychological study of misbehavior by soldiers captured by the communists during the Korean War, started by blaming American society for failing to instill in young American men "a set of moral values and the strength of character to live by them." It ended by condemning the U.S. Army for not identifying and correcting this shortfall, conveniently overlooking the existence of the army's Character Guidance Program and mandatory instruction on numerous civics and ethics topics in weekly troop information and education lectures. Korean War bibliographer Paul Edwards correctly states that the majority of men in the ranks in 1950 differed markedly from their World War II antecedents but errs in identifying how. "Most of those who entered the service at this time were interested in adventure, but of the peaceful type; they thought in terms more of occupation duty than of war." Edwards's argument rests on the unproven assumption that Occupation troops by definition lack both skill and will for combat.[8]

The dominant explanation, formulated before the end of 1950 and accepted by most historians and policy makers since, attributed tactical failure on the battlefield to a series of related factors, the combination of which supposedly preordained a U.S. military defeat. First, the U.S. Army lacked sufficient personnel to man the billets authorized in the defense budget for fiscal year 1950. Second, the Truman administration and the American public placed greater faith in the nation's atomic monopoly than on large numbers of combat troops for national security, allowing them to embrace fiscal measures that hamstrung attempts to sustain readiness. Third, the belief in the supremacy of American military institutions created by the victory in World War II and the atomic monopoly provided a false sense of security regarding potential threats and allowed many military leaders to deemphasize conventional readiness.[9]

Although these factors form only a partial explanation, uniformed observers in the early 1950s embraced them as the proximate causes for their problems in Korea. In the opening weeks of fighting, soldiers heaped scorn on the Truman administration and Secretary of Defense Louis Johnson in particular for his fiscal austerity. One lieutenant poignantly declared, "I hope that guy Johnson is satisfied. I hope all those politicians are happy with the way they saved money on the Army." Unmentioned in the press at the time was the near universal support Johnson had enjoyed in reducing defense spending right up to June 25, 1950.[10]

Upon retiring as army chief of staff in 1955, Gen. Matthew B. Ridgway simplistically blamed Generals Eisenhower and Bradley for acquiescing in "the shameful dissolution of the American military" in the wake of Allied victory in 1945, an act that left the Army in "a state of shameful readiness." Ridgway also attacked the Army's decision to implement reforms recommended in 1945 by the Doolittle Board. According to Ridgway, the effects of this program "undermine[d] discipline" and eroded "that priceless element" of military effectiveness—"the officer-enlisted man relationship based on mutual respect."[11]

Taking a different approach, Gen. J. Lawton Collins blamed both poorly implemented training programs undertaken by General Walker as well as the budget constraints imposed by "Secretary of Economy" Johnson. Writing in 1969, Collins conveniently minimized his own role as chief of staff from 1949 to 1953 in forcing those constraints on the Army. Not only was this a disingenuous attempt to evade responsibility, but it also flatly contradicted his own firsthand report regarding Eighth Army's combat readiness made to the secretary of the army after visiting the Far East. Shouldering some of the blame himself, General of the Army Omar Bradley in his second memoir stated that not arguing more forcefully in 1948 and 1949 for a realistic defense budget "was a mistake . . . perhaps the greatest mistake I made in my postwar years in Washington." While a true statement, it does not exonerate Bradley for failing to follow through with his 1948 congressional testimony. Before being elevated to serve as chairman of the Joint Chiefs of Staff, the acclaimed "G.I. General" had earnestly demanded a dramatic expansion of the army to "tide us over an emergency and permit rapid mobilization of the reserve forces if necessary."[12]

Triumph of the "Fehrenbach School"

Despite early attempts to identify the true nature and extent of the "defeat" in the opening weeks of the Korean War, most Americans erased the entire war from their consciousness. In time, the war's veterans accepted and even began to reflect this treatment. As the veterans concentrated on building their lives, the war receded from the foreground of their experience to a degree unmatched by the readjustment to civilian life of any other generation of veterans before or since. Furthermore, the Truman administration's decision to minimize the war's impact on the economy ensured that it never assumed more than marginal importance to most Americans' lives. In the absence of a vigorous debate on the subject, novelist and veteran T. R. Fehrenbach's 1963 book *This Kind of War: A Study in Unpreparedness* established in the minds of two generations the impression that the U.S. Army of 1950 "couldn't fight its way out of a wet paper bag" and survived only through the efforts of the U.S. Marine Corps. Fehrenbach's dismal portrayal of the Eighth Army's performance in the summer of 1950 as an unbroken series of failures and his sweeping generalizations about undermanned, ill-trained, poorly equipped, and indifferently led units eliminated the distinction between operational and strategic blunders committed by those serving at theater level and higher and tactical failures by soldiers and officers in the field. Notwithstanding this distortion, Fehrenbach's became and remains the standard interpretation of the Eighth Army's performance in 1950.[13]

The army acceded to Fehrenbach's assessment because it had already embarked upon its own campaign of self-flagellation in 1961 with the publication of Roy E. Appleman's *South to the Naktong, North to the Yalu*, the initial volume of the U.S. Army's official history. Appleman, an army field historian in Korea, believed that there was "no reason to suppose that any of the other three Occupation divisions in Japan would have done any better than did the U.S. 24th Division." He boldly asserted that "they showed the same weaknesses"—without his having conducted more than superficial research into the training background or level of preparation of any unit. Similarly, reviewer Col. Charles W. McCarthy found Fehrenbach's work "full of lessons for all ranks and ages; full of examples, both good and bad, which should be emulated or avoided." However, McCarthy could only point to examples of tactical or strategic decisions, not to any successes or failures in the preparation of a unit for war, because neither Fehrenbach nor Appleman before him had bothered to research that aspect of the issue.[14]

Subsequent authors amplified Fehrenbach's arguments in their own publications. In 1967 Russell F. Weigley rightly described the U.S. Army of 1950 as a "postwar force" shaped by the experience of the last war and quite unprepared doctrinally to fight a limited war. However, he erred by attributing battlefield failure in Korea to "faulty execution by troops who were too lightly trained, too loosely disciplined, and too lacking in motivation to match the determination of the enemy." In effect, Weigley synthesized *This Kind of War* and *In Every War but One*. Two decades after Weigley, Clay Blair's more balanced work, *The Forgotten War: America in Korea, 1950–1953*, correctly laid some of the blame on the senior leadership in the Eighth Army for painting too optimistic a picture of training and readiness but retained much of Fehrenbach's thesis regarding what constitutes readiness. In Blair's view, Truman and Johnson "had all but wrecked the conventional forces of the United States" by forcing economies onto the service that prevented any realistic readiness. In particular, Blair faulted Johnson's stringency for producing untrained soldiers (the product of a basic training program shrunk from seventeen weeks to eight) and junior leaders (lieutenants commissioned in 1950 reported immediately to their units because no funding existed for branch training) and to enlisted pay so miserly that the army was forced to accept draftees, who made "disgruntled, indifferent or even hostile soldiers." Blair's analysis ignored the fact that by 1950 over 99 percent of first-term enlisted soldiers were volunteers. Blair also overlooked the fact that the decision to close the army's Ground General School and branch basic officer courses came from the army itself, not the Truman administration, and only indirectly resulted from fiscal concerns.[15]

Predictably, General MacArthur objected to the impression created by Appleman's volume of the official history because he felt Appleman's interpretations facilitated the creation of a "pernicious myth" regarding the fighting ability of the American soldier:

> "It [*South to the Naktong, North to the Yalu*] is unduly weighted by innumerable alleged incidents of individual and organizational cowardice on the part of the Army, many of them dealing with the smallest actions, down even to patrols. The perspective becomes so warped that overall and strategic purposes are at times almost completely obliterated. The impression produced by the work in its present form cannot fail to be demoralizing upon the Army. . . . I cannot state too strongly my belief that the emphasis given in the book to the spiritual weakness underlying our military effort in Korea is not justified by the facts."[16]

Such sentiments should not be seen simply as examples of MacArthur's attempting to burnish his own reputation. Indeed, had he left the accusations of "spiritual weakness" unchallenged, he could have attributed the disastrous American military experiences in the summer and autumn of 1950 to flawed execution by troops unequal to the task, rescuing his own reputation as well as those of Lt. Gen. Edward N. Almond and Maj. Gen. Charles Willoughby. It is a measure of MacArthur's character that he stood up for the individual soldier of the Eighth Army without Ridgway's posturing and declined an opportunity to advance his own reputation at the expense of his soldiers.

Having triumphed over even MacArthur's protests, the Appleman/Fehrenbach orthodoxy received renewed emphasis following the collapse of the Warsaw Pact in 1989 and the defeat of Iraq in 1991. In January 1992 Gen. Gordon R. Sullivan declared his intention to break with an American tradition by executing a post–Cold War force reduction that would retain a well-trained, well-led, combat-ready army. Sullivan promised the nation that under his watch there would be "No More Task Force Smiths." Doubtless General Sullivan did not aim to denigrate American soldiers of any era and sought only to capitalize on Task Force Smith's value as a metaphor. Nevertheless, the most insidious effect of his mantra was to further damn the American soldier of 1950.[17]

Cautious Reappraisal

Despite the boost that Sullivan's official embrace provided to the "Fehrenbach School," a growing group of scholars, led by Allan Millett and Bruce Cumings, believe the Eighth Army narrowly achieved a decisive strategic victory in the late summer of 1950. Their interpretations divide American involvement in Korea into two wars: the successful war against the North Koreans and the stalemated war against the Chinese.[18] Many veterans support this thesis on the grounds that the two enemies differed fundamentally in terms of manpower, tactics, equipment, training, and logistics. A natural corollary to this interpretation is a general skepticism surrounding the universal condemnation of the Eighth Army of 1950.

Three studies from the early 1990s began the trend toward a revision of the historical record, although they focused very narrowly on the single issue of institutional racism in the U.S. Army. In 1991 Charles M. Bussey reopened old wounds with *Firefight at Yechon: Courage and Racism in the Korean War* by blaming institutional racism, not unreadiness, for the 24th Infantry Regiment's infamous reputation in combat. Two years later Lyle Rishell's *With a Black Platoon in Combat: A Year in Korea* offered a supporting argument from the perspective of a white officer who had commanded units in the 24th. By sponsoring the publication of *Black Soldier, White Army: The 24th Infantry Regiment in Korea* in 1996, the U.S. Army Center of Military History lent official weight to the revisionists' argument. Most importantly, however, *Black Soldier, White Army* was the first serious attempt to delve into the archival records and compare unit readiness as it was understood and reported at the time. Not surprisingly, the resulting evidence contradicted virtually everything written previously.[19]

Looking at the problem from a wider perspective, Richard Wiersema compared regimental combat effectiveness across the entire Eighth Army in the opening weeks of the Korean War. He argued that the poor performance of units initially sent to Korea resulted from an institutional failure to provide adequate resources for combat and an incomplete understanding of the situation in Korea on the part of senior leaders such as Maj. Gen. William F. Dean, Brad Smith's division commander. Consequently, understrength battalions found themselves occupying frontages more appropriate to full-strength regiments; that they succumbed to division-strength North Korean attacks should have surprised no one. Although Wiersema wrongly concluded that Dean and MacArthur knowingly accepted the potential for defeat in their initial troop deployments, he correctly identified the genesis of the negative impression of Task Force Smith. Wiersema argued that previous writers' fixation with the successful landings at Inchon on September 15, 1950, prevented them from properly assessing the Eighth Army's defeat of the KPA on the banks of the Naktong River in August and September, an operational victory that General MacArthur compared to Stonewall Jackson's 1862 Shenandoah campaign in terms of its strategic importance.[20]

Long before the appearance of these works, however, soldier-journalist-historian S. L. A. Marshall began a campaign to oppose the indiscriminate slandering of the army and its soldiers. Marshall spent three months in Korea in 1950–51 assessing the Eighth Army against his own experiences with American soldiers in both world wars. His findings refuted the "bad soldier" myths then current and were published in several newspapers and journals in 1951. Within days of arriving in Korea he had castigated media correspondents for their defeatist and exaggerated coverage of the Chinese intervention in November 1950: "For God's sake quit writing stories aimed to doom your country and its cause." Marshall's subsequent report appears to have made no impact, however. Because Marshall focused on the soldier, he was out of step with the military leadership of the time. He was also disconnected from the contemporary "overemphasis on technology" at the expense of consideration of the human element, especially the common infantryman. Official acceptance of Marshall's ideas suffered in the post-1953 era from the army's institutional preference for gadgetry and organizational experimentation rather than concentration on fundamentals. Hence, he failed to make a lasting revision of the "bad soldiers" myth.[21]

Moreover, the deeply contrasting picture of U.S. Army and Marine Corps performance first painted by Fehrenbach and amplified by subsequent historians continues to resonate among both military leaders and the general public. Thus, simultaneously with General Sullivan's poor choice of historical analogy, Army War College student Col. William J. Davies faithfully reproduced the Fehrenbach thesis cloaked as a leadership study, arguing that within the postwar army "the basic failure was one of institutional environment and values." Fehrenbach's interpretation achieved semiofficial status in 1994 when the Association of the United States Army reprinted *This Kind of War* through its affiliated press, Brassey's. As a result, Fehrenbach's work remains today the dominant point of departure within the U.S. Army regarding its performance in Korea, surpassing all other accounts—including the official histories—in terms of exposure among soldiers and their familiarity with its arguments. Even in popular and quasi-scholarly works, the Fehrenbach thesis reigns supreme. In its latest incarnation Robert Bateman claims that "most of the occupation army in Japan" looked like the 7th Cavalry Regiment, when in fact that unit labored under significant hardships unknown to most other regiments. Moreover, Bateman combines reminiscences of "stability" phase veterans with those of the "readiness" phase, distorting the record and eroding the credibility of his argument.[22]

As the following chapters demonstrate, the true state of readiness in the

Eighth Army in mid-1950 defies generalization or labeling. The record indicates that some units had progressed to a fairly complex level of training, and all veterans of the period remain defiantly proud of their regiments in spite of decades of criticism. This work is therefore more than simply a narrative discussion of training proficiency. It is also an argument in favor of rehabilitation and redemption, for revision of the "traditional narrative" that condemns the troops of the U.S. Eighth Army for the reverses of the summer of 1950.

Postwar or Prewar Army?

THE U.S. Army in 1950 was a shadow of its former self. From a peak of nearly 8.5 million uniformed members in 1945, its strength as of June 26, 1950, stood at 591,487 soldiers. Organized into ten combat divisions, eleven separate regiments, and a host of smaller support units and military advisory missions, the force lacked almost 40,000 of its authorized 630,201 soldiers. It boasted just one combat-ready division, the lightly armed 82nd Airborne, as a strategic reserve. International crises in early 1948 led to strong bipartisan support for limited rearmament. Congressional reauthorization of Selective Service encouraged army leaders to plan for a total strength of 900,000 officers and men in twelve divisions by the end of fiscal year 1949.[1] By early summer of 1948, however, fiscal concerns again trumped considerations of strategy and readiness. In effect, President Truman acquiesced in congressional allocation of $3.1 billion in additional funds for defense "but was unwilling to let the Services spend it." Simultaneously, Truman decreed that planning by the Department of Defense should in no way contemplate establishment of "a 'structure' which would require in excess of $15 billion to maintain during the fiscal year 1950." The result was a reversion by the Regular Army to a situation similar to the post–National Defense Act of 1920 days of skeleton units unable to sustain readiness but theoretically capable of rapid expansion in time of war.[2]

The fact that an expansible army is by definition not an expeditionary army went unmentioned by Secretary of the Army Kenneth C. Royall despite congressional testimony to the contrary by Army Chief of Staff Gen. Omar Bradley. Nevertheless, Bradley and his immediate subordinates accepted what they hoped would be a short-term readiness gap in return for promises of executive support for universal military training (UMT). This controversial proposal would have created a pool of over three million potential soldiers by 1958. However, President Truman balked at the political and financial cost of implementing UMT, and Congress failed to override him. Thus, the Joint Chiefs were forced to accept a limited implementation of the draft to make up its shortfalls.[3] Other austerity measures followed. Within the army's divisions, infantry regiments lost one of their three battalions; field artillery battalions lost one of their three firing batteries. No regiment possessed men or equipment to operate its organic tank company, and divisional tank "battalions" in the Far East Command consisted of just a single company of poorly armed and armored M24 Chaffee light tanks, not the M26 Pershing medium tanks stipulated in their tables of organization and equipment. Significantly, the U.S. Army's leadership forced these changes on operational units without reducing mission requirements or revising tactical doctrine—a factor of crucial importance in the first weeks of the Korean War. Hence, although organizational changes based on combat experience in World War II made the post-1947 infantry division much more lethal than its World War II antecedent, fiscal restraint limited divisional strength to a peacetime ceiling of 12,500 soldiers instead of the required 18,900. Within units in Japan these artificial ceilings were unevenly distributed. Since administrative requirements remained constant even as personnel requirements fluctuated, strength reductions fell most heavily on maneuver units, not headquarters elements.[4]

From September 1945 to April 1949, Occupation duties required the full attention of the maneuver formations of the Eighth Army. This reflected General MacArthur's requirement that Eighth Army units first discharge these duties, then provide general support of U.S. policies within the theater and only then take steps to prepare for combat in case of a general emergency. In the early months of the Occupation these duties included the maintenance of law and order, crowd control, the disbanding of the Imperial Japanese Army, and the repatriation of forced laborers. Missions expanded in 1947 and 1948 to include supervision of elections, mounted "presence" patrols in the countryside, and the seizure of property looted by the Japanese from foreign nationals before 1945.[5] This was no small task; in just one month U.S. soldiers recovered over 1,050 kilograms of silver bullion and 7,954,040 kilograms of foreign coins. Many officers with combat experience in World War II were unhappy with the army's new imperial mission, which one of them derisively termed "tax-collecting." For officers and senior noncommissioned officers life in Japan quickly came to resemble the colonial existence of interwar Panama or the Philippines, while junior soldiers viewed life in Japan as an adventure—especially since the Japanese economy afforded even a lowly private the opportunity to experience luxuries beyond the reach of the average Japanese family.[6]

This Eighth Army, a postwar force consisting of understrength divisions with paper battalions fully engaged in what are now called "stability operations," ceased to exist on April 15, 1949. Earlier that spring, General MacArthur reoriented the nature of the Allied Occupation of Japan. No longer would the principal function of the Eighth Army be to remind the Japanese who had won World War II. In accordance with new strategic realities the "stern rigidity" of the immediate postwar period now gave way to an era marked by "friendly protective guidance" as the United States sought to re-create Japan as a pro-American economic bulwark in Asia. This shift resulted in part from realization that current war plans for a conflict with the Soviet Union would require a competent force to defend Japan against an attack launched from either the Soviet Union or Korea. The impact of this change on the Eighth Army was immediate. The relaxation of Occupation controls "released hundreds of officers and enlisted men for return to military duties and enabled the command to give increased attention to the development of both administrative and combat efficiency."[7] In short, Eighth Army shook off its postwar lethargy and began focusing on potential future conflicts.

Simultaneously, Eighth Army's G-1 staff made its first rational attempt to stabilize personnel assignments within the Eighth Army's subordinate units. Of the more than one hundred thousand soldiers in Japan in early 1949, nearly half had entered the service before V-J Day. Their experiences and memories of the Occupation closely corresponded with descriptions of life in Japan as an adventure in which readiness for combat took a back seat to civil operations and recreation. By the end of 1949, however, "all [sic] of these veterans of the 1945 period had completed their tours and had been replaced." The implications of this turnover become clear when one considers three other facts. First, the "stability and reconstruction" phase of the Occupation lasted almost four times as long as the "defense of Japan" phase. Second, the Far East Command labored under a continually descending personnel ceiling that fell faster after 1948. Therefore, the number of new personnel in the Far East whose memories of the Occupation might have reflected a greater focus on readiness was not as large as those who remembered the easy times. Third, the soldiers who participated in the "defense of Japan" phase became casualties at a tremendously high rate in the summer of 1950. This fact further reduced the number of available veterans who could knowledgeably discuss Eighth Army's readiness.[8] As a result, the collective voice of these veterans has never been heard, drowned by the clamor raised by a disparate group of journalists, academics, soldiers, and politicians united perhaps only in their determination to control the debate for their own purposes.

The Need for Readiness

As a result of the shift in U.S.-Japanese strategic relations in the winter of 1948–49, Eighth Army suddenly found itself searching for a new mission. In the forty months following the Japanese surrender on September 2, 1945, Eighth Army served as General MacArthur's executive agent, implementing the provisions of Allied policy toward defeated Japan. A good deal of Eighth Army's role had been implicit; the selective employment of large formations of heavily armed soldiers to quell labor unrest and monitor political assemblies underscored the unequal relationship between Americans and Japanese. This role became unnecessary with the Truman administration's adoption of NSC 13/2 on December 10, 1948. This policy document codified an ongoing devolution of administrative responsibility from Allied military government authorities to Japanese civil authorities. Already on July 28, 1948, the military government staff sections of the Eighth Army were eliminated; their functions were transferred to regional Civil Affairs teams. Unlike the military government units, the Civil Affairs teams reported directly to Headquarters, Supreme Command Allied Powers, reducing significantly Eighth Army's role in administrative and surveillance operations. In time even the term *military government* was officially proscribed, discarded as a "misnomer": "In keeping with the changing aspect of the Occupation, it is considered propitious to change these designations to titles more nearly descriptive of the real functions of these agencies."[9]

The reduced mission requirements did not lead to calls for a reduction or elimination of the U.S. military presence in the Far East. The most important reason for this was the Cold War. The Truman administration and many congressional leaders feared that the continued economic, social, and political unrest in many Asian countries in the wake of World War II left those nations vulnerable to Soviet influence. Tensions with the Soviet Union rose precipitously in May 1948 as a result of the Berlin blockade and the deposition of the Beneš government in Czechoslovakia. France and Britain, once principal players in Great Power politics, found themselves reduced to supporting roles by three decades of war and recession. Moreover, news from China told of a steadily deteriorating Nationalist military situation that ended in the fall of 1949 with the Guomindang's expulsion from the mainland. In these circumstances any appearance of U.S. retreat was believed to be dangerous. Joint Staff planners in Washington feared above all that retrenchment in Asia would lead the Soviets to misjudge U.S. resolve and stumble accidentally into World War III. And in Japan FECOM G-3 planners underlined both the danger to U.S. forces posed by Communist organizations "who either by overt or covert methods may be expected to further USSR objectives" and "the difficulty in opposing their activities by direct United States military operations." As a result, the Joint Chiefs of Staff repeatedly urged the Truman administration to maintain or even expand the number of U.S. bases in Asia, both to stabilize regional allies as well as to create a defense in depth against possible Soviet aggression.[10] Even so, the idea of retaining significant numbers of ground forces outside the United States was relatively new in 1949. The immediate challenge for Lt. Gen. Walton H. Walker and his subordinates concerned keeping the men of four infantry divisions gainfully employed. Their long-term challenge was to safeguard the American position in the Far East while also defending Japan itself. The best way to accomplish both tasks was to visibly enhance the combat readiness of the Eighth Army through an intensive and long-duration training program.

The question of focus for any training program had already been settled. The defense of the Japanese home islands became the principal mission of the Eighth Army in July 1949 with the publication of Change 7 to Occupation Instruction Number 5. For the American military, distractions related to Occupation duties were now limited to the retention of a capability to "re-establish military controls if needed" instead of close daily supervision of Japanese government and society. Freed from much of the stability and security requirements of previous months, commanders at all levels could now focus their attention on defending Japan from a potential Soviet attack.[11]

To guide Eighth Army planners in devising a ground forces training program to meet anticipated contingencies, Maj. Gen. Charles Willoughby and his G-2 (Intelligence) staff section at FECOM produced and periodically updated an estimate of the capabilities and intentions of potential enemies, principally the Soviet Union. In addition, the FECOM G-3 (Operations) section as well as the multiservice Joint Strategic Planning and Operations Group (JSPOG) produced their own assessment of potential threats. The conclusions presented by these groups allowed planners at the operational level (Eighth Army) to identify those tactical-level tasks that the infantry divisions, regiments, and battalions would have to accomplish successfully in order for the United States to achieve its overall strategic goals. These estimates and the training scenarios derived therefrom were repeatedly tested by the Eighth Army staff through a series of command post exercises (CPXs) held from November 1949 through May 1950. All of the exercises were predicated on a Soviet invasion and American defense of northern Japan. Division-level defensive missions developed by the CPX experience reveal the close linkage between contemplated engagements and training scenarios. For example, given the known capabilities of the Soviet army and navy, the most likely course of action open to Josef Stalin was an invasion of Hokkaido by a combination of airborne and seaborne forces. To counter this, the 7th Infantry Division planned to defend Chitose Airdrome and the Otaru and Aomori-Ominato beach areas, augmented by reinforcements from other divisions in Japan as needed. The 1st Cavalry Division (Infantry) would defend the Kanto Plain and key U.S. Air Force installations near Tokyo, while the 25th Infantry Division would defend against diversionary airborne or amphibious assaults on western or central Honshu. The 24th Infantry Division would spread itself thinly across both Honshu and Kyushu, but was not to expect much contact given the extreme distance of this area from Soviet bases in the Far East.[12]

Training Directive Number Four

General Walker's training program complemented MacArthur's desire that all services' training should lead to "the establishment of a cohesive and integrated naval, air, and ground fighting team."[13] The first step was to build a capable ground force that could take advantage of the capabilities offered by naval and air forces. Walker's staff subsequently outlined a series of progressive training events designed to increase the readiness of combat units in Japan. Eighth Army Training Directive Number Four, published on April 15, 1949, marked the end of the postwar era for American soldiers in Japan. Although the first objective of training remained "to prepare all individuals and units for occupation duties," the new training program stipulated that the conduct of training "must stress that *every soldier,* regardless of assignment, has as his primary duty the obligation to fight or support the fight." If they had ever existed, the easy days of Occupation were gone, replaced by a new sense of purpose as unit commanders, noncommissioned officers, and soldiers strove to rebuild their units' abilities to fight, survive, and win in combat. The new directive required all subordinate units to complete individual military occupational specialty (MOS) training and tactical evaluations at the squad, platoon, and company/battery/troop level by December 15, 1949. Battalions and squadrons were to be certified by mid-May 1950, with regimental combat team exercises complete by the end of July 1950. Walker expected to certify his four divisions as combat ready by the end of 1950. In addition, he ordered one battalion from each division to complete air transportability training and one regiment per division to complete amphibious assault training by October 31, 1950. Former Army Vice Chief of Staff Peter Clainos, in 1949 the commander of the 1st Battalion, 7th Cavalry Regiment, recalled that the new directive brought about an immediate change of emphasis

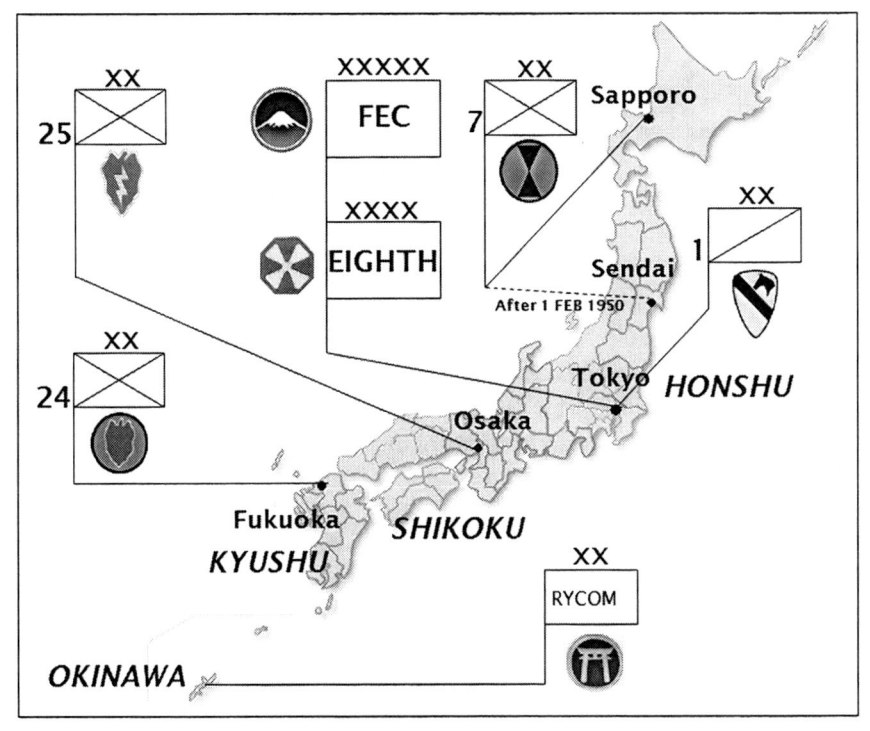

Division of Occupation zones of responsibility under the U.S. Far East Command, 1949–50. The southern divisions were grouped under I Corps, while the two northern divisions reported to IX Corps until those units' inactivation in March 1950.

within the 1st Cavalry Division. By early summer he and his contemporaries "were breaking our necks to make these units combat ready."[14]

Walker's plan was orthodox but ambitious. Significant obstacles threatened the progress of any training program in the post-1945 army, including insufficient funds for operations and maintenance, a critical lack of suitable maneuver training areas, and a crippling shortage of equipment of all types. Though not unique to Japan, the combination of these factors made training in Japan particularly problematic. Walker, known as Gen. George S. Patton Jr.'s favorite corps commander during World War II, expected compliance from his corps and division commanders. His physical appearance and abrasive personality earned him the nickname "Bulldog" from press correspondents and subordinates. He lost no time in setting his personal imprint on the Eighth Army. Immediately after taking over from Lt. Gen. Robert L. Eichelberger in September 1948, Walker divided the staff to separate the functions of the Occupation from those that dealt with training and readiness.[15]

With Eichelberger's departure the last of the senior veterans of MacArthur's Pacific campaigns left the Far East. Aside from his personal staff who had been with him at GHQSWPA (except Willoughby), the Supreme Commander found himself surrounded by "Europeans," generals who were protégés of Eisenhower, Bradley, and Collins. Although Walker's status as an outsider did nothing to ease the tension between MacArthur and the Joint Chiefs, Bradley's choice of Walker to command Eighth Army made sense. Before commanding XX Corps in Europe in 1944–45, Walker supervised the training of several divisions as commander of the Desert Training Center at Camp Irwin, California. After the war Walker commanded Fifth U.S. Army. This Chicago-based unit oversaw the reestablishment of a trained Organized Reserve Corps in the Great Lakes region following demobilization. Thus, Walker arrived in Japan with a wealth of training experience unsurpassed in the U.S. Army.[16]

Foundation of Sand?

Publication of Training Directive Number Four did not mean that training had heretofore been ignored in Japan, any more than it had been in the rest of the Army. However, the turbulent personnel situation that persisted throughout the U.S. Army prevented much advancement beyond individual training. During the stability phase of the U.S. Occupation, commanders had used their training programs to enhance discipline and unit cohesion. As late as January 1949, a 7th Division training memorandum's low expectations envisioned unit-run programs designed to produce "alert, well disciplined individual soldiers thoroughly qualified in requisite basic military subjects and techniques and capable of performing any assignment in the squad, section or platoon commensurate with their rank." The program of instruction stressed individual tasks such as drill and ceremonies (six hours); camouflage and concealment (two hours); first aid (six hours); inspections (ten hours); and interior guard duty (three hours).[17] Other divisions had similar aims.

In addition, two other factors plagued unit commanders as they formulated training plans: the relative youth of the force and the relatively low aptitude scores of the replacements sent to FECOM. Both factors reflected the significant demographic differences between the World War II army and its post-1945 successor. By the end of 1949 over 50 percent of soldiers were twenty-one years old or younger (some not yet eighteen) and had never before been away from home—a 150 percent increase from 1939. In terms of discipline, this presented commanders with a continuous challenge as immature and well-paid American youths swelled the ranks of the U.S. Army in the late 1940s. All units subsequently found themselves encumbered by the administrative requirements of imposing judicial and nonjudicial punishments on offending soldiers. For 1949, the 25th Infantry Division reported conducting 599 "368" boards to separate undesirable soldiers, 90 general courts martial, 633 special courts martial, and 1,920 summary courts martial. The division historian attributed the spike in discipline problems to the sudden "influx of poorly educated, partially trained unintelligent youngsters of 18 and 19" years of age.[18]

This was by no means a problem unique to American units in the Far East or anywhere else in the world. Even in the British Commonwealth Occupation Forces, many veteran soldiers lamented the lack of discipline and character of new replacements, whom the Australians in particular quickly tagged as "loud-mouthed larrikins and law-breakers."[19] Also, although average educational levels army-wide in 1948 equaled two years of high school, a large percentage of white soldiers assigned to FECOM in the late 1940s scored in the lowest two categories on the Army General Classification Test. In some infantry regiments a plurality of soldiers scored in the lowest two intellectual aptitude categories. This trend found its analog in officer assignments as well. Academic rank and commissioning source determined whether an officer received a posting to Europe, the United States, or the Far East. Few if any newly commissioned lieutenants volunteered to serve in an area where they were prohibited from bringing their families for at least eighteen months. As one member of the West Point Class of 1946 observed, except for volunteers only the lowest-performing cadets received assignments to Occupation units in Korea or Japan. Hoping to attract high-quality officers for duty in the Far East, the Army offered Reserve officers the opportunity to remain on active duty in their current grade if they accepted duty with Occupation forces in Korea. But as one veteran of this era remarked, most of these officers had risen from the ranks fighting against the Japanese (and Koreans) and had little desire to do more than serve out their time while waiting for separation, retirement, or acceptance as a Regular Army officer. Among other implications, this meant that complex tasks required repetitive drills in order for soldiers to learn them while officers of uneven quality and motivation supervised training. Coupled with the rapid changeover of personnel within units, this reinforced an already established emphasis on individual-level Occupation-driven training needs at the expense of collective combat training. As a result, one summary of activities for 1948 highlights training in communications, clerical skills, supply procedures, and driving skills—jobs of much greater immediate importance in the Occupation than the ability to defend against an infantry-tank assault.[20]

Despite the difficulties and challenges posed by the shift in emphasis, most officers appear to have welcomed the change. Officers with combat experience embraced the new training program because they strongly believed in the importance of sustaining what the U.S. Army finally codified in 2003 as "the warrior ethos."[21] Lt. Col. Wayne Hardaman, G-3 of the 25th Infantry Division, put it more bluntly: the elimination of most Occupation-driven missions meant that "training became the *sine qua non* instead of the ugly duckling" in the Far East. The 1st Cavalry Division conducted its first internal test of unit-based individual training as early as January 1949, when members of the division G-3 staff section evaluated the replacement training program of the 271st Field Artillery Battalion. The division's monthly summary anticipated an increase in such inspections for two reasons. First, several subordinate organizations had embarked upon a basic training program in late 1948 and were nearing completion. Second, the flow of replacements between FECOM and the Zone of the Interior (that is, the United States, "ZI" in official shorthand and GI slang) constituted an uncontrolled hemorrhage. The January 1949 1st Cavalry Division monthly summary estimated an "approximate seventy per cent influx of new personnel in the past six months." The division G-3 acknowledged that high turnover meant any proficiency gained through internal training programs would quickly be lost through attrition. To compound the problem, few of the new replacements were NCOs: "The new men are practically all new soldiers requiring further training in the basic military subjects prior to any specialist training or duty in assigned positions."[22] Therefore, before any long-term increase in readiness could be achieved, the U.S. Army would have to enter a prolonged period of relative stability. That required a firm commitment from the Truman administration regarding force structure and personnel levels, a commitment that Harry S. Truman's uniformed subordinates were unable to provide in the summer of 1949.

The "Hollow" Army—An American Tradition

Prior to U.S. mobilization for World War II, individual units conducted their own basic training programs. The rapid expansion of the army following the 1940 reinstatement of Selective Service and federalization of the National Guard created tremendous problems for the officers charged with creating an effective ground combat force. In late 1941 Gen. George C. Marshall established Headquarters, U.S. Army Ground Forces (AGF), a separate command that directly supervised the training of tactical units in preparation for shipment overseas, while the Army Service Forces (ASF) handled the administration of basic training to soldiers who would be sent overseas as individual fillers. AGF exercised supervisory authority over the replacement training centers using inspection teams from within its staff. This dual-track training system resulted from the failure of the replacement training center system to keep up with the demands of the army's mobilization for the war effort. An unforeseen but welcome consequence of this duplication effort, however, was the overall higher level of competency within a given MOS of replacement training center graduates compared to soldiers trained by their parent units. This disparity resulted principally from the economies of scale and degree of specialization of training cadre that the training center concept provided compared to divisional organizations. AGF recognized the value of the training center approach and sought to retain it following the end of World War II.[23]

Having created the citizen army for the emergency, the War Department naturally turned to AGF to demobilize that army when its services were no longer needed. By late 1945 AGF operated twenty-four centers across the nation with the aim of reducing end strength while balancing force structure requirements. Despite prodigious progress a backlog inevitably developed, and domestic politics rather than military necessity soon dictated that demobilization take precedence over retention of manpower, skilled or otherwise. Pre–V-J Day plans to retain a combat-ready Regular Army of two and a half million men quickly fell victim to a widespread campaign to "bring the boys home." Having already shown no hesitancy to confront the Truman administration on other issues, Republican congressmen used the demobilization issue to paint the War Department and the Truman administration as coconspirators in an attempt to foist peacetime conscription and perpetual deficit spending upon the nation. Soldiers played a significant role in fomenting this discord. In early 1946 American soldiers around the world staged public protests over a War Department–directed slowdown of demobilization. The largest of these, held in Manila on January 6 and 7, attracted between eight and ten thousand soldiers.[24]

Hoping to silence critics and stem the wholesale separation of trained leaders and specialists, Army Chief of Staff Gen. Dwight Eisenhower defended the pace of demobilization by attributing a planned slowdown to faster-than-anticipated separations in late 1945 and growing doubt "that the Army which did so much to win the victory will be left fit to preserve it." He also estimated that at a minimum the future Regular Army should number 1,500,000 men in order to meet anticipated Occupation requirements and also provide the expeditionary capability that the Truman Doctrine implicitly required. Unfortunately, in the same month as Eisenhower's plea for caution, the War Department implemented a provision to immediately separate all men with two years' military service. The inclusion of another easily met criterion for demobilization meant that Eisenhower's desire to slow the pace of discharges to maintain a combat-ready force was impossible to fulfill. When the dust settled at the conclusion of demobilization on June 30, 1947, army strength stood at just 684,000.[25]

Rapid demobilization destroyed the U.S. Army's effectiveness, as it had following every major American war since 1783. In the Far East demobilization played havoc with attempts to maintain readiness. The 1st Cavalry Division processed 75,411 enlisted and NCO departure and accession transactions from July 1, 1945, through May 31, 1947.[26] In other words, in just twenty-two months the equivalent of three times the *wartime* authorized enlisted strength of the division came to Japan and left again. Faced with such high turbulence no commander could hope to sustain even a veneer of combat effectiveness.

Logistics and maintenance units suffered crippling losses in the weeks and months following V-J Day as a result of the individual demobilization program. First priority for return to the United States was accorded to those soldiers who had accrued high point scores or had completed two years of military service. The relative safety of rear-area units during actual combat meant that they suffered very little turnover during the war. Because of that, however, the vast majority of their personnel immediately became eligible for demobilization at war's end, with predictable effects on their ability to execute their support functions. Nor was this an isolated problem. In Italy, the 313th Engineer Battalion of the 88th Infantry Division ceased to exist except on paper as a result of individual separations—by September 1945 the entire battalion consisted of eight officers and fifty-six enlisted soldiers of all ranks. One second lieutenant who arrived in Japan in December 1945 found himself signing the morning reports of two engineer companies in different battalions.[27]

Attempts to correct the problem in the fiscal year 1947 budget by basing personnel estimates on anticipated requirements failed because of Harry Truman's penchant for funding national defense using the "remainder method"—using revenue to pay for all other expenditures and dedicating the remaining amount for military appropriations regardless of the consequences. Selective Service was temporarily extended in 1945 and again in 1946, but only after political pressure forced the War Department to lower its estimate of future end strength requirements to 1,070,000 by June 30, 1947. Coupled with reduced service obligations (men conscripted after June 1946 served only eighteen months) and draft immunity for fathers, the army experienced a tremendous demographic change. Erroneously believing that high postwar voluntary enlistments resulted from civic feeling, the War Department acquiesced to the lapse of conscription in 1947 only to see a precipitous drop in enlistments once the threat of the draft disappeared. By mid-1948 the U.S. Army had just 538,000 active-duty soldiers, a majority of whom had entered service within the last two years.[28]

Hasty demobilization and reduced recruit accessions in the 1946–48 period placed a tremendous strain on AGF's training centers. Believing in the superiority of centralized basic training, AGF continued to operate six replacement training centers in the postwar period, but the unsettled personnel situation reduced their effectiveness to near zero. After having increased basic training to seventeen weeks during World War II, AGF shortened it to thirteen weeks at the close of hostilities and then to eight weeks in January 1946 in an attempt to meet the ravenous appetite for replacements in the occupied areas. Even this failed to maintain a sufficient flow of replacements, and AGF resorted to sending partially trained or even untrained men directly to the theater. In Japan, Eighth Army established its own basic training center in early 1947 at Atsugi. One company commander, a second lieutenant on loan from the 46th Engineer Battalion, recalled that the first group of inductees were "almost right off the streets . . . three to four weeks away from home, [and had undergone] no training."[29] Although the Eighth Army's Replacement Training Center soon went away, the problem of poorly trained soldiers and a lack of NCOs did not. It was simply beyond the power of Eighth Army to control while also fully engaged in Occupation missions. Only after most of those duties became the responsibility of Japanese civil and police administrations could American soldiers again devote their time to becoming proficient at their wartime tasks.

Nor could AGF by itself solve the problem, because force structure and personnel authorizations originated in the executive branch with virtually no input from Army Staff. During the early 1948 crisis period the army received authorization to expand over the course of fiscal year 1949 to 900,000 soldiers. Two additional centers opened to train the anticipated 300,000 recruits. Less than a year later these two installations were closed down when the Truman administration imposed severe austerity measures on the Department of Defense for the remainder of FY 1949 and for its upcoming appropriation for FY 1950. Already exceeding the revised 1949 authorization of 677,000, the army was forced to halt draft inductions completely and limit new enlistments and reenlistments, virtually shutting off the flow of replacements (trained or otherwise) from the ZI to the Occupation commands. The volatility of the personnel situation would plague Eighth Army throughout its quest to transform itself from an occupying "stability" force to a trained and effective combined arms organization. One significant benefit, however, was that, army-wide, by the end of 1949 fewer than one percent of enlisted soldiers were draftees, a situation that persisted until the outbreak of war in Korea. For this reason commanders could at least leverage the voluntarism and cooperative spirit of their soldiers without worrying about the adulterating effects of cynical draftees on unit morale.[30]

Stemming the Tide of Personnel Turbulence

Despite the enormous problems posed by the personnel situation, commands at every level in the Far East embraced the challenge of adjusting the professional focus from Occupation to combat readiness. A significant step forward occurred in early 1949. The Far East Command G-1 staff implemented a program designed to mitigate the effects of sustained high personnel turbulence. The Constant Flow Program aimed to level gains and losses across the entire Eighth Army, thereby reducing the chances that any single unit would suddenly lose a significant number of trained soldiers in any given month. The plan envisioned the arrival and departure of 2,700 white soldiers and 440 black soldiers each month—still a significant level of turbulence but one with which the training base in the United States could cope. In approving the program General Walker ordered that manning levels of all four divisions of the Eighth Army be aligned as closely as possible. As a result the bloated 1st Cavalry Division, an organizational dinosaur of two brigades of two regiments each, finally became a triangular division. The 12th Cavalry Regiment (1,275 soldiers) was transferred bodily to the 7th Infantry Division and reflagged as the 32nd Infantry Regiment. The three remaining regiments of the 1st Cavalry also slimmed down to conform to infantry regiment tables of organization, and the division received the parenthetical designation "infantry." Between March 1 and May 15, 1949, an additional 1,000 soldiers were sent to the 7th Division, along with 2,100 to the 24th Division and 1,275 to the 25th Division. Although Constant Flow provided only enough replacements to man the infantry divisions at their reduced peacetime levels (12,500 instead of 18,900), the program did finally restore some predictability to force levels in the Far East. Following a recommendation by the Army Inspector General that sufficient replacements be shipped to Japan to facilitate training, the replacement centers quickly complied by sending 3,000 soldiers to the Far East above and beyond the requirements of Constant Flow.[31]

Unfortunately for FECOM and Eighth Army, all of these replacements were still products of the eight-week basic training cycle. Staff officers from the Office of the Chief, Army Field Forces (OCAFF; Army Ground Forces became Army Field Forces in 1948 when Gen. Mark Clark took over for retiring Gen. Jacob Devers), fully recognized the deficiencies of the eight-week cycle but were powerless to change it until the army's budget and manpower requirements stabilized. In response to complaints from the field regarding recruit training and to eliminate "wasteful duplication" of the training effort by field units, OCAFF recommended to General Collins that basic training again be expanded to thirteen weeks' duration. As finally adopted for fiscal year 1950 (which began on July 1, 1949), the new program provided for a fourteen-week program of 560 instructional hours. Significantly, the new cycle devoted 23 percent of total instruction time to weapons training and 16 percent to physical fitness training activities.[32]

The major shortcoming of this expanded training program lay in its failure to impart anything beyond basic soldier skills to new recruits, who received no specialty training or MOS designation. Responsibility for training individual soldiers to perform the duties of their assigned MOS remained at the unit level; the replacement centers would not assume that obligation until July 31, 1950. Despite the OCAFF historian's comment that the new Mobilization Training Plan (MTP) 21-1 "was not wholly satisfactory," the fact remains that it was a considerable improvement over what had gone before. It doubled the time spent on weapons instruction, nearly doubled the amount of time devoted to physical conditioning, tripled the amount of time spent under field conditions, and included instruction on subjects left out of the eight-week program entirely, such as night training and hand grenade and rocket launcher familiarization.[33]

Rushed into publication to meet a March 7, 1949, implementation deadline, MTP 21-1 had no significant impact before the end of 1949. In a report covering an inspection of training in Japan, Col. F. M. Harris of OCAFF noted that so few graduates of the expanded program had arrived in Japan as of October 1, 1949, that "an overall assessment of the improvement" could not be made. Moreover, FECOM continued to receive what many officers felt was a disproportionate number of low-aptitude soldiers as measured by scores achieved on the Army General Classification Test (AGCT). As of September 30, 1950, over 41 percent of privates in Eighth Army scored 89 points or less (out of 163) on their classification test. The number of low-aptitude NCOs was not as high but still significant: 35 percent of corporals and 28 percent of sergeants fell into the two lowest achieving groups. Although this situation boded ill for the competency of certain technical specialists, it did not automatically mean that collective training in infantry units would appreciably suffer. Moreover, despite the perception of some officers in Japan that FECOM received a disproportionate share of low-aptitude soldiers, the army's own inspectors found similar percentages in Europe. In the period September 1, 1948, though March 31, 1949, a total of 34,713 white replacement soldiers arrived at the Marburg Replacement Depot. More than 65 percent of them were twenty years old or younger, and almost 48 percent of them scored in the lowest two AGCT achievement categories.[34]

The personnel turbulence in the Army between 1945 and 1949, the dramatic downward trend in the average age of soldiers following World War II, and the inability of the force's training base to sustain even a minimally competent replacement pool resulted from problems beyond the U.S. Army's ability to control. In the immediate postwar period political expediency trumped rationality in the demobilization process. No consensus existed on the size of the future Regular Army establishment within the Defense Department, let alone between the executive and legislative branches of the U.S. government. President Truman's lifelong distrust of professional officers would have prevented him from giving the Joint Staff a considered hearing even if they had spoken with one voice. Finally, army leaders themselves were for long periods distracted by the interservice conflicts that were inflamed rather than reduced by the creation of the Defense Department. Only the growing challenges of the Cold War coupled with the creation of the North Atlantic Treaty Organization and gradual rehabilitation of former enemies allowed officers at the highest levels to redirect their energies toward rebuilding and sustaining combat readiness. What they found was an organization that had already begun at lower levels to address a growing gap between stated national strategic goals and the army's ability to achieve them.

3

The Bumpy Road from Rhetoric to Readiness

IN the spring of 1949 the U.S. Army's inspector general, Maj. Gen. Louis A. Craig, visited Eighth Army to check its state of training. In a subsequent report to Bradley, Craig identified significant shortfalls in Eighth Army's readiness. Noting a general lack of skill on the part of junior soldiers, Craig laid some of the blame on the replacement training system and rated divisional readiness as low. However, he reserved the bulk of his criticism for officer leadership, not soldier proficiency. Many officers with whom he spoke felt that they had been abandoned, a feeling reinforced by the scattering of stations across Japan, and some felt little urgency to implement training programs. Drawdown-induced tensions between Regular and Reserve officers threatened to derail any attempt to build readiness. Reserve officers on active duty in combat arms units believed they were denied the same opportunities for advancement as their Regular Army brethren. Their voiced resentments appeared to Craig as manifestations of a lost professionalism or worse. Moreover, the IG found that service units in particular were blissfully ignorant of even the rudiments of military training. In view of these problems, it is not surprising that Craig took issue with FECOM's adoption of a forty-hour training week when so much work needed to be done.[1]

In an attempt to repair the political damage Craig's report would do to MacArthur's reputation, Maj. Gen. Edward M. Almond wrote a rebuttal to his friend Maj. Gen. Harold R. Bull, the director of organization and training on the Army Staff. Addressing his letter "Dear Pinky," Almond quoted recent guidance from the Department of the Army regarding adoption of a forty-hour work week over five or five and a half days, and again cited the low AGCT scores of "an extremely high percentage" of recent replacements as an obstacle to training progression. Almond made no mention of the other shortcomings identified by Craig in his report.[2]

Almond would have better served his boss by forwarding to Bull a copy of Walker's Training Directive Number Four. Eighth Army's training guidance for the coming year provided detailed instructions for the training of both maneuver and support units. Alternately, he could have included the summary report compiled by a member of the FECOM G-3 staff concerning a tactical demonstration conducted on June 17, 1949, by the 1st Cavalry Division. This report outlined the short-term problems incurred by the leveling of units in preparation for Constant Flow, which in turn "tended to level off training, putting those battalions which were well along in training back into basic and small unit" phases of training. The demonstration unit, the 8th Cavalry Regiment, had previously spent four weeks at the maneuver training area at Camp McNair on the slopes of Mount Fuji concentrating on squad and platoon collective tasks. The observer reported good control of squads, adequate use of indirect fires, and high soldier enthusiasm. The report recommended additional training on the use of cover and concealment and on better coordination of infantry and armor units during offensive operations.[3]

This report underlined the effects of failing to provide branch-specific training to new recruits prior to their arrival in the Far East. Although OCAFF acknowledged this shortcoming, it was not corrected until July 1950. Until then it was the responsibility of the gaining unit to provide any individual specialized training required for job performance as well as to integrate the new soldier into his unit as a member of a team. Individuals trained at the replacement centers in the United States received no exposure to advanced subjects even under the revised fourteen-week program. Basic training as then conducted was designed "to give an adequate foundation on which to build individual and unit branch training." This limited scope sought only to develop "willing obedience" and "soldierly qualities" in the recruit.[4] The actual training and certification of soldiers in particular military occupational specialties was left to the unit. This outlook placed a greater burden on units than on the training centers. The centers could focus all efforts on the initial transformation from civilian to soldier, while units were obliged to meet three simultaneous objectives: "first, to teach individuals how teamwork produces an effective combat unit; second, to develop cadres on which fighting units can be built; third, to produce in minimum time, smooth working units which are ready for combat."[5]

Such a system presupposed a lengthy period of mobilization following any outbreak of war, during which mobilized reservists would make up any personnel shortfalls in the regular force. It also reflected the inefficient division of training responsibilities between the Army Staff's Directorate of Organization and Training (DOT) and the Army Field Forces (AFF). According to the DOT's Training Circular Number 7, *Army Training*, the director of organization and training retained overall responsibility for training policy while AFF was limited to a supervisory role. The growing gulf between Army Staff and AFF conceptions of the purpose of basic training can be seen by comparing the two agencies' official statements. Training Circular Number 7 envisioned a generic unit training regimen in which no particular subject or task received more emphasis than others. Moreover, combat effectiveness was not a goal of this program. In order, its priorities were leadership, discipline, appearance and conduct, and maintenance and supply economy. By contrast, OCAFF believed that basic training and all individual training "has two purposes: first, to teach men to fight; and second, to teach men to instruct others how to fight." A September 1949 clarification of the inspection function of AFF failed to rectify the basic issue of control over training. Thus, units were left to their own devices in reconciling the gap between low soldier proficiency upon arrival from the replacement centers and the critical focus of inspectors from OCAFF. Some commands established their own consolidated basic training commands, such as the 7720th Replacement Training Depot at Marburg, Germany, and the 5th Regimental Combat Team Provisional Training Company at Schofield Barracks, Territory of Hawaii.[6] In contrast to this approach, General Walker looked to the World War II mobilization experience as his guide.

Through Training Directive Number Four, Walker explicitly sought to return to the wartime model of unit-based training with which he was most familiar. To maximize the effectiveness of this program, division commanders were ordered to enroll all replacements who had arrived in the Far East within the last twelve months in regiment-operated basic training programs. At the end of this phase, commanders were expected to report completion by all enlisted personnel of AFF Mobilization Training Plan 21-1 as well as certification of a sufficient number of NCO instructors to train personnel on MOS-specific individual and small-unit collective training tasks directly related to wartime requirements. The primary goal of this second phase was the creation of "smooth working squads, platoons, and companies which are ready for combat in the minimum time." The function of training in the third phase envisioned the combination of well-trained squads, platoons, and companies "into coordinated battalion and regimental combat teams capable of effective use of any or all types of weapons or equipment available . . . and to provide training in tactical and logistical functions under simulated combat conditions by means of field exercises and training tests."[7]

The progressive training plan envisioned by Training Directive Number Four deviated somewhat from the wartime model. In the wartime mobilization period, AGF had expected the entire training cycle to last no more than twelve months. Walker relaxed this timetable for Training Directive Number Four, directing only that readiness be certified by specific dates, December 1950 in the case of division-level proficiency. Corps commanders were free to repeat training at the battalion and regimental level as frequently "as deemed necessary to qualify units to accomplish training objectives set forth" in the directive.[8] This latitude ensured that commanders would not feel rushed to push their units through "gates" simply to meet deadlines, but rather would feel free to fail units that demonstrably were not ready to progress to higher levels of training.

Concurrently, Walker directed that subordinate commanders conduct an "overhead inventory" of service unit requirements. Doing so allowed the Eighth Army G-1 to eliminate wasteful diversions of manpower by establishing provisional service companies "containing Engineer, Signal, and MP cells, within spaces available to Eighth Army, for each of the 19 tactical posts, camps, and stations in Eighth Army." To the various infantry unit commanders, this meant official support for training all assigned infantrymen as infantrymen. Though isolated special platoons remained, the majority of men previously serving as *ad hoc* truck drivers, military policemen, and maintenance and repair men could now be reintegrated into combat formations. Training Directive Number Four facilitated this transition by allowing for contract civilian labor "to relieve troops of housekeeping details" wherever practicable. Walker also ordered commanders to minimize the impact of "necessary fatigue and administration" duties in order to maximize attendance at training events. These measures reflected statements made during an Eighth Army staff conference in March of 1949 acknowledging that "the depleting of combat units by special duty assignments and overhead activities is an insidious impediment to training . . . [and] must be kept to an absolute minimum." Even soldiers afflicted with venereal diseases, heretofore confined prior to disciplinary action, would now participate in training as fully as their medical condition allowed.[9] A subsequent Far East Command Headquarters clarification of the training policy ordered commanders at all levels to continuously reevaluate their Occupation missions to "reduce to the absolute minimum" the number of military forces engaged in noncombat training tasks and further directed that "no combat-type unit will be assigned, other than temporarily, missions incompatible with its final objective of becoming an effective part of the next higher combat team."[10]

In addition to lobbying successfully for an extension of basic training, AFF won support for changes to the manner in which major commands reported their readiness to the Army Staff. Prior to publication of General Collins's memorandum codifying the supervisory functions of AFF, units outside the United States had no requirement to report their readiness. Units in the Zone of the Interior did report their training status, but to the Comptroller of the Army, not to either the G-3's Director of Organization and Training or to AFF. By December 1949 OCAFF had begun drafting a new strength and readiness report. The AFF historian believed the new report "constitute[d] a complementary sphere of activity to OCAFF's development of a comprehensive system of inspections." This new report was just being studied by the Army Staff when the Korean War broke out in June 1950.[11]

Eighth Army anticipated this requirement by over a year. On June 22, 1949, General Walker ordered all subordinate units of the Eighth Army to submit regular combat effectiveness reports.[12] These provided higher unit commanders with a snapshot assessment of subordinate unit readiness. Submitted quarterly, reporting units provided details of training activities, personnel strengths, and equipment readiness and serviceability and also provided feedback regarding hindrances to effective training and commanders' assessments of unit morale. These reports provided a framework for assessing unit progress toward readiness as it was understood at the time, unfiltered by the later experience of combat in Korea. The reports cumulatively show units proceeding, albeit fitfully, along a prescribed path toward a goal that many commanders as well as individual soldiers eagerly embraced as an alternative to the postwar constabulary mission. They also bear an unmistakable similarity to the operational readiness report adopted by OCAFF in 1950.[13] Far from resting on its Occupation laurels as so many of its detractors have claimed, Eighth Army demonstrably led the U.S. Army in reaching more realistic assessments of unit readiness and potential combat effectiveness.

Career Management and the Training Program

Just as Eighth Army began its training program in earnest, other developments within the Army Staff threatened its potential effectiveness. Although not part of the Army Reorganization Act of 1950, concurrently enacted career management policies reflected desires by senior leaders to avoid forever a return to the "many outmoded provisions, long since discarded" of the interwar years. Some of the proposed revisions proved beneficial, while others clearly detracted from organizational effectiveness by valuing bureaucratic efficiency over unit readiness.[14] They illustrate how deeply the War Department's experience with operational research during World War II had affected the middle ranks of the officer corps, leading many logisticians and personnel specialists to place greater faith in standardization and templates at the expense of common sense and previous experience. These reforms originated in a desire to avoid a return to a pre-1941 centralized and stratified structure that was not amenable to "immediate expansion and instant readiness for combat—defensive or offensive." They also reflected a general trend in the U.S. Army toward improving readiness. Proponents of centrally directed career management envisioned the peacetime training of leaders who in an emergency could be "advanced in accordance with a sound plan to positions of vastly expanded responsibility and authority." In practice, however, much of what was implemented removed discretionary promotion and assignment authority from local commanders and placed it in the hands of the G-1 staff in Washington, D.C., which simplistically equated institutional education and command assignments as interchangeable components of professional development without regard for the effects of a "ticket-punching mentality" on unit effectiveness.[15]

Beginning with fiscal year 1949, the Department of the Army applied its Career Guidance Program to the NCO and warrant officer corps. The G-1 staff expected the new program would facilitate the creation of "a broadly qualified well-rounded noncommissioned and warrant officer corps which in time of emergency will provide trained cadre for mobilization" and expansion of the force. Conceptually, career management meant that enlisted soldiers would move along a prescribed assignment path designed to impart technical proficiency across a wide range of skills within a clearly defined career field. Proficiency exams would measure not just readiness for promotion, but also whether a soldier retained his current rank if he failed to continue advancing. Six months after implementation of proficiency-based promotions, all enlisted soldiers and warrant officers would be required to pass the MOS competency exam for their current grade. Those who failed this exam would be reduced one grade and be required to pass the proficiency test for that lower grade within another six months. The seven-tier enlisted pay grade structure remained intact, but technical specialist designations disappeared. Those soldiers rated as technicians under the old system often suffered reductions in rank and pay under the automatic conversion to the new rank hierarchy.[16]

Despite these short-term frustrations, rationalization of enlisted promotions introduced a measure of stability within the infantry regiments owing to an official emphasis on "systematic and progressive" assignments in order to provide "continuous opportunities to qualify for advancement." From their first days in uniform, soldiers classified as infantrymen now had a clear understanding of the requirements for advancement. Soldiers who mastered the basics of infantry tactics and weapons became eligible for promotion to sergeant after passing the required proficiency exam and could expect to wear sergeants' stripes "far more rapidly than in the old Regular Army." The new program met with the cautious approval of the editors of *Infantry Journal*. Their editorial for February 1948 expressed the hope that the shift to merit-based promotions would create a climate in which "the Army [would] maintain an unceasing watch for the inept and rid itself [of] the incompetent and the inept."[17] In practice, however, the Career Guidance Program meant that unit rosters carried the names of senior NCOs nominally filling leadership positions within platoons and companies but actually performing duties at headquarters staffs, division-operated schools, or other locations. Such duties may have increased an NCO's promotion potential, but it also kept many qualified NCOs from interacting with younger soldiers. It also prevented units from receiving additional qualified noncommissioned officers to replace them, since the replacement system was a zero-sum process. Thus, many units in the Eighth Army could not fully exploit the training skills and combat experience possessed by diverted NCOs and required junior NCOs or even privates to execute leadership duties beyond their experience or training. Moreover, few of these "borrowed" soldiers returned to their parent organizations when war broke out in June 1950. The implications of a lack of leadership depth at the small-unit level in combat went unaddressed even in otherwise combat-focused units like the 25th Infantry Division.

Old soldiers were quick to criticize the new program. One company first sergeant, who held a reserve commission and had commanded a tank company during World War II, lamented the perceived injustices of the new system, which seemed to value education over ability and duty variation over unit cohesion. As he recounted, a visit from a personnel classification specialist meant that "the next thing the company commander knows one of his good platoon sergeants is up in headquarters turning the mimeograph machine." He went on to argue that the spike in discipline problems in the post-1945 army resulted from too few sergeants with the ability to "make a certain number of bull-headed privates see things the Army way." In a lively rebuttal, a G-1 staff officer explained that "the Classification system was designed to inventory the Army's manpower resources so that they could be used as needed—or trained for use if they didn't possess the required skills." He ended poorly, however, using a typically bureaucratic argument that the U.S. Army's personnel problems resulted not from an out-of-touch staff but from "the failures of commanders to understand and use [the classification system properly]."[18]

The new one-size-fits-all approach to personnel management worked even less well when applied to officers for fiscal year 1950. Revisions to officer assignment policies resulted in part from changes in how the Army promoted and eliminated officers. Among other changes, the Officer Personnel Act of 1947 implemented automatic promotions for company and field grade officers based on time in service and eliminated commissioning officers into a specific arm or service. Henceforth, "officers will be appointed in the Regular army without reference to branch. . . . Officers will be members of the arms or services by virtue of assignment, not appointment."[19] Elimination of branch-specific appointments was a logical prerequisite of a centralized officer assignment program. Originally intended as an oversight mechanism for use by the various branches, career management acquired a reputation as a vehicle to correct perceived promotion discrepancies between combat arms officers and those of the support branches. The director of the agency responsible for this program envisioned "a certain degree of specialization based on previous experience" unconstrained by considerations (such as branch-specific training) that would limit the assignment of any officer "to perform [only those] tasks appropriate to their grade and experience." Moreover, the Career Management Branch within the Department of the Army reserved the right to intervene on behalf of officers "who fail to receive appropriate assignments" that would facilitate career progression.[20] This outlook rejected the logic of branch-based consecutive assignments in favor of "substitut[ing] greater opportunities for capable officers to gain wider experience in broad command, staff, and technical duties." The most insidious result of this program was the installation of unqualified, overage, or even physically infirm officers as infantry and artillery battalion or regimental commanders as rewards for previous service. Many of these officers spent World War II as technical or administrative specialists far from the front lines and assumed their postwar commands with no combat experience, let alone experience in preparing units for war. Senior observers in FECOM alerted AFF to the problem in the fall of 1949, noting that "certain officers with a directed MOS for command duty arrive in FEC after long periods of other than command duty covering both war and postwar experience. Certain of these officers display a 'rustiness' in matters pertaining to command duty and training experience which . . . reflects in the progress of their units."[21]

OCAFF inspectors agreed with this assessment and reported to Gen. Mark Clark, the commanding general of AFF, that Eighth Army required additional infusions of competent leadership at the regimental level and below.[22] A subsequent inspection team amplified earlier criticisms in light of experiences in Korea less than a year later: "The detrimental effect of the career [management] program on combat efficiency is an inescapable corollary of the program as a whole, which seeks, by variations in assignment, to produce well-rounded and versatile officers. It is essential that current officer assignment procedures be modified to the extent necessary to provide our key combat units with officers trained or experienced" in leading troops in combat at the battalion and regimental level. This observer mission recommended the complete suspension of career management "for the duration" of the war in Korea and a revision of assignment practices before reimplementation in order to allow repetitive tours.[23]

The U.S. Army G-1's staff reacted defensively to such charges, vividly demonstrating the compartmentalized nature of policy development on the Army Staff in the late 1940s. In a letter to the army's G-3, Col. E. A. Chazal of the G-1 staff defended the systematic rotation of officers into command positions for which they were demonstrably unqualified by training or experience: "Present assignment policies are sound. . . . [Career management for officers] requires that officers be assigned to duties commensurate with their grades and in accordance with [their] need for particular training as indicated by their career patterns. . . . *It would be injudicious to restrict command assignments to trained or experienced officers* . . . [since that would] stagnate the progress of younger officers."[24]

Recognizing the futility of open resistance to career management, the Infantry School at Fort Benning, Georgia, sought to mitigate the officer assignment program's most deleterious effects. In March 1950 the Chief of Infantry directed the creation of a new course designed to "bring the upper brackets of field-grade officers up to date" regarding training and operations. School officials hoped to "reblue" senior officers (colonels and lieutenant colonels) "who have been away from troop duty for a long time . . . before going on troop duty with a directed MOS of 1542 (unit commander)."[25] Unfortunately, the outbreak of war in June 1950 prevented the new program from influencing readiness in any command. In retrospect, the assignment of patently unqualified officers to maneuver unit command billets for their retirement tour must be seen as one of the single most damaging policies implemented by the U.S. Army between 1945 and 1950.

Equipment Readiness

If the army could at times be its own worst enemy concerning personnel stability, it definitely proved itself capable of achieving significant results with virtually no new obligated funding for procurement in the years following World War II. The huge equipment surplus left over from the war gave the Truman administration and the army the confidence to limit procurement in the postwar years to food and medicine. Even before Japan surrendered, U.S. industry had begun scaling back its output of war material, and FECOM received no new tanks after September 2, 1945. And in fact, new procurement should not have been necessary. Sufficient stocks of all types had arrived in the Pacific Theater before V-J Day to sustain a credible ground force for several years. And yet, by 1950 equipment shortages covered the entire spectrum of items from vehicles to weapons to repair parts to even uniforms and boots in some units.[26]

Postwar demobilization practices lay at the heart of Eighth Army's equipment readiness in 1950. As previously noted, logistics units suffered debilitating losses of trained personnel upon the conclusion of hostilities, and there simply weren't enough soldiers to collect, transport, inventory, store, and maintain the hundreds of tons of military equipment purchased for the Pacific war. The tremendous costs anticipated for recovery of war material from depots scattered on islands across the Pacific Ocean further reduced enthusiasm for any systematic attempt to preserve military equipment. As a result, in the two years following V-J Day, many of the army's supply depots were either abandoned or systematically dismantled in accordance with the provisions of the 1944 Surplus Property Act.[27] Construction material and vehicles made their way to China, the Philippines, and other Pacific Rim governments in exchange for small fractions of their real value. Other materials were simply dumped into the sea. The elimination of stocks at Logistics Base Buttons in the New Hebrides through creation of an underwater reef of "jeeps, six-wheel drive trucks, bulldozers, semi-trailers, fork lifts, tractors, bound sheets of corrugated iron, unopened boxes of clothing, and cases of Coca-Cola" was by no means unique.[28] Many depots were created for campaigns that never occurred; their stocks sat unused because it was "clearly uneconomical to use second-hand [sic] equipment and material . . . when new material was available," if only because of the time and cost involved in loading and unloading of cargo.[29] In 1946 Congress transferred control of overseas stocks of surplus material from the War Department to the Department of State. The intent of this legislation was to improve U.S. access to foreign universities by trading surplus material for foreign currency credits that could be applied to tuition expenses.[30] Other amendments to the Surplus Act authorized owning agencies to dispose of property to local governments, private individuals, and veterans. The multifaceted disposal program depleted the force's inventory of serviceable goods in a relatively short period of time.

Recognizing an impending crisis, FECOM logisticians received authorization from General MacArthur to implement Operation Roll-Up in mid-1947. Operation Roll-Up collected vehicles, weapons, ammunition, spare parts inventories, tools, clothing, and communications equipment from throughout the Pacific, refurbished and repackaged these items, and then either stored or reissued them. By early 1950 Roll-Up was a major operation, responsible for processing "4,000 engines, 3,000 transmissions, 2,800 transfer cases, 5,875 axles, 11,500 steering gears, . . . 1,900 trucks, 100 sedans, 5,000 batteries [and] 20,000 tires."[31] In addition to providing much-needed equipment to units heavily committed first to Occupation duties and then to training, it also provided the means by which Japanese workers could acquire skills directly applicable to an economic recovery. Indeed, the program could not have succeeded without the use of Japanese labor, owing to the severe shortage of trained specialists within the U.S. Army. Moreover, the use of Japanese workers supervised by a small American staff enhanced the fiscal advantages of the program, since the cost of a uniformed American technician far exceeded that of a Japanese industrial worker. As Gen. Urban Niblo, the FECOM ordnance officer, reported in May 1950, "By rebuilding our vehicles in Japan with Japanese facilities and labor and American supervision and know-how, we save one-fourth the cost, if the vehicles were rebuilt in the United States. When we add in the cost of shipping these vehicles from the Zone of the Interior to the savings in rebuild costs, the effectiveness of the program becomes even more apparent."[32]

Operation Roll-Up became a model for other U.S. Army overseas commands as they struggled with barebones budgets in the late 1940s. Not surprisingly the most successful copycat scheme was the European Command's Triple-R [Rebuild, Reclaim, and Repair] program. Like Roll-Up, Triple-R relied on German labor under U.S. Army supervision and used preexisting industrial facilities. From April 1947 until October 1949, Triple-R refurbished 38,000 vehicles, 300,000 tires, and thousands of tons of engines, tools, spare parts, and uniforms. In all, equipment valued at $220,000,000 in postwar appropriations estimates was returned to service at a cost of only $45,000,000.[33]

Although not an unqualified success, Operation Roll-Up laid the foundation upon which Japanese industry quickly expanded to support major United Nations combat operations in Korea. The most tangible benefit of Roll-Up was the renovation of large amounts of combat equipment, items that in 1950 were "in substantially better condition than would otherwise have been the case." As one veteran directly involved in Roll-Up recalled, "Upon complet[ion of] repair of the vehicles, [they] were issued the same as new, including new paint jobs."[34] Already in 1948, the Sugita Ordnance Plant was rebuilding an average of twenty-five Jeep engines each day, while a floating rubber reclamation effort called the Tire Barge produced seventy recapped tires daily. An officer who served in the 64th Field Artillery Battalion stated that when his unit began training in earnest in 1949, some of the howitzers and other equipment were still coated with Cosmoline applied by Roll-Up technicians after completion of the rebuild process. Moreover, although the vast majority of the equipment in his battery had seen combat service, it was still in good shape, and there were "plenty of parts locally" for maintenance purposes.[35]

Unfortunately, this was not a universal experience. A mortarman from C Company, 21st Infantry Regiment, stated that Task Force Smith owed its defeat to poor equipment readiness, not a lack of training. "Under training was not the problem. It was the equipment we had. I was in the mortar section, [and] after the second or third round [fired on July 5, 1950] the base plate broke." Retired Col. Carl F. Bernard, in July 1950 a lieutenant in the 21st Infantry who fought with Task Force Smith, remembered similar problems: "Many weapons had been condemned as 'unfit for combat' by our division ordnance inspectors. One example: a sergeant and I had taught a class on flame-throwers the month before we debarked for Korea, but we had to cannibalize all eight weapons in the Regiment to get two that worked. All had been used hard by the [50]3rd Parachute Infantry Regiment on Corregidor five years earlier."[36] A soldier levied from the 7th Infantry Division to fill up the 25th Infantry Division reported to his new unit with his 7th Division-issued rifle. "About a year earlier [while still assigned to F Company, 32nd Infantry Regiment] he had paid an ordnance sergeant $5.00 for a new rifle barrel but [the NCO] installed it in a dim light and screwed it up" so that the front sight post was ten degrees off center. Another 7th Division veteran recalled that when he arrived in Japan in 1949, the weapons available for replacements "were in bad shape. Most of the rifles were worn out junk the 11th A/B [11th Airborne Division] left behind." Clearly there were limits to what the reclamation effort could do in terms of supplying the needs of a modern army training for high intensity conflict. Moreover, these effects lasted the duration of the Korean War. Upon surveying his division after thirty days in command in April 1953, Maj. Gen. Arthur Trudeau of the 7th Infantry Division declared that most of his vehicle fleet had reached the limits of rebuild life and could not support mobile offensive operations.[37]

However, arguments blaming the soldiers of Eighth Army for failing to maintain their equipment are simply not valid. Eighth Army's poor equipment readiness resulted directly from the failure of the Truman administration in general and the army's leaders in particular to provide adequate funds for research, development, and acquisition or maintenance of all types of material in the postwar period. The dependence upon Japanese labor to make up for American military personnel shortfalls within maintenance units meant that when those units deployed either for training or for combat in Korea, their ability to accomplish their wartime mission became problematic, since the Japanese workers stayed behind. Even when such units remained in their normal facilities, the workload was "far in excess in comparison to the amount of mechanics authorized by TO&E."[38] American soldiers and officers, however, made the best of a poor situation while hoping for the best. As the FECOM G-4 reported, "The serious implications of committing troops to combat with inadequate service support with resultant reduced combat efficiency and increased consumption of material (through inability to maintain or evacuate and repair) were recognized and accepted in the same manner as was the commitment to combat of regiments lacking battalions."[39] In other words, officers and soldiers in the field recognized that they had been given a mission for which the troop-to-task equations had not been computed properly, but they recognized that they had no recourse but to execute that mission to the best of their ability, in hopes their senior leaders would find a solution. Instead, the Joint Chiefs meekly submitted to further budget cuts for fiscal year 1951 in the mistaken belief that the U.S. economy could not support greater outlays for national defense.

Physical Fitness

Many discussions of combat in Korea characterize American soldiers as physically weak and "roadbound." These are actually two distinct criticisms. The second condition resulted from doctrinal changes made by U.S. Army leaders after studying their experience in World War II. The first relates only distantly to doctrine and is of questionable veracity. Nevertheless, historians and soldiers have for decades blamed "easy Occupation life" for supposedly sapping the stamina from the men of Eighth Army. Such arguments rest on one of two assumptions: either every soldier arrived in Japan at the peak of physical condition and lost it during the daily execution of Occupation duties, or the force failed to raise the physical condition of the men in its charge to minimum requirements and consequently left them unprepared for the rigors of combat. In fact, neither assumption is valid.

During World War II, almost 18 million military-age males were examined for possible induction into the armed services. Of these, nearly seven million were rejected as unfit. Approximately 0.1% of these rejections resulted from dental problems deemed too severe to repair. Another 4.8% of white examinees were rejected for "psychoneurotic disorders."[40] The other 95% failed to meet the minimum musculoskeletal physical health standards stipulated by the Selective Service Act of 1940. Many rejected men suffered from defects caused by nutritional deficiencies or poor medical care during the Great Depression. The soldiers inducted into the military between 1945 and 1950 had all likewise lived through the Depression. The fact that demographically many of the army's postwar enlisted men came from economically depressed areas of the United States calls into question the charge that soft Occupation duties ruined the physical hardiness of otherwise healthy young men. More likely, disadvantaged youths identified military service as a way to improve their physical and economic health simultaneously. Moreover, as during World War II, the number of marginally qualified men who were accepted for service fluctuated on a monthly basis. Draft quotas were levied according to the number of fully qualified men who earned service deferments in order to attend college. As the Joint Chiefs found to their chagrin, the incentive for healthy middle-class youths to enlist disappeared once Selective Service was allowed to lapse in 1947. As a result, relatively few of the men who entered the ranks in the late 1940s were high school all-American athletes.

Questions about the general fitness of American youths had already surfaced in the mid-1940s during debates on the virtues of Universal Military Training (UMT). In 1943, the Chief of Athletics and Recreation of the Services Division of the U.S. Army painted an uninspiring picture of American manhood at the War Fitness Conference: "Our physical [education] programs in high schools have been a miserable failure.... Many of our boys have perished because of the accumulation of fatigue, the lack of endurance, stamina, and certain abilities.... Physical education through play must be discarded and a more rugged program substituted."[41] In 1947 Bernard Brodie estimated the total number of physically fit males aged eighteen to twenty-five at about 6,800,000. But because so many of the upper-age cohorts had already seen service in World War II, there was a dangerous dearth of manpower capable of meeting the physical standards for induction into the military. UMT would ameliorate this situation by providing both instruction on physical education and practical application through conditioning programs and athletics. In addition, trainees would experience "outdoor life, good food, complete sanitation"—the latter two items presumably lacking in the homes of many potential inductees. Public support for UMT echoed this argument. One high school principal lamented the public school system's inability to affect public health. In his view, "a year of training under Army methods, for boys around 18 or 19 years of age, will do more than twelve years of public school patty-cake physical education."[42] Congress' failure to enact UMT meant that the potential second- and third-order health benefits of the program never advanced beyond conjecture.

Even if few of the recruits in the late 1940s were in peak physical condition, it is simplistic to blame the service for failing to improve their overall fitness. Army leaders knew the value of physical conditioning and advocated a progressive physical training program to raise and maintain the strength and stamina of its soldiers. Physiological studies conducted on Army Air Forces cadets in 1941 revealed that although an eight-week conditioning program produced significant improvements in the subjects' physiques, failure to continue the program beyond the study period soon eliminated any benefits gained. These findings corroborated earlier studies of "substandard" conscripts in Europe before World War II, aged sixteen to twenty-one, that demonstrated the potential of even a moderate exercise regimen to increase overall fitness when properly incorporated into a soldier's lifestyle. After World War II, however, basic training became progressively shorter because of the increased need for individual replacements during demobilization. Recruits who might have benefited from the increased physical activity at the replacement training centers under the wartime fourteen-week program were, after undergoing the post-1945 eight-week program, "not sufficiently indoctrinated to withstand the inactive period of pipeline experience [that is, the period between leaving basic training and reporting for duty in Japan] and had lost much of the benefit of basic training before arriving in the Far East Command."[43]

This was hardly the fault of the army, however. Army doctrine for physical training in 1950 aimed to produce "teamwork, aggressiveness, confidence, resourcefulness, a will to win, unit solidarity, and the ability to think and act quickly under pressure." Furthermore, the manual's authors recognized that postwar recruits, accustomed to "the softening influences of our modern machine civilization," would need more emphasis on this aspect of their transition from civilian to soldier than ever before. Included as an appendix was a model conditioning regimen and strength maintenance program for unit commanders to follow. Unfortunately, a significant number of officers in the post-1945 U.S. Army remained skeptical of the value of dedicated physical training. Many believed that physical fitness was a benefit of, not a prerequisite to, realistic combat training. One officer remarked in the pages of *Infantry Journal* that "once a man has been conditioned a sports program will maintain a high enough degree of physical efficiency." The patrician Gen. Maxwell Taylor believed that tennis offered greater benefits in less time than a rigorous and focused physical training program.[44] Nevertheless, enough evidence existed to demonstrate the effectiveness of unit-run fitness programs which deemphasized intramural sports in favor of battle-focused training such as running, calisthenics, and foot marches.

Army physical fitness training doctrine supported those officers who believed that fitness was an organizational imperative and not a personal choice. Since physical training remained the responsibility of the company commander in 1948, Army Field Manual 21–20 laid out in considerable detail the mechanics of increasing individual and unit fitness and the use of testing to measure program effectiveness. By administering a physical fitness test at measured intervals, unit commanders could determine both the immediate fitness level of their soldiers and what intermediate and long-term conditioning goals would be attainable. The five-event test outlined in the field manual stressed the different components of physical fitness to ensure that the scores of soldiers who habitually concentrated on a single aspect (for example, running or weight lifting) would not skew the results for the unit as a whole. Testing was not simply a drill to produce reportable statistics: "The purpose of testing is to find out the condition of the troops and then to do something about the deficiencies revealed." During the fourteen-week basic training program recruits could expect to be tested at least three times, and every twelve to fifteen weeks thereafter. The field manual's authors recommended institution of a physical fitness competition at the regimental level to "stimulate interest in physical fitness and motivate all men to improve their condition." Competition would also facilitate instilling a lifelong interest in physical fitness, a still-evolving concept in the United States in 1950.[45]

American society stood at the junction of two lifestyles in the immediate postwar period. The physically challenging and rather unforgiving environment of the first half of the twentieth century was quickly giving way to one in which physical frailties could be mitigated through labor-saving devices at home and work, by social programs enacted under the New Deal, and through improved medical care (both preventive and curative.) The U.S. Army anticipated this shift in 1946 when it published FM 21–20. However, revolutionary top-down doctrinal change is difficult to accomplish speedily within a large bureaucratic organization. It is possible that many commanders paid only lip service to the ideals of physical fitness training as outlined in the field manual. Recognizing that possibility does not automatically mean that the army itself is culpable in the lowered physical readiness of specific units. Where the army can be faulted is in failing to specify a method whereby commanders could be held accountable for the physical fitness of their units and for not demanding a uniform application of doctrine. There was no regulatory requirement for periodic fitness tests. In the end, company commanders were free to design their own fitness programs with almost no guidance from senior officers. As a result, physical fitness levels varied greatly by division, regiment, and even among companies in the same regiment—not because Occupation life was easy, but because of insufficient understanding and application of the doctrine on the part of unit leaders at every level.

4

The 27th Infantry Regiment, 25th Infantry Division

FORMED in 1901 for service in the Philippines, the 27th Infantry Regiment earned the nickname "Wolfhounds" in 1918. That year the 27th Infantry served as part of the U.S. Siberian Expedition sent to guard the estimated one billion dollars' worth of military supplies sent by the Western Allies to keep Russia fighting Germany in the summer of 1917. With the signing of the Treaty of Brest-Litovsk by the revolutionary government under V. I. Lenin in March 1918, the Allies moved to repossess the aid to prevent its use by the Bolsheviks or the Germans. One of two U.S. regiments sent to Vladivostok, the 27th so tenaciously pursued Bolshevik raiders that a Red Army officer tellingly compared them to the Russian wolfhound, an aggressive animal much favored by the former aristocracy.[1] Based at Schofield Barracks, Territory of Hawaii, in the interwar years, Wolfhounds soldiers led the U.S. Army into World War II by firing at Japanese aircraft on December 7, 1941, from their barracks roof. The regiment landed on Guadalcanal on December 29, 1942, as part of the 25th Division's relief of the 1st Marine Division and fought its way up the Solomon Islands throughout 1943. Refitting in New Zealand, the regiment then sailed for the Philippines, landing on Luzon on January 10, 1945. With the Japanese surrender on September 2, 1945, the regiment became part of the designated Occupation force. First stationed at Kagamigahara Airfield in Gifu Prefecture, in mid-1947 the regiment moved to Osaka and established its home at Camp Sakai on the grounds of the former Japanese Naval College.[2]

CHAPTER 4

Making Men into Soldiers

By mid-1948 the regiment consisted of the regimental headquarters company and a single understrength battalion, a victim of the postwar demobilization process. With the publication of Training Directive Number Four and the implementation of Constant Flow, however, the 27th began filling out its ranks. The 2nd Battalion was reactivated in April 1949, filled out with transfers from the 1st Cavalry Division. Colonel John W. Childs, the regimental commander, designated Company E of the 2nd Battalion as the unit responsible for administering the initial thirteen-week basic training program to all those soldiers transferred from the 1st Cavalry Division with less than one year of service along with all recent replacements. Transferred men possessing significant experience were apportioned to the several companies of the regiment. The initial phases of basic training lasted from late April to mid-June 1949, when the trainees traveled to Anogohara Training Area for field training. After an additional four weeks of instruction and practical exercises, evaluators from the 25th Infantry Division's G-3 staff section assessed the training proficiency of the new recruits in mid-July. After completing these tests, the trainees were then dispersed among the rifle companies of the regiment. All companies then conducted familiarization training and firing for the new men with the .30-caliber light machine gun, M1919A4. Although each platoon was authorized only one light machine gun, this weapon constituted a large percentage of a platoon's firepower. As such, all soldiers were expected to be proficient in maintaining and operating the weapon in order to replace wounded or dead gunners.[3]

The regiment moved to the Eighth Army's largest training area, Fuji-Susono Maneuver Area, in early August. There, the rifle companies conducted initial training for all men in squad and platoon tactics and continued to train new men on the light machine gun. In addition, the rifle companies' 60-mm mortar sections, the headquarters company's 81-mm mortar platoons, and the regimental heavy mortar company's 4.2-inch mortar platoons conducted gunners' proficiency training and examinations. Just before returning to the regimental base at Camp Sakai, elements of the regiment and its supporting artillery unit, the 8th Field Artillery Battalion, conducted a combined-arms live-fire demonstration to "acquaint new members of the regiment with the amount and effect of concentrated fire of an Infantry Regiment."[4]

Although the regiment returned to Camp Sakai at the conclusion of the firepower demonstration, training did not cease. Soldiers new and old were cross-trained in all individual and crew-served weapons, and the heavy weapons companies (D and H) conducted "crew drills day in and day out." The new men, now thoroughly integrated into their units, faced one final individual task before collective training could begin. Advanced marksmanship instruction took place at Camp Sakai in early September along with continued training in rifle squad battle drills.[5]

Units placed a great deal of emphasis on weapons training, for obvious reasons. Teaching a man to shoot underscores his transition into the military. Although having previously undergone several hours of instruction on basic rifle marksmanship, becoming an expert with the service rifle involves the mastery of a body of knowledge unique to the military and is accompanied by repetitive drills and rituals even today. Recruits who failed to score the minimum number of hits to rate a qualification badge were known as "bolos" to their peers and received a great deal of extra attention from their NCOs. For this reason, successful attainment of an "expert" rating has long been a significant milestone on the journey from civilian to soldier.[6] The field fire portion of advanced marksmanship training was conducted at Wakayama and Anogohara training areas. The remoteness of these locales further limited the number of potential distractions that might compete for soldiers' attention. Moreover, qualification of two battalions' riflemen would be a time-intensive project based on contemporary training doctrine. Although preliminary instruction for the .30-caliber M1 rifle required only four hours and could be given to groups as large as a company (205 enlisted men, six officers), timed familiarization fire required approximately twenty minutes per rifleman, in addition to time allocated to confirming the weapon's zero. This did not include a minimum of thirty minutes per man for completion of the qualification tables.[7] Thus, even on multistation firing ranges, a battalion would require several days to qualify all its personnel. This allowed soldiers not involved in firing or working on various range details to continue to practice individual, squad, and platoon tactics as time allowed, facilitating the establishment of unit cohesion and proficiency starting at the most basic level.

As a further inducement to use the available time efficiently, units cycled through Shinodayama, Uji, and Aebano Maneuver Areas upon completion of record firing. There, elements of the regimental headquarters staff certified the squads using Army Field Forces Training Test 7–1 as their guide. Among the evaluated tasks in this test, the squad was required to react properly to receiving incoming mortar or artillery fire, destroy a machine gun in a bunker, and assault an enemy position. All three tasks involve a great deal of coordination and teamwork and challenged the leadership abilities of the squad leader as well as the knowledge and skills of the individual soldiers.[8]

As the rifle squads undertook their certification, the Heavy Mortar Company, commanded by 1st Lt. Bertram Bishop, conducted technical training for all mortar crews in the regiment. Bishop already enjoyed a reputation as a man capable of creating good training opportunities with scant resources. Constrained by scheduling conflicts with other mortar and artillery units that did not always permit him to fire his mortars on an impact area, Bishop often took his crews to the seashore. There, the crews fired the mortars into the sea using the jagged Japanese coastline for reference points.[9]

The regimental medical company also participated in the training program. In October the company established a battalion aid station at Shinodayama Training Area for "a demonstration in care and evacuation of wounded men."[10] In addition to observers from the division staff and the 24th and 35th Infantry Regiments, a training inspection team from OCAFF observed this event. After spending more than thirty days reviewing training execution at all levels throughout Japan, the team noted that of the four divisions in Eighth Army, "the training being conducted by this Division [the 25th] is considered the most uniformly effective of any observed. More emphasis [is] placed on practical work than in other units; training aids are used to a greater extent; training is conducted outdoors and in the field to a greater extent; and the disposition of units is such that training can be, and is, supervised closely by the Division Commander and his staff."[11] The inspectors' observations make clear a sustained high level of activity. Moreover, the scale and scope of training indicated decentralized execution, allowing regimental and battalion commanders wide latitude in directing retraining or progression to more advanced tactics. Throughout October the training focus for the 27th Infantry remained at the platoon level, with most companies receiving favorable remarks from the observers for their execution of approach marches, defensive positions, and attacks. Deficiencies were noted, perfection being then as now an unattainable standard. The types of deficiencies, however, indicate problems with leader development that only further training and experience at higher levels of collective training could remedy. As many veterans indicated, the individual soldiers embraced tactical training. "In spite of the attractions [of Japan] . . . the men took tactical training seriously and tried to do the job right."[12]

From November 3 to 24, 1949, the 27th Regiment conducted an intense period of higher level collective training events as envisioned in Training Directive Number Four. Rifle platoon and company tasks for evaluation included occupation of a defensive position, a withdrawal and repositioning during hours of darkness, and a hasty attack in conjunction with tanks as part of a battalion reserve. In addition to unit training, "all units less Medical [C]ompany fired the prescribed rocket launcher course." The culmination of training occurred near the end of the three-week period when both 1st and 2nd Battalions completed three defensive and three attack live-fire exercises.[13]

The 27th Infantry Regiment thus ended 1949 having fulfilled the requirement to complete company-level certification by December 15, 1949. Other units throughout Eighth Army did not meet this deadline, however. As early as mid-September, I Corps staff officers warned that shortages of certain types of ammunition and weapons systems would hamper achievement of training goals by infantry units as well as specialized company/battery level units.[14] Other units in Eighth Army were forced by the exigencies of maneuver area scheduling to invert their training programs and conduct battalion-level training before individual or squad and platoon certification.[15] Responding to the need to increase usable terrain, Eighth Army engineers expanded the Fuji-Susono Maneuver Area in November 1949, effectively combining into one large area the formerly separate I Corps and IX Corps training areas. In addition, Major General William Kean, 25th Infantry Division commander, decided to use Fuji-Susono whenever the division could secure time there, regardless of season. This meant that some units in the division would conduct their training and testing "despite the bitter cold and driving winds encountered there during the winter months." Even as Kean's staff implemented this decision, however, attempts were made to find alternate sites owing to the huge costs involved in moving a regiment to Fuji and back to their base. At $45,000 per round trip per regiment, and based on training conducted thus far, the G-3 and G-4 staff sections estimated it would cost the division in excess of $500,000 for all units to complete the required training—a prohibitive amount. Moreover, Fuji-Susono lay ten hours by rail from the 24th Infantry Regiment, and sixteen hours from the 27th Infantry Regiment as well as division headquarters.[16] All attempts to secure adequate alternatives ultimately proved fruitless, however, and the 25th Division's training remained focused at "Fuji-San."

From Platoon to Battalion Proficiency

The year 1950 opened without any hint of the coming catastrophe in Korea. Service journals concerned themselves with the mundane and ordinary topics of peacetime service. None of the articles in the first three issues of *Military Review* for 1950 made any mention of Korea as a potential theater of operations. *Infantry Journal* ran a prescient article in the January issue describing the Finnish Army's *motti* tactics ("cutting, slicing, and encircling the enemy") that perceptive Eighth Army soldiers would have recognized several months later. The March issue of *Infantry Journal* ran two additional articles that in hindsight proved prophetic. First, Capt. Donald E. Rivette argued for the retention of towed antitank guns on the Table of Organization and Equipment of infantry regiments in the face of superior Soviet armored formations. Second, Col.

John G. Van Houten seconded S. L. A. Marshall's recent arguments about minimizing the load carried in battle by the average infantryman in order to reduce fatigue (and thus fear).[17]

In Japan, the soldiers of the 27th Infantry Regiment packed their bags again in preparation for a crowded training schedule after devoting a portion of their Christmas leave to entertaining local Japanese orphans. In an attempt to maximize the number of training days available to all units, Eighth Army assumed control of all maneuver training areas in Japan large enough to accommodate maneuvers at battalion or higher level. On January 20, 1950, the training section of the Eighth Army's G-3 staff published a comprehensive schedule of all "major field training exercises and combat firing tests to be conducted by Eighth Army units during the first six (6) months of the current calendar year." The 27th Infantry Regiment's itinerary included battalion field exercises at Shinodayama Maneuver Area from January 9 to 30, 1950; battalion field exercises at Aebano Maneuver Area from February 13 to March 27, 1950; battalion combat firing tests from April 10 to 24, 1950, at Fuji-Susono; and regimental combat team exercises from June 5 through 30, 1950, at Fuji-Susono.[18]

Second Battalion moved to train first, since 1st Battalion had spent the week after Christmas 1949 training at Aebano, presumably because no one else wanted it at that time of year. Lieutenant Colonel Harold B. Ayres, after only a month as battalion commander, must have hoped to gain a thorough assessment of his unit's strengths and weaknesses by devoting several days to each of the battalion's principal wartime tasks. After conducting a week of preparatory training at Camp Sakai, the battalion moved to Shinodayama on January 11, 1950. For the next four days 2nd Battalion conducted battalion-level training—most likely starting out slowly to allow Lieutenant Colonel Ayres to explain his objectives and expectations to his subordinates. On January 17, Ayres's battalion conducted a deliberate attack, integrating the fires of Lieutenant Bishop's Heavy Mortar Company into the overall fire support plan. Transitioning to a deliberate defense, the battalion focused on preparation of positions, conducting a counterattack from a defensive position, and conducting a defense in order to delay a superior enemy force.[19]

On January 5, 1950, Lt. Col. Edward Grenelle turned over command of 1st Battalion to Lt. Col. Gilbert J. Check in a traditional ceremony conducted at Camp Sakai. Moving to Anogohara Training Area, 1st Battalion followed a training sequence similar to 2nd Battalion's. From January 14 to 21, 1950, 1st Battalion conducted a deliberate defense and a defense to delay a superior enemy force, using the jeep-mounted regimental intelligence and reconnaissance (I&R) platoon to simulate enemy tanks. From January 21 to 25 the battalion trained on offensive tasks, including a deliberate attack, battalion acting as an advanced guard for the regiment and battalion reserve conducting a counterattack as part of a regimental defense. Training ceased on January 25, 1950, in order to form the battalion as an honor guard for General Collins, then touring the Far East to gauge the progress of combat training and readiness in the infantry divisions.[20]

After a short period of rest and refitting at Camp Sakai, including a regimental parade for Major General Kean, both battalions returned to Shinodayama on 6 and 7 February. For the next sixteen days they trained again on their primary wartime tasks of attack and defense, rotating through Aebano Maneuver Area to conduct exercises with live ammunition. Significantly, both battalions trained to defend as a separate unit as well as to conduct night attacks on fortified positions. In addition, 2nd Battalion practiced operating as a flank guard for the regiment in a retrograde operation.[21]

Observers from the 25th Infantry Division G-3 conducted basic proficiency tests of both battalions at the Fuji-Susono Maneuver Area in March 1950. Moving by rail on 6 March, both battalions began their field exercises with reviews of past training. Eighth Army evaluators observed 1st Battalion on March 12 and 13 and 2nd Battalion on March 19 and 20. Again, the regimental I&R platoon acted as the "enemy" force for both iterations. Apparently giving favorable ratings, Eighth Army evaluators scheduled both units for reinforced battalion combat firing tests, in which the infantry battalions, supported by mortar fires from the Heavy Mortar Company and artillery fires from the 8th Field Artillery Battalion, would certify their proficiency and readiness for combat.[22]

Adjustments and Assessments

On April 3, 1950, Eighth Army published Training Directive Number Five. This directive superseded the previous year's edition but offered little substantive change. The most obvious difference between the two concerned the attention to Occupation duties. Training Directive Number Four had acknowledged the continuing requirement for certain Occupation-driven personnel absences, and subsequent guidance directed "commanders [to] carefully and continually scrutinize occupational duties and other conditions that interfere with training, and . . . reduce or eliminate them whenever possible."[23] The new directive made no mention of Occupation requirements: "Within Eighth Army the training mission has first priority. Duties not authorized in tables of distribution or tables of organization and equipment will be reduced to bare essentials and will be rotated among individuals." For the Eighth Army in Japan, life had a single purpose in 1950: "*To gain and maintain the highest possible state of combat effectiveness.*"[24]

In the Combat Effectiveness Report covering the first quarter of calendar year 1950, Colonel Childs summed up his regiment's training accomplishments thus far: "Battalions completed approximately 75% of battalion-phase testing; reinforced battalions completed preliminary combat firing tests; specialist and technical training [completed] in addition to support missions; assault teams trained with rifle and heavy weapons companies; completed refresher training for replacements." In what may have been a veiled complaint regarding the submission of the still-new Combat Effectiveness Report itself, Childs identified "administrative burden" as the most significant obstacle to training. Using the formula laid out in the previous year's implementing memorandum, Colonel Childs scored the 27th Infantry Regiment at 592 points out of a possible 750, similar to assessments made by the commanders of both the 24th and 35th Infantry Regiments.[25]

Colonel Childs apparently did not consider the training obstacles reported by his two battalion commanders significant enough to forward to his higher headquarters, or else he decided that some of them could not be solved in time to influence the completion of the regiment's training. Lieutenant Colonel Check carefully outlined many of his concerns, mostly regarding the distance and suitability of the training areas frequented by the battalion. He considered Aebano, Anogohara, Shinodayama, and Fuji too remote and lamented the expenditure of time traveling to and from those areas. He also considered both Shinodayama and Uji training areas too small; safety limits at Uji prevented live firing by more than a single squad (eleven men) at one time. Regarding equipment, Check noted that his battalion possessed only two of its authorized four 75-mm recoilless rifles in the heavy weapons company, and none of the rifle companies possessed any of their three authorized 57-mm recoilless rifles. Recoilless rifle sections in the weapons platoons of rifle companies carried the World War II–vintage 2.36-inch rocket launcher in lieu of the more lethal 3.5-inch rocket launcher. Of greater significance than equipment shortages, though Check declined to highlight them, were personnel shortages. He reported a total of 686 enlisted men and 28 officers present for duty of an authorized 858 and 37, respectively. Nearly 60 enlisted men, officially assigned to the battalion, remained absent because of school requirements, confinement on disciplinary charges, illness, or detached duty. Two captains and three lieutenants assigned to the battalion actually worked at 25th Division headquarters, and senior noncommissioned officers executed leadership duties normally carried out by lieutenants in seven platoons throughout the battalion. Lieutenant Colonel Check gave his battalion an overall score of 797 points out of a possible 1000, noting that morale in the battalion was high "owing to the increasing interest of the men in the type of Battalion Team Training they are undergoing

... [and] several new officer replacements whose interest and enthusiasm for their work have assisted in raising the morale of the troops as well as our training standards." Typical of such junior officer enthusiasm are the recollections of Posey L. Starkey, a lieutenant in D Company since July 1949. Starkey found the opportunities at Fuji exhilarating: "We didn't talk about grazing fire—we actually did it. We walked FPL's and drew range cards based on real terrain. And, we were away from the distractions of Sakai and garrison life."[26]

Lieutenant Colonel Ayres's report for 2nd Battalion contrasts sharply with Check's. Identifying only those issues capable of resolution at the regimental level, Ayres noted the shortage of recoilless rifles but cited the "frequent detail of personnel to non-training activities (boards, courts, schools, committees, TDY/DS)" as the most serious obstacle to completion of training. Second Battalion having been reactivated only in March 1949, personnel problems appear to have plagued it for its entire existence prior to the Korean War. With just 664 enlisted soldiers present and 44 others assigned but absent, the battalion lacked 198 authorized soldiers in its ranks. Proportionally, officer shortages exceeded enlisted shortfalls. NCOs filled most platoon leader positions, and lieutenants commanded all companies owing to a shortage of eight captains. Similarly, equipment shortages were more severe than in 1st Battalion, with only one of four 75-mm recoilless rifles on hand (and that one a prototype T21 model), two 60-mm mortars missing, and the ubiquitous 2.36-inch rocket launcher issued in lieu of all individual and crew-served antiarmor weapons in the rifle companies. Still, Ayres noted an improvement in morale, attributing it to the "more active and interesting phase of training, creating more unit identity and teamwork." Indeed, a healthy competitive spirit quickly developed between the two battalions, resulting in near parity for such reportable statistics as expert rifle marksmen and expert mortar and machine gun crews. In addition, both battalions boasted fourteen of fifteen certified platoons and twenty-five of twenty-seven certified squads. In addition to tactical training and weapons proficiency, the two battalions reported 650 and 517 soldiers, respectively, trained for movement by air transport. Surprisingly, however, neither commander presented a laundry list of broken or unserviceable weapons or vehicles. The list compares favorably with a similar operational readiness report for any light infantry battalion in the U.S. Army of the 1990s.[27] Evidently the soldiers found it possible to maintain that equipment they did possess in working order.

April provided little respite from the training schedule for any unit in Eighth Army, and the 27th Infantry typified the experience of the infantry regiments. Of course, not all of the activity occurred in the maneuver areas. On April 8, 1950, Major General Kean held a division review, requiring the presence on parade of every unit in the 25th Infantry Division not actually engaged in testing.[28]

Following this disruption, 1st Battalion and elements of the Heavy Mortar Company moved by rail from Camp Sakai to Fuji-Susono on April 11, 1950. The regimental I&R platoon served as the "aggressor force" for the duration of the testing period. There, in conjunction with elements of the 8th Field Artillery Battalion (simultaneously undergoing its own combat-task certification), 1st Battalion executed its combat firing tests in both offensive and defensive mission scenarios. The battalion received "satisfactory" ratings for each mission and departed for Camp Sakai on April 17, on the same train that brought 2nd Battalion to Fuji-Susono.[29]

Second Battalion failed to meet the standard established by 1st Battalion in the performance of the tests, receiving a "low satisfactory" rating for its performance of the defensive mission and an outright "unsatisfactory" for its conduct of the offensive mission. To compound this black mark on the regiment, no other battalion in the 25th Infantry Division received lower than a "satisfactory" rating on either mission. No documentation detailing the battalion's shortcomings appears to exist, but the failure to meet the established training standard must have been related to the greater personnel shortage in 2nd Battalion, exacerbated by the relatively low level of experience among the assigned officers.[30]

With the 1st Battalion, 35th Infantry, coming into Fuji-Susono for its own tests, 2nd Battalion had no chance to conduct an immediate retest, and the battalion returned to Camp Sakai in preparation for a previously scheduled air transportability exercise. While 2nd Battalion deployed to Itami Air Force Base from May 4 to May 8, 1950, and thence back to Fuji-Susono, the remainder of the regiment reverted to individual task training and small arms qualification at the Wakayama and Shinodayama ranges. Passing both combat firing tests the second time, 2nd Battalion fell into the rotation of units to the rifle ranges beginning May 22, 1950. The regimental headquarters, after conducting a command post exercise on May 18 and 19, returned to Camp Sakai for a regimental parade on May 20, 1950.[31]

Welding the Final Seams

The 27th Infantry conducted decentralized training over the first week of June 1950. Machine gun crews moved to Fuji-Susono by truck to conduct familiarization and qualification firing, while the rifle companies again conducted small arms firing tables and squad maneuver training at Shinodayama. Each battalion also reported conducting a series of foot marches in the vicinity of Camp Sakai. The entire regiment deployed to Fuji-Susono on June 17 and 18 in preparation for the Eighth Army–graded regimental combat team exercises scheduled for June 21 through July 21, 1950.[32] The regiment was in the middle of its evaluation when word came of the North Korean invasion of South Korea.

Few members of the regiment believed war in Korea was imminent, a feeling shared by soldiers throughout the Eighth Army. Even Maj. Gen. William F. Dean, commander of the 24th Infantry Division (and formerly Commanding General, U.S. Army Military Government in Korea) initially believed that the Republic of Korea (ROK) Army would be able to withstand the Communist invasion. However, late on Friday, June 30, 1950, after completing the live-fire portion of the evaluated task, battalion in night defense, the entire regiment received orders to return to the Fuji cantonment area. No explanation was given to the men, "but we knew something was astir." Their suspicions were confirmed the next day when the regiment returned to Camp Sakai without completing the RCT-level evaluation. Orders from Eighth Army to the commanders of the 1st Cavalry Division and the 7th Infantry Division to transfer men to the 24th and 25th Infantry Divisions quickly dispelled any last-minute hopes of sitting out the war.[33] On July 7, 1950, the 27th Infantry moved to Kyushu, staying in barracks formerly occupied by the 24th Division before departing for Korea from the Japanese port of Moji. For the Wolfhounds, the time had come to put into practice what they had learned over the course of the past year.

5

The 31st Infantry Regiment, 7th Infantry Division

THE 31st Infantry Regiment was activated and organized on July 1, 1916, at Manila, Territory of the Philippines. For two years the regiment remained in the Philippines on routine garrison and training duties. In 1918 the regiment joined the 27th Infantry Regiment as part of the American Expeditionary Forces in Siberia and adopted the regimental nickname "Polar Bears." Within a few months the commander of the Siberian Expedition, Maj. Gen. William S. Graves, abandoned the unworkable neutrality policy urged on him by President Wilson and authorized combat operations against the Bolsheviks. The most active fighting for the 31st Infantry occurred in the vicinity of the Suchan coal mines—decisive terrain, since they constituted the region's only source of coal to keep the Trans-Siberian Railway functioning. In forty-two battles and engagements, sixteen Polar Bears officers and soldiers received the Distinguished Service Cross for gallantry in action against Red forces. When American forces withdrew in 1920, the 31st Infantry returned to Manila, where it remained for the next twelve years.

In early 1932 President Hoover ordered American forces to China to protect American lives and property during the "Shanghai Incident." The 31st Infantry arrived in China in February and stayed until July. Although the Polar Bears observed several battles between the Chinese and Japanese, they were never directly engaged. The unit returned to the Philippines following the Song-Hu Armistice signed in May by the Chinese and Japanese governments.[1]

The only Regular Army formation in the Philippines on December 7, 1941, the 31st Infantry initially served as part of Gen. Douglas MacArthur's reserve force. Withdrawing to the Alangan River after the battle of Abucay Hacienda in January 1942, the regiment remained in reserve until April. Just before its final battle the adjutant reported a total effective strength of 160 men of an original 2,100. The majority of these men passed into Japanese captivity when Major General King surrendered the Luzon force on April 9, 1942. The night before, the regimental colors were buried in a field atop Mount Bataan to prevent their capture by the enemy.[2] With General King's surrender the regiment was removed from the active rolls of the U.S. Army.

On January 19, 1946, the army reactivated the 31st Infantry Regiment. Personnel and equipment of the former 184th Infantry Regiment, 40th Infantry Division, formed the nucleus of the unit when the latter unit was mustered out of federal service and its colors returned to the California National Guard. The ceremony took place on the parade ground at Camp Seobingo in Seoul, the headquarters of the 7th Infantry Division. The 31st Infantry became a part of the 7th Infantry Division and spent the next thirty-five months conducting counterguerilla operations along the 38th Parallel. From December 1948 to June 1949 the 7th Division conducted a phased move from Korea to Japan. The 31st Infantry replaced the 187th Glider Infantry Regiment of the 11th Airborne Division, taking over the latter's headquarters at Camp Crawford near Sapporo on the northern island of Hokkaido. Camp Crawford also housed the 7th Infantry Division headquarters, the 57th Field Artillery Battalion (105-mm), and the division's motorized reconnaissance company.[3]

Reconstitution

Personnel policies applied during the drawdown of U.S. troops in Korea meant the regiment arrived in Japan severely understrength. Although still a three-battalion regiment, only the 2nd and 3rd Battalions completed the trip from Seoul to Sapporo; the 1st Battalion remained on Honshu to relieve the 511th Parachute Infantry Regiment of the 11th Airborne Division. Upon the completion of movement from Korea and the establishment of the regimental headquarters at Camp Crawford, the regiment numbered approximately seventy officers and eighteen hundred enlisted men.[4]

Several adjustments in personnel strength and authorizations occurred over the first several months of 1949. First, on February 1, 1949, 1st Battalion was removed from regimental control and established at Hachinoe, Honshu, as a separate unit reporting directly to the division commander. Next, on March 20 the regiment reorganized under the 1948 "N" series Table of Organization and Equipment. The new TO&E eliminated the regimental cannon company and reduced the overall strength of the rifle companies. This allowed for some personnel consolidation but did not bring any unit up to even the reduced authorizations in force at the time. Finally, in May approximately eight hundred replacements reported to the 31st Infantry Regiment. More than 60 percent of these men were intratheater transfers, mostly from the 1st Cavalry Division. The remaining three hundred or so were new recruits. The influx of personnel allowed the regiment to activate the Heavy Mortar Company as well as fill the regimental medical company. Unfortunately, the new body of men reflected an army-wide trend. Few of the transfers were noncommissioned officers; most were first-term enlisted men awaiting completion of their mandatory terms of service.[5]

Chronic shortages of NCOs plagued every unit in the U.S. Army in the late 1940s. For the 7th Infantry Division, however, policies applied when the division moved to Japan exacerbated the problem. Because the move was treated as an administrative transfer, permanent change-of-station policies were applied to individuals, not the division. As a result, rifle companies especially were inadvertently stripped of their most experienced enlisted leaders. "Officers and enlisted men with less than five months' service in [the Far East] at the time of the move were left behind [that is, in Korea to help finish the drawdown of the U.S. military occupation], no consideration whatsoever being given to grade, organization, or job assignment."[6] As a result, when the 31st Infantry Regiment arrived in Japan, it was not a unit. It was a collection of individuals with disparate backgrounds, perspectives, and experiences. To rectify this the leadership of the regiment decided that the early and earnest application of a training program would be the best way to build cohesion and a corporate identity.

Arriving in northern Japan at the beginning of winter, the regiment made cold weather training the first priority. Accordingly, the regiment established a Ski Cadre Instructors' School in Nagano to train unit representatives on tactics, techniques, and procedures for conducting military operations in arctic or subarctic conditions.[7] The graduates of this school returned to their units and provided general instruction regarding winter cross-country movements and outdoor survival. Initial training events were hampered by a shortage of equipment, but by late February the rifle companies from 2nd Battalion had all conducted snowshoe marches in the vicinity of Camp Crawford.[8] In March both 2nd and 3rd Battalions added overnight bivouacs to their cold weather training programs. During these exercises, enlisted soldiers honed their individual navigation skills with compass and map while the battalion leadership conducted a terrain walk of a defensive position. Conspicuously absent was any attempt at collective training at any level.[9]

April 1949 was a transitional month for units across Eighth Army, but especially so for the 31st Infantry Regiment. During this month, 2nd and 3rd Battalions conducted their last basic winter exercises for the year. The emphasis for these exercises lay in operating and sustaining the units under tactical conditions. Battalions established field trains for logistic support, commanders stressed wire and radio communications over the use of runners, and individual units moved by cross-country foot march between training events.[10] Simultaneously, staff officers and NCOs from the G-3 section of the IX Corps staff traveled to Camp Crawford. On April 8 they tested every enlisted man in the regiment using the newly standardized Mobilization Training Plan produced by OCAFF. The results of the dual-format test vividly demonstrated a near universal challenge facing unit commanders in the post-1945 U.S. Army. Although the men did quite well at hands-on proficiency examinations, most scored poorly on the written portion of the exam. As the regimental historian explained in the unit's annual history, the disparity could be "directly attributed to the fact that the average grade completed in school by the men of the regiment was 8.23 years."[11] Such an assessment corresponds exactly to the problems facing the other regiments profiled here. As early as 1947 Eighth Army had required all soldiers to meet minimum educational standards, but the turbulent personnel situation ensured a continual supply of undereducated replacements.[12] The 7th Infantry Division's first training memorandum published in Japan echoed this requirement, mandating a minimum of four hours' instruction each week during the duty day for any soldier unable to read and write at a fifth grade level.[13] Nevertheless, due in no small part to the overall success of the IX Corps tests and the ongoing literacy training program, the Regimental S-3, Lt. Col. Ralph E. Leighton, stated that "the Thirty First Infantry Regiment during the last month has passed the boundary marker. No longer is it a group of individuals wearing as part of their uniforms the crest of a regiment. It is a team. The change has been slow in coming; now that it is here, we are prepared and are ready for any tactical mission that may come."[14] Though clearly an exaggeration, Leighton's boast did acknowledge that the regiment had entered into a new phase and focus of training. Leaving the basic training phase behind them, the Polar Bears now began an intensive period of weapons training.

As stated earlier, weapons training is a significant milestone in the professional development of a soldier. It is a proficiency with weapons that sets a soldier apart from civilians and ultimately is one of a handful of factors that will determine survival or death on the battlefield. Acknowledging this, the 31st Infantry Regiment dedicated a full five weeks in April and May 1949 to weapons familiarization and qualifications training. This period placed a tremendous strain on the lower-level leadership of the regiment. By doctrine, sergeants teach soldiers how to shoot. Although every soldier received some rifle marksmanship training even during the eight-week basic training course, such instruction never obviated the need for reinforcement and further development. Unfortunately, as a result in part of the effects of the NCO Career Guidance

Program, the 31st Infantry still suffered from a chronic shortage of capable noncommissioned officers at the squad and platoon level. To work around this, battalions conducted their preliminary marksmanship instruction (PMI) in large groups using lecture and demonstration rather than by squads under the tutelage of their sergeants. Hands-on training commenced on May 27, 1949, with "landscape firing" using .22-caliber rifles (a cost-saving measure) to reinforce the four fundamentals of marksmanship prior to range firing with military weapons. In addition to this, the new soldiers in the training companies received instruction on all small arms organic to the rifle platoon, including the M1 rifle, the M1911A1 pistol, and the M1918A2 Browning automatic rifle. The men also completed the "A" record firing course for the M1 carbine.[15] Perhaps because of the extra effort made by the leadership involved, only thirty soldiers in the entire regiment failed to qualify with their assigned weapon at the completion of training in June 1949.[16]

Growing Leadership at the Tip of the Spear

Just as the regiment began its transition away from basic training, it received almost eight hundred new soldiers, nearly half of whom still possessed only eight weeks' basic training. Rather than further diffuse the already scarce supply of noncommissioned officers, Col. John D. Miller, regimental commander since March 14, 1949, followed the example set by the Wolfhounds and established two provisional training companies. Although directly contravening guidance from 7th Division headquarters, segregation of the new men made sense.[17] It made the best use of limited training resources and cadre while still allowing the bulk of personnel to progress in their training. It also allowed for the immediate development of a sense of unity and cohesion among the new men as well as creating a "leadership laboratory" for the Regimental Leadership School. The Regimental Leadership School was established at Camp Crawford on February 28, 1949 by acting regimental commander, Lt. Col. Marion W. Schewe. Schewe's decision resulted from guidance issued by Maj. Gen. William F. Dean, commanding general of the 7th Infantry Division during the move from Korea to Japan, who recognized that the shortage of noncommissioned officers posed a potentially crippling problem for the reconstitution of the division. In Training Memorandum Number 1 he urged subordinates to foster and develop junior leaders: "There is a singular opportunity for all ranks to display and exercise sound progressive leadership, not only in the accomplishment of the occupational mission, but in the training mission as well. The outstanding leader will be exemplified by the well trained squad, platoon, company and battalion for which he is responsible."[18]

The initial leadership class numbered thirty-four candidates, of whom all but three completed the course.[19] Expectations that the new school's output would make up the regiment's leadership shortfalls proved short-lived, however. As the months progressed, the focus of the program of instruction shifted from general leadership instruction to an emphasis on squad leader duties and responsibilities. Simultaneously, the school reduced the number of candidates accepted for training, operating on the premise that better results would obtain from "emphasis being placed on developing men who have potential, instead of trying to develop the potentials of the men coming into the school." As an indication of the seriousness with which the regiment's leaders took the school's mission, over 25 percent of enrollees were relieved from the fourth class because of their unwillingness or inability to perform as squad leaders.[20] Clearly, Colonel Miller and his subordinate commanders focused on quality, not quantity, and were willing to accept a lower-than-anticipated output in exchange for long-term benefits to the unit.

Accepting fewer NCO graduates from the leadership school meant that the chain of command within regiment would also have to accept that near-term progress on the training program would necessarily be slow. During June 1949 the regiment's training focused on the first rungs of collective training: training individuals to act as members of squads and crews. The scarcity of trained NCOs and the diversion of the best ones as cadre for the leadership school forced commanders to acknowledge that in many cases the sergeants actually conducting training "did not have the least idea of what they were supposed to do as squad leaders, or indicate that they knew any tactics at all."[21] Battalions implemented their own squad leader training programs to augment the instruction provided at the leadership school, but with minimal success initially. Not until late 1949 did the regiment's monthly summaries indicate that squad leader proficiency had improved to the point that it facilitated higher-level collective training at the platoon, company, and battalion level. Until that time unit commanders endured untrained or unmotivated NCOs or even privates as squad leaders.

The new men assigned to the provisional basic training companies completed their indoctrination and were reassigned throughout the 2nd and 3rd Battalions during June 1949. No sooner had this occurred than a new personnel problem arose: high turnover of the old Korea hands. Already in June the regimental adjutant predicted that the personnel policies that governed the unit's transfer from Korea in late 1948 would come back to haunt the regiment. Departures would continue to increase and "will definitely reach [their] apex sometime toward the last of this year. This will of course present some serious difficulties when the key personnel start leaving the regiment all at one time."[22]

Because the restrictions on reassignment of personnel from Korea to Japan had prevented soldiers with relatively little remaining overseas time from moving with the regiment, most of the personnel who qualified for transfer to Japan became eligible for return to the Zone of the Interior within twelve months of their arrival on Hokkaido. As a result, both noncommissioned officers as well as privates with leadership potential soon began leaving the 31st Infantry Regiment in numbers sufficient to threaten the entire training program.

The situation was alleviated somewhat by the reorganization of the infantry rifle squad. By reducing squads from twelve men to nine, sergeants were no longer stretched as thin as they had been and could devote more time to individuals as well as the group.[23] The bigger problem remained that of NCOs diverted from squad leader or platoon sergeant positions to nonleadership duties because of the new demands of the Career Guidance Program. The Far East Command G-1's rosy assessment of total NCO strength within the command at the end of 1949 did not correspond to reality within the average infantry battalion. While it may have been beneficial to keep personnel transfers to a minimum from a budgetary and administrative perspective, forcing units to keep on their rolls NCOs from whom they received no leadership or training benefit only inhibited the attainment of combat readiness. Moreover, although corporals perform vital work at the squad level, they typically do not possess sufficient experience to function well at higher levels of responsibility, so the aggregate increase in corporals from 6,500 to 18,000 over the course of 1949 meant little.[24] Finally, the scarcity of NCOs across FEC should have impelled strength managers to direct the best quality soldiers to the combat arms units. In reality, soldiers with the highest aptitudes as measured by AGCT score were skimmed off at every level of the replacement process, leaving the least trainable for combat arms battalions. The situation became so intolerable that General Almond felt compelled to intervene. Noting that "the subordinate commands are extremely short of individuals with high mental qualifications and overburdened with those possessing the lowest potential," he prohibited GHQ's staff sections from screening projected replacements and directed that they accept personnel without prior consideration of GCT score or civilian skill.[25] Unfortunately this directive came too late to influence Eighth Army's training programs before the outbreak of the Korean War, and training progression in the 7th Infantry Division continued to suffer from a general lack of effective leadership at the most critical levels.

The months of July and August were devoted to practical applications of squad training. As a component of the first phase of training, General McAuliffe directed that each infantry squad and platoon "be developed into a fighting team capable of operating intelligently and vigorously . . . in the execution of all types of battle missions under varying conditions."[26] For the 31st Infantry Regiment, this meant a series of short field exercises punctuated by battalion-level alerts to train company-level leadership on wartime/emergency tasks. First, all rifle squads in the regiment practiced conducting squad combat firing tests according to the requirements of Army Field Forces Training Test 7–1. This took place over ten days in early August at Shimamatsu Maneuver Area, approximately twenty-five miles south of Camp Crawford, during which time the two battalions established bivouacs under field conditions. The major problems identified by the evaluators from the regimental staff included poor control of movement, an ignorance of how to use terrain effectively during movement, and failure by the leaders to inform soldiers fully of the situation and their responsibilities before mission execution. Second, a series of company-size alerts trained both company and battalion leaders on their particular roles within the overall Eighth Army plans for the defense of Japan. The regimental S-3 expressed satisfaction with the ability of the companies to execute their missions once they arrived at the designated location but identified preexecution coordination of transportation as a subject of concern.[27] By the end of August 1949 all rifle squads had successfully passed the official combat firing tests—by all accounts a minor miracle, given the institutional weakness of the regiment's NCO corps at the time.

Team Building

For three days the Polar Bears stood down from the training program to celebrate their first Organization Day since 1941. Colonel Miller chose "America's Foreign Legion" as the official theme of the thirty-third anniversary celebration, emphasizing the fact that the Polar Bears were the only Regular Army unit never to have served within the continental United States. Moreover, he sought to enhance unit pride by claiming the title "First American Unit in Tokyo" as a result of the regiment's humanitarian deployment to that city from Manila following the 1923 earthquake. He further highlighted the 31st Infantry Regiment's possession of the only "peacetime" battle award ever made—the Yangtze campaign streamer affixed to the regimental colors for service in Shanghai in 1932.[28] Miller's remarks were obviously designed to inculcate a sense of pride in unit among individual soldiers as well as foster a corporate identity among the men as a group. Also, just as in other regiments, intramural competition and award of "bragging rights" played a big role in developing esprit de corps.

Before Organization Day, Colonel Miller authorized the establishment of an Honor Company plaque to be awarded monthly "to the company with the best record for the month, based on the lowest number of Courts-Martials [sic], Venereal Disease, and Delinquency Reports plus the best showing in parades and inspections."[29] As much a tool for developing company-grade leaders as an award for collective achievement, the plaque served much the same function as the honor streamer used by the Wolfhounds. Indeed, as the regimental adjutant recorded, "using such trophies has seemed to have proven itself in many places." For the Polar Bears, it appears that such measures were timely and appropriate. Incidents of indiscipline had risen sharply from June to July 1949. The number of soldiers reported delinquent or AWOL in July rose 77 percent over the June 1949 number, from seventy-four to ninety-six. Similarly, soldiers tried by summary courts-martial (typically conducted at the company level) rose 61 percent over June's totals (thirty-four compared to twenty-one), and special courts-martial (for serious or violent crimes) doubled from five to ten. Finally, the number of soldiers who contracted a venereal disease and sought treatment from the regimental medics increased 63 percent, to thirty confirmed cases in July.[30] Although the division summary for July contains no analysis on the reason for the sudden increase, two factors can certainly be assumed. First, the sudden influx of first-term enlistees as replacements, typically eighteen- or nineteen-year-old boys with money in their pockets and away from home for the first time, must have been a boon to the local economy (both licit and illicit). Second, the shortage of NCOs meant that many of these young men lacked the supervision that could have kept them in line both on and off duty. As a result, many of them, having absorbed little to no sense of responsibility during their cursory military socialization at the stateside replacement centers, abruptly encountered military regulations and military justice only after having committed their transgressions. Obviously, Colonel Miller's remarks at the regiment's Organization Day were an attempt to instill in these new men a sense of pride and responsibility, one that would at least curb their passions.

Athletic competitions provided an officially sanctioned outlet for the pent-up energies of the young men in the regiments throughout the army. The 31st Infantry Regiment did particularly well in identifying soldiers with sports experience or potential and then motivating them to perform better than their peers in other units. As a result, Polar Bears teams won seven of eight regimental-level competitions conducted by the 7th Infantry Division in 1949, including football, basketball, and rifle and pistol marksmanship during the division small arms tournament.[31] In the latter event, Lieutenant Colonel Bolland, 2nd Battalion's commander, won the individual first place slot for both M1 rifle and M1911A1 pistol competitions.[32] The regiment's accomplishments regarding athletics are especially noteworthy compared to those of the 27th Infantry. In the 7th Division there was no policy of excusing team members from training in order to practice their sports. All athletic activities—including competitions—were conducted after the conclusion of the duty day.[33]

Building Combat-Ready Battalions

The period September–December 1949 saw a sustained period of training activity for the 31st Infantry Regiment. Given the requirement to complete battalion-level certification by the end of the calendar year and the certainty that winter weather would severely hamper the conduct of training, the IX Corps G-3 accelerated the testing schedule for all units. All maneuver training unit tests were to be completed by December 3 at the latest.[34] For the Polar Bears, this meant the elimination of a full two weeks of preparatory training time from the schedule. As a result, Colonel Miller ordered his battalion commanders to maximize their time in the field to eliminate time wasted moving to and from training areas and firing ranges. According to the regimental history, 90 percent of all training conducted during this period occurred in a field setting—hardly the type of pseudotraining normally attributed to the Eighth Army in this period.[35] Indeed, maneuver units of the division reported that Occupation missions ceased to be their responsibility beginning in August, allowing commanders to focus entirely on training for combat.[36] In the infantry regiments of the division, the increased operations tempo delivered not just better training—no distractions or breaks meant that soldiers retained instruction better—but also improved both morale and discipline. As Maj. Lester K. Olson, the regimental S-3 since June, noted in his training summary for September, "throughout this period with an increased workload, the men of the regiment have maintained themselves with an even higher morale and 'esprit-de-corps.' It is believed that this has come about through the realization by the men . . . that the only way the tests will be completed successfully is to work together."[37] Although Major Olson's observation may reflect a certain cynicism regarding soldier motivation, it does demonstrate that the men of the regiment accepted the necessity of training to standard, if only for the short-term goal of achieving a reprieve from living under field conditions.

The intensified training period began with the administration of the army's five-event physical fitness test. Following this, the regiment's two battalions moved out to two medium-sized training areas to conduct platoon-level training and testing. Rifle platoons were measured against the provisions contained in Army Field Forces Training Test 7–2. The graded exercise outlined in 7–2 required the platoon to conduct an attack against a prepared defensive position. Specifically evaluated performance measures included the platoon leader's field order, movement of the platoon to the assault position, emplacement of supporting fires, conduct of the assault, and consolidation and reorganization of the platoon upon successful seizure of the enemy position.[38] Of eighteen rifle platoons in the 31st Infantry Regiment at the time, four failed the test initially—more than 20 percent. Again, evaluators' comments indicate that the lack of strong NCOs at the squad and platoon level lay at the heart of unit shortcomings. Fire discipline among both assault and support elements, level of detail and specificity of squad leaders' orders, and knowledge and use of terrain to conceal movement were the reasons most often cited for failure. Following additional training time, the four weak platoons were retested and found sufficiently capable to earn a passing grade.[39] Other testing conducted in September included both day and night evaluations of the regimental intelligence and reconnaissance platoon and machine gun and 81-mm mortar platoon tests for the battalions' heavy weapons companies. As indicated by the concluding paragraph in the regimental S-3's monthly summary, the month's testing provided a much more realistic measure of the effectiveness of training thus far than the rosy picture painted by the former S-3 at the end of April: "Plans for October will include . . . 81mm mortar platoon retests, [and] MG platoon retests."[40]

As with the squad tests in August, much of the problem with the different platoon tests can be attributed to a weak NCO corps. However, as indicated above, personnel turbulence began to affect training proficiency seriously in the regiment at this time. As the Constant Flow Program gained momentum in identifying and shipping eligible soldiers back to the Zone of the Interior, units in the 7th Infantry Division suffered crippling losses in terms of cohesion and effectiveness. Much of the benefit of the weeks of training conducted between May and September was lost because of the rotation process. Moreover, the accelerated training and testing schedule forced Colonel Miller to shut down the Regimental Leadership School during the first week of October in order to return the NCO cadre to their platoons and companies. Finally, as the OCAFF training inspection team noted in its report, almost none of the replacements received in the Far East up to October 1949 received more than eight weeks of basic training. Because of the continued shortage of NCO replacements, it is easy to agree with the regimental adjutant's gloomy forecast that by the end of 1949 the training program would of necessity revert to basic training in order to accommodate the large number of replacements.[41]

In keeping with General MacArthur's desire to build combined arms experience at every level, September concluded with a combined arms live fire exercise (CALFEX) conducted by elements of the 31st Infantry Regiment and the 31st Field Artillery Battalion. This firepower demonstration served two purposes. First, it gave recently arrived replacements a clear impression concerning the amount of firepower available to an infantry regiment. Second, it helped both units in preparing for follow-on battalion-level testing. Just like the infantry regiments, the field artillery regiments undertook their own training and testing program and were formally evaluated on their fire support proficiency during infantry battalion combat firing tests. As a result, the artillery battalions also maximized the time they spent in the field. In addition to the CALFEX, the 31st Field Artillery Battalion fired two live immediate suppression missions in support of company-level maneuvers by the Polar Bears. In all, the artillery battalion fired more than eight hundred rounds of standard 155-mm high explosive ammunition during September's training.[42]

As the regiment prepared to support the battalions during their own upcoming tests, Colonel Miller also looked to train his own headquarters. When 2nd and 3rd Battalions conducted a week-long bivouac at Shimamatsu Maneuver Area, the regiment's service and headquarters companies deployed as well to support them. This first field deployment of the entire regiment quickly revealed some potentially crippling basic equipment shortages. Without sufficient lister bags for potable water storage the regiment was forced to transport five-gallon cans to and from Camp Crawford daily. Given the conditions of most roads in rural Japan in 1949 this would have significantly increased the maintenance requirements for the regiment's truck fleet and also consumed extra fuel that the regiment could ill afford. Also, the regimental S-4, Capt. Theodore S. Staiger, reported that the 1948 Table of Organization and Equipment didn't provide enough tents even for the reduced strength of the regiments in Japan in 1949. Commanders were forced to choose between protecting the health of their soldiers or the serviceability of their equipment and supplies. Soldier morale also plummeted because of the increased wear and tear on personal equipment as a result of the accelerated training tempo. By the end of September, no replacement boots in the most common sizes could be found anywhere in the division, and the two pair of fatigues issued to each soldier proved insufficient to provide immediate access to clean and dry uniforms at the end of the training day. These supply shortfalls were partially remedied by the end of October with the issue of an additional fatigue uniform to each soldier, but boot repair and replacement remained a problem well into the opening weeks of the Korean War.[43]

October was devoted to preparation for battalion tests. In addition to closing the Regimental Leadership School, all Occupation missions except those directed by the Division G-3 were discontinued "to allow the maximum number of men to train together."[44] Rehearsals of battalion tasks were interspersed with training and testing of the rifle companies according to Army Field Forces Training Test 7–10. This comprehensive examination evaluated the companies in both offensive and defensive scenarios, acting both as part of a larger unit and acting independently. Elements of the battalion heavy weapons companies as well as the regimental heavy mortar company and the 31st Field Artillery Battalion fired in support of the live-fire portions of the evaluation. Additionally, battalions retested those 81-mm mortar platoons and machine gun platoons that had failed the official tests in November and certified the rifle companies' 60-mm mortar sections.[45]

From October 8 to October 11, 1949, Col. F. M. Harris's OCAFF inspection party observed training activities throughout the 7th Infantry Division. Interspersed with quite specific but appropriate comments on the relative tactical skills of observed units are some very caustic comments about what in the field army was labeled "chickenshit." For example, inspectors who visited the 31st Infantry faulted the unit for "a general lack of smartness on the part of individuals" and "laxness in saluting during off-duty hours." On the whole, however, the 31st earned high marks for its training and administration and received an overall rating of "very satisfactory."[46]

Second Battalion was in the middle of practicing attack problems for the upcoming tests when the inspectors arrived at Shimamatsu Maneuver Area. Commenting on a battalion-level approach march movement to contact, OCAFF's representatives found the problem well-planned and satisfactorily executed. The next day, the battalion's Company F conducted a live-fire attack supported by a battery of 105-mm howitzers from the 57th Field Artillery Battalion, an exercise that the inspectors termed "excellent" in its planning and execution. Of particular note, the inspectors praised the company commander and battalion staff for their conduct of a postexercise critique led by the umpire group. Significantly, the deficiencies noted during execution resulted primarily from leadership failures at the company and platoon level (for example, unclear company order, misoriented platoon leaders) and not from errors of omission or commission by NCOs. The inspection team evidently did not see any training conducted by units of the 3rd Battalion, except for a guard mount by Company L, which impressed the visitors with its alertness and smartness of appearance. Other elements of the regiment that came under the eyes of the inspection team also earned high marks. The I&R platoon's training on patrolling and observation post procedures was "well prepared and effectively presented," while the medical company's training on field expedient first aid rated "excellent" for being both "interesting and effective."[47] No evaluated unit in the regiment earned less than a "satisfactory" rating, unlike several units within the 7th Infantry Division.

Both 2nd and 3rd Battalions executed their reinforced battalion combat firing tests during the period November 4–9, 1949, supported by the 57th Field Artillery Battalion, undergoing evaluation according to AFF Training Test 6–2.

To add realism to the battalion-level tests, F-80 jet aircraft from the 49th Fighter Wing flew several sorties of close air support for each battalion using dummy ordnance. Having earned a "very satisfactory" rating from the IX Corps evaluators, 3rd Battalion returned to Camp Crawford to conduct marksmanship instruction and qualification November 10–17. Third Battalion also executed an emergency deployment readiness exercise. Alerted on November 21, the battalion moved by rail from Camp Crawford to an abandoned airfield near Chitose on southern Hokkaido. There 3rd Battalion established a defensive perimeter designed to defeat a notional attack by Soviet paratroopers. In the meantime, 2nd Battalion, having failed its graded exercise, conducted a seven-day review of all training from squad to battalion level. Returning to Shimamatsu Maneuver Area on November 30, the IX Corps staff certified the battalion as combat ready on December 2. Both battalions returned to Camp Crawford during the first week of December and prepared to implement their winter training programs. In true Polar Bears fashion the Heavy Mortar Company passed its training test on December 15 despite a strengthening winter storm, and all replacements that had arrived since the late summer fired their weapons for record in the last days before Christmas 1949.[48]

Two Steps Forward, One Step Back

The year 1950 dawned clear and cold on Hokkaido. Soldier morale rose during December and early January, with fewer cases of indiscipline than in previous months. Although the regimental historian attributed this rise to the general festiveness of the holiday period, it could also have had something to do with the canceling of a regimental combat team exercise originally planned for December 21–24. Severe weather kept the soldiers indoors for the remainder of the year; the regimental S-3 hopefully rescheduled the exercise for January 26, 1950. In the interim the two battalions of the 31st Infantry concentrated on cold weather training and movement with skis and snowshoes in the first three weeks of the year, while the regimental staff prepared for a command post exercise. During this renewed emphasis on individual training, Capt. Richard J. Hertel of Company E began field tests of a unique piece of equipment—the "gunboggan." Hoping to improve cross-country mobility of crew-served weapons in heavy snow, Captain Hertel had several oversize plywood sleds constructed, to which crews fastened their .30-caliber light machine guns. In addition to making his gun crews much more mobile than previously, affixing the tripod legs to the sled enhanced the weapons' stability when fired. Evidently the gunboggan exceeded expectations, because the regimental S-3 recommended its use by 57-mm and 75-mm recoilless rifle crews as well.[49]

The Polar Bears interrupted their training program to welcome a new regimental commander in February. Colonel Richard P. Ovenshine became the third regimental commander in eleven months at a ceremony conducted at Camp Crawford on February 2, 1950. Ovenshine had extensive experience on divisional staffs during World War II and had briefly commanded the 165th Infantry Regiment of the 27th Infantry Division during the initial Occupation of Japan.[50] Concurrently with Ovenshine's assumption of command of the regiment, he also became the commander of Camp Crawford. The 7th Infantry Division's headquarters relocated itself from Camp Crawford to Sendai on northern Honshu Island with an effective date of February 2, 1950. The removal of the division's headquarters units considerably relieved the crowded living conditions at Camp Crawford. The move also placed the division headquarters much closer to Eighth Army headquarters in Tokyo.

For the remainder of the month the primary focus of training remained individual winter skills, culminated by a regimental ski and snowshoe meet on February 25. This event combined military skills such as land navigation, marksmanship, and first aid with winter survival and cross-country movements. Although it was rated a successful conclusion to this phase of training, the regimental S-3 failed to identify the winning soldier or even to which company he belonged. In addition, the regiment also conducted a two-week refresher course for all platoon sergeants, with an emphasis on leadership principles and how best to impart instruction on tactical tasks. By placing the month's training program in the hands of the squad leaders, the platoon sergeants were given enough time to get reacquainted with the basic responsibilities of their jobs.[51]

With the coming of March warmer weather beckoned, and squad- and crew-level training began in earnest. After spending much of their instruction time indoors, the light machine gun sections of the rifle companies and the 60-mm and 81-mm mortar platoons deployed to firing ranges in the vicinity of Camp Crawford for ten days of live-fire practice and qualification. In addition, the 57-mm antitank crews of the rifle companies conducted familiarization fires with the M9 2.36-inch rocket launcher. Additionally, all replacements who had arrived since December conducted familiarization and qualification firing with either the M1 rifle or M1/M2 carbine. At the end of the month the several units of the regiment conducted physical fitness tests—more as a gauge to see how much had been lost during the winter than as a measure of proficiency, according to the regimental historian. Finally, two other significant training events occurred in March. First, cadre from the Eighth Army Air Transportability School at Yokosuka Air Force Base traveled to Hokkaido to train the regiment on air movement. Staff officers from regimental and battalion staffs attended a seventeen-hour course designed to acquaint them with the basics of airframe load planning, while all enlisted soldiers and company-grade officers attended a twelve-hour hands-on proficiency course on the loading and securing of cargo and personnel. The ATS cadre finished their training with a demonstration of the resupplying of a rifle company using an L-5 airplane. The second training event was a two-week squad leader refresher course patterned after the previous month's platoon sergeant training. Again taught by the Regimental Leadership School cadre, the focus remained on the principles of leadership, effective instruction, and the duties and responsibilities of squad leaders in a tactical setting. Imparting this information to the appropriate audience would be a key factor in the regiment's upcoming field exercise.[52]

During the last three days of March, the entire 31st Infantry Regimental Combat Team deployed from Camp Crawford to Shimamatsu Maneuver Area. Regimental combat team firing exercises were graded events designed as culmination training events at and below regimental level. To qualify for progress to division-level integrative training, regimental combat teams needed to earn at least a "satisfactory" score from Eighth Army umpires. Joining the Polar Bears infantrymen were the 57th Field Artillery Battalion (105-mm towed howitzers), a battery of the 31st Field Artillery Battalion (155-mm towed howitzers), the 15th Engineer Battalion, the 7th Medical Battalion, and a company from the 77th Tank Battalion. The focus of training was proper execution of one offensive and one defensive mission. This was the first time that the entire RCT had trained together as a unit, although the constituent parts had been actively engaged in raising their combat readiness since the previous summer. The lack of previous practice at integration showed, however. As the Division G-3 described it, the exercise showed a "definite need for further training of the communications platoon, command post procedures, and passive air defense measures." The G-3 observer caustically concluded that the 31st RCT needed to devote a good deal of attention to training as a team and not as a grouping of individual units. The 31st RCT earned "unsatisfactory" ratings on both missions.[53]

As a result of this disappointing showing Colonel Ovenshine directed that the entire month of April be used for retraining. Units would review all subjects trained since the previous summer, beginning with basic individual tasks and progressing through all levels of collective training to include battalion maneuvers. In addition, two RCT-level command post exercises were conducted, on April 5 and 13, that included leaders and staff from all subordinate and supporting units in order to eliminate the command and control problems that had so frustrated the G-3 observer in March. When the soldiers from the rifle companies were not engaged in collective training, the battalions employed them in the construction and use of an improved rifle marksmanship range. Unlike existing static ranges, the new range employed life-sized targets at unknown distances. Instead of lying prone in the open, the firer on the new range now had to acquire and engage his target from a number of positions while remaining behind cover. The unorthodox range received the endorsement of the division commander for its focus on combat realism.[54]

"Train As You Fight"

What had begun as a trickle in December became a flood by April, severely hampering the retraining effort. In April 1949 alone the 31st Infantry Regiment lost over two hundred experienced officers, NCOs, and soldiers; the regiment received fewer than thirty replacements. The 7th Infantry Division now began to feel the full effects of the faulty personnel policies put in place for the move from Korea. While the other three divisions of Eighth Army enjoyed predictable personnel situations by April 1950—though turnover was still higher than desirable—the 7th Infantry Division experienced a turnover rate more analogous to the immediate postwar demobilization period. Under the circumstances it is remarkable that the maneuver units made any progress in training. And to make matters for the 31st even worse, the regiment was forced to suspend training for several days in midmonth in order to repatriate fifty-six Japanese soldiers from their Soviet captors. The fact that this mission was most easily executed by the Polar Bears because of their proximity to the Soviet Union probably offered slight comfort to the regiment's leadership, who were focused firmly on the RCT exercise retest.[55] Despite these distracters, when the 31st RCT again took to the field for the retest, it demonstrated sufficient proficiency at all levels to earn "very satisfactory" ratings on both graded missions. The Division G-3 observer recorded that this exercise, conducted May 8–11, "showed a vast improvement over the March test, proving the results of five weeks of intensive combat team training which the 31st had undergone prior to this retest."[56]

The combat effectiveness reports submitted by the two battalion commanders for the second quarter of calendar year 1950 indicate a continued emphasis on fundamentals. These reports, dated June 26, 1950, demonstrate that combat effectiveness was not so much a goal as a continuous process. Although not articulated in any Eighth Army or divisional order, the training program was designed to allow unit readiness to fluctuate. So long as units remained within a "band of acceptability," they retained their ratings, but it was understood that in many cases subordinate organizations would have to review or repeat training in order to account for personnel turnover. Reflecting this, the 31st Infantry Regiment's training schedules for May and June 1950 continued to emphasize progression from individual and small-unit skill to large-scale collective proficiency. In May, 2nd Battalion devoted the bulk of its training time to squad and platoon training. The battalion intelligence and reconnaissance platoon passed its day and night patrol tests (Army Field Forces Tests 30-1 and 30-2, respectively) during the third week of the month, in between squad firing tests conducted May 14-18 and 25-26. In addition, the rifle companies' light machine gun teams (M1919A4/6, .30-caliber) fired the qualification table again on May 29. During the next month the entire battalion underwent the Basic Medical Skills Test (Army Field Forces Test 8-1) from June 7 to 9, and the rifle platoons executed graded firing tests from June 15 to June 19. Similarly, 3rd Battalion accomplished all squad firing tests and I&R platoon evaluations as well as advanced individual marksmanship (firing tables 8 and 9) and the rocket launcher familiarization course for selected personnel.[57]

As in the 27th Infantry, the two battalion commanders of the 31st Infantry offered very different subjective evaluations of the obstacles to the accomplishment of the training mission. Lieutenant Colonel Robert R. Summers of 2nd Battalion made personnel issues the focus of this section of the report. In priority he listed a shortage of officers in general, a shortage of competent NCOs, and constant turnover among enlisted personnel as the chief problems preventing the achievement and maintenance of a high state of readiness. Summers's leadership team lacked one major and five captains, and five rifle platoons had no officer; the same situation affected the battalion intelligence section. Lieutenant Colonel William R. Reilly, commanding 3rd Battalion, attributed his battalion's shortcomings not to leadership or personnel problems but to resource shortfalls. Limited training areas during the winter and a shortage of winter gear for soldiers, the complete absence of 57-mm recoilless rifles, and the advanced age of his other crew-served weapons ranked as his three most significant obstacles. Reilly as well lacked his second field grade officer but was better off with lieutenants and captains. Both officers also reported an almost complete lack of antitank capability. Like every other regiment in Japan, the 31st Infantry made do with the 2.36-inch rocket launcher in lieu of both the 75-mm and 57-mm recoilless rifles. Regarding the 75-mm piece, 2nd Battalion did actually have two of the weapons on hand, but both were listed as unserviceable, having been received without sights or mounts. Third Battalion had nothing but rocket launchers. As well, antiarmor teams in the rifle squads carried the obsolete 2.36 instead of the more-powerful 3.5-inch rocket launcher then in very limited production. Both battalions reported a relatively high state of vehicle readiness. Second Battalion reported every on-hand vehicle as mission-capable. Similarly, 3rd Battalion reported all on-hand vehicles operational but noted that they still lacked four quarter-ton trucks (jeeps).[58]

On the whole the two battalions appeared no worse off than any other infantry battalions in Japan (or army-wide) on the eve of the Korean War. The

31st Infantry Regiment as constituted on June 25, 1950, was a far cry from the loose aggregation of individuals shipped from Korea to Japan eighteen months previously. The unit had indeed developed a sense of pride and cohesion and had markedly improved the ability of individual soldiers as well as the platoons, companies, and battalions to engage in combat successfully. Unfortunately for the 7th Infantry Division, the assumptions made in Tokyo regarding the scale of the North Korean threat required that the infantry regiments of the division give up many of their trained soldiers, NCOs, and officers. When the 7th Infantry Division was itself alerted for deployment to Korea in July, it had to be rebuilt hastily with fillers from the United States (a mixture of new recruits and recalled reservists) augmented by thousands of Koreans with little or no military experience in their own or anyone else's army. Nevertheless, the men of the 31st Infantry adapted quickly to their changed circumstances and fought well during their initial battles following the Inchon landings, including seizure near Osan of Hills 113 and 92, the site of Task Force Smith's valiant stand against the KPA 4th Division back in July. As with the 27th Infantry, this success was no accident and can be attributed to the continuity of leadership at the regimental and battalion level and the presence of a trained core of personnel within the rifle companies. Colonel Ovenshine had commanded the regiment during its most intensive field training phase. His battalion commanders had likewise been active participants in the training of their battalions, as had the principal staff officers at battalion and regiment. Because of their institutional knowledge of the strengths and limitations of the regiment, and the fact that Colonel Ovenshine had focused his efforts on RCT teamwork in April and May, the September attacks along the Suwon-Osan highway were well-executed combined arms battles. In fact, because of the careful orchestration of supporting elements, including naval aviation, to suppress the KPA defenders, the 31st RCT captured the two hills with minimal casualties while counting over one hundred enemy dead.[59] No "untrained" or "soft Occupation" unit could have accomplished this; nor could such proficiency have been developed in the scant weeks since the division had been alerted, since much of that time had been spent aboard ship. One can only conclude from this action that the officers and men of the 31st Infantry Regimental Combat Team had done their job to the best of their ability in meeting General Walker's training program goals, an accomplishment for which previous commentators and historians have given them too little credit.

6

The 19th Infantry Regiment, 24th Infantry Division

THE 19th Infantry Regiment traced its origins to President Lincoln's March 4, 1861, expansion of the Regular Army. As part of the Army of the Ohio the regiment "saw the elephant" for the first time during the second day's fighting at Shiloh on April 7, 1862. Assigned to the Army of the Cumberland for the remainder of the war, the regiment fought at Murfreesboro, Chattanooga, Chickamauga, and Atlanta. The 19th Infantry earned its nickname—"The Rock of Chickamauga," subsequently shortened in army jargon to "Chicks"—for its heroic defense of the left front of the Union XIV Corps despite having run out of ammunition and suffering over 75 percent casualties. At one point in this battle, command of the regiment devolved to a second lieutenant, all other officers having been wounded or killed by the deadly rebel fire. In honor of that fact, members of the regiment memorialized September 20 as the regiment's organization day, and command of the regiment was officially conferred on the most junior second lieutenant for the day—a practice known as "earning his eagles."

Following the Civil War the 19th Infantry served as part of the army of occupation during Reconstruction, participated in campaigns against the Ute and Cheyenne Indian tribes in the West, and patrolled the Texas-Mexico border in the 1880s and 1890s. With the outbreak of war with Spain in 1898 the regiment was ordered to Georgia to train contingents of volunteers. Although the regiment did not participate in the Cuban campaign, one of its officers, 1st Lt. Andrew S. Rowan, earned immortality for successfully carrying President McKinley's message of support to *insurrecto* leader Calixto Garcia. The 19th

Infantry did participate in General Shafter's pacification of Puerto Rico before shipping out to the Philippines in 1899. For three years the 19th Infantry helped put down the Philippine Insurrection, then it returned to the United States. Just three years later, however, a Moro insurrection on Mindanao brought the regiment back to the Philippines, this time for nearly nine years of counterinsurgency warfare. The regiment returned to the United States again in early 1914 only to be deployed once more, this time to Vera Cruz, Mexico. The first U.S. Army unit to land in Mexico, the Chicks were among the last U.S. forces to be removed from the city.

With U.S. entry into World War I, the 19th Infantry became an organic unit of the 18th Division but saw no service in Europe. In 1922 the regiment was transferred to the Hawaiian Division. For the next twenty-one years the regiment served in a tropical paradise, mixing garrison training and security with labor requirements as the men of the unit helped finish construction of Schofield Barracks. After December 7, 1941, the regiment remained on Oahu to guard against a possible Japanese invasion until early 1943, when it moved to Australia with the rest of the 24th Infantry Division.

Relative latecomers to combat in World War II, the Chicks saw their first action only in July 1944 in New Guinea as part of the amphibious assault at Tenahmerah. The Chicks returned to fight in the Philippines for the third time in less than fifty years as the first wave of an amphibious assault on Leyte on October 20, 1944. Assault landings on Mindoro and Luzon quickly followed in 1944 and 1945. In its final action of the war the regiment earned a Distinguished Unit Citation for its assault landing on Mindanao and swift capture of the city of Davao.[1]

The regiment participated in the Occupation of Japan from the beginning, starting on the island of Shikoku and moving to the island of Kyushu in May 1946. Relieving the 6th Marine Regiment there, the Chicks built a new camp at Beppu and christened it Camp Chickamauga. For the next two and a half years the strength of the regiment slowly dwindled, until by December 1948 there were only fifty-seven officers and 883 enlisted men and NCOs on the rolls for the whole regiment. The entire 3rd Battalion was inactive except for a skeletonized headquarters company, and all of 2nd Battalion was inactive except for a caretaker staff in the headquarters company and Company E (which served as the regimental military police company). First Battalion possessed only Companies C and D as manned, effective units to execute the entirety of the regiment's Occupation duties. Division headquarters had detached Company B to use as school support cadre at the division specialists' school at Kokura. Given the dismal level of manning it is not surprising that the regimental adjutant characterized training as nonexistent at that time. One unit history summed up the regiment's entire training program for 1948 as "physical conditioning and reviewing the basic skills of the soldier."[2]

Prior to the publication of Training Directive Number 4, all four infantry divisions in Eighth Army were reorganized under a revised Table of Organization and Equipment. For the infantry regiments, this meant a reduction or transfer of capabilities from functional companies to the rifle and weapons companies. For example, the former cannon company became the heavy mortar company, and the antitank company (equipped with towed 37-mm and 57-mm guns) became a medium tank company. Also, the regimental medical detachment became the medical company to make up for the loss of two medical companies at the division level. None of the reorganizations by themselves had any impact on potential combat effectiveness. Additional infusions of personnel would be required for that to occur. Hence, with the adoption of the Constant Flow Program and the one-time shipment of an additional three thousand replacements to FECOM in the spring of 1949, the regiment was able to begin manning its new specialty organizations. By the end of the year only the tank company and one complete battalion were inactive; all other elements of the regiment were manned at close to the reduced levels authorized under the Truman administration's FY 1950 budget.[3]

The Pace Quickens

As in the other divisions, the shortage of qualified NCOs at the squad, platoon, and company level posed a challenge for the 24th Infantry Division. Consequently, Maj. Gen. Anthony C. McAuliffe (since April commanding his third division in four years) approved the establishment of the 24th Infantry Division Potential Noncommissioned Officer School. Conceived and overseen by the division G-3, Lieutenant Colonel Kreidberg, the Potential NCO School was designed to improve the technical competence of promising young soldiers and also equip them with some ability to present instruction in an organized and efficient manner. Elements of the program of instruction directly complemented the needs of the division, including twelve hours devoted to "Methods of Instruction," and forty hours of "Practical Work as Acting NCO Instructors." Gaping holes also existed, however. Eight hours each were devoted to "Dismounted Drill" and "Standards and Procedures for Inspections," but only one hour to "Combat Leadership" and two hours to "How the Leader Builds Morale, Discipline, and Esprit de Corps." And although each student received eighteen hours' instruction on small arms, there was no field training and therefore no opportunity to exercise NCO leadership at the tactical level under field conditions. Thus, although some aspects of the school's curriculum directly benefited units preparing to undergo a rigorous training program, very little of what was taught paralleled requirements for maneuver units in combat.[4]

Further evidence of a lack of focus surfaced in the 24th Infantry Division's Training Memorandum Number 8, published on May 17, 1949. Although this document stressed that units should minimize the amount of static, "lecture-type" instruction, the remainder of the memorandum discussed only the execution of dismounted drill and ceremonies. Given that drill was perhaps the only collective training conducted during the lean years of 1947–48, it is not altogether surprising that commanders and staff officers continued to focus on it to the exclusion of all else. Drill did offer some long-term benefits for the tactical training program by emphasizing teamwork and discipline. Also, the demand for "perfection ... in every detail" boded well for individual soldiers about to undergo the first serious field exercises in their short careers.[5] The overall thrust of the document, however, leads inescapably to the conclusion that almost six weeks after publication of General Walker's Training Directive Number Four, at least one set of leaders at the division level failed to fully appreciate the seriousness with which General Walker and General MacArthur viewed the need to increase combat readiness in Eighth Army.

By mid-July 1949, however, the 24th Infantry Division had begun training in earnest. The division G-3's Training Memorandum Number 10 outlined the phases of training, delegated authority for conducting proficiency tests, and reiterated the importance of conducting hands-on individual and collective training over lectures and briefings. Reflecting the division's late start, Major General McAuliffe authorized units to remain in the basic/individual training phase until mid-September 1949. The final four months of 1949 would then be devoted to small-unit proficiency (squad through company training). Combined arms training at battalion and regimental level would begin in January 1950 and would continue through March, with six weeks of testing and certification to conclude no later than May 15, 1950. To provide an additional incentive for individual soldiers, the division G-3 directed all three regiments to execute testing for award of the Expert Infantryman's Badge to all MOS-qualified infantrymen during the last two weeks of the individual training phase. A mark of individual achievement and distinction, award of the Expert Infantryman's Badge also earned the winner an additional five dollars per month.[6]

The division staff provided more guidance on training less than a month later. Training Memorandum Number 12 outlined a master training program for infantry regiments, battalions, and companies to follow when constructing individual unit training schedules. During the period September 17, 1949, to February 25, 1950, soldiers of the division's three infantry regiments could expect to complete 107 hours of squad training, 125 hours of platoon training, 132 hours of company training, and 215 hours of battalion-level collective training with other arms. All of this was designed to prepare each battalion to execute I Corps–administered reinforced combat firing tests at any time between February 25 and May 15, 1950. The 19th Infantry was tentatively scheduled for its tests from April 17 to April 22. In addition to collective training, the Division G-3 directed minimum levels of mandatory instruction on air transportability (30 hours), drill and ceremonies (33 hours), inspections (24 hours), troop information (23 hours), and physical training (115 hours). By the end of August 1949 it would have been clear to even the dullest private that the concept "easy Occupation duty" no longer applied to the 24th Infantry Division.[7]

Having begun 1949 with much of its organization inactive or manned at cadre status only, the 24th Infantry Division's personnel strength slowly increased throughout the year. Enlisted strength almost tripled between January 1 and November 1 (4,279 to 11,824), while the number of commissioned officers doubled from 346 to 648, only 19 short of full manning at peacetime authorizations. To accommodate the anticipated influx of replacements and minimize unproductive "pipeline" time in Japan, the division commander authorized creation of a provisional replacement company in July 1949. Made a permanent organization in September, it functioned efficiently enough to limit transient time to seventy-two hours or less from arrival in the division area of responsibility to arrival at unit of assignment. The 19th Infantry benefited greatly from the increase in personnel. Beginning the year with just 54 officers and 1,104 enlisted men and NCOs, by July the 19th Infantry boasted personnel strengths of 90 and 2,150, respectively. Nor did the Department of the Army's curtailment of service obligations for draftees after twelve months' service (implemented in November 1949) appreciably affect the regiment's manning levels. At the end of the year there were 104 officers and 2,129 enlisted men and NCOs assigned to the regiment.[8]

Rebuilding and manning the regiment did not occur smoothly, however. Although Col. Charles P. Lynch served as regimental commander from March 1948 to October 1949, there was little continuity among subordinate commanders. Five different officers commanded 1st Battalion during 1949; 2nd Battalion had an identical experience. All staff primaries at the regimental level changed at least once during 1949, and company command resembled a revolving door for senior lieutenants. Given this level of turbulence within the regiment's leadership, the division G-3's emphasis on basic skill proficiency for individuals and small units becomes much more understandable. With so many officers new to their positions it made no sense to immediately embark upon large-scale maneuvers for which no unit or leader was prepared.

CHAPTER 6

Back to Basics

Although the 24th Infantry Division published its training guidance somewhat later than the other three divisions of Eighth Army, some divisional units had initiated individual training independently early in 1949, including the 19th. One hundred four recruits from Company A passed their division-administered basic training tests in January 1949. The following month the remaining active companies of the regiment (less Company B) completed a seventeen-week basic training program. An attempt by Lt. Col. Henry C. Britt, commander of 1st Battalion, to conduct small unit training began on February 20 but was discontinued because of personnel turbulence and organizational changes.[9] By March the number of new replacements had increased to the point that Colonel Lynch directed that F Company be used as a provisional training company to provide a three-week refresher course for approximately 250 newly arrived soldiers. By the end of April, 1st Battalion was again engaged in small-unit training while F Company, H Company, and the regimental headquarters company all completed their basic training refresher courses and certified all personnel according to OCAFF's standards as outlined in Army Field Forces Training Test 21–1.

The reestablishment of long-dormant company organizations, the assimilation of new personnel from within both the Far East Command and the Zone of the Interior, and the discovery that much of the organizational property was unserviceable required the regiment to devote most of June to the repair and refurbishment of facilities and equipment, with relatively little time left for training. Also, residual Occupation requirements continued to place demands on some units of the Eighth Army. The 19th Infantry conducted six reconnaissance patrols and one mounted platoon-sized patrol in force during the month of June. Finally, humanitarian and civil defense missions following Typhoon Della (June 20–22) further reduced the time available for training. During this period, however, the regimental S-4 section worked hard to set the conditions for success in the upcoming training cycle. After receiving their initial issue of 75-mm recoilless rifles in May (one weapon each to Companies D and H), Maj. Edward B. Lord, the regimental S-4, arranged to have every weapon in the regiment examined for wear by the 24th Infantry Division G-4 section. Those identified as unserviceable were exchanged for replacements issued by the division.[10]

The arrival of additional personnel in May and June allowed Colonel Lynch to activate the Heavy Mortar Company and Company G. These two units, along with Company E, began a short refresher training period for their newly assigned soldiers similar to that conducted by Company F. Company H had already begun such a program upon its activation in April, joined by Company B, which the division commander returned to control of the regiment that month. In July a further influx of personnel (seventeen newly assigned lieutenants and 145 enlisted men) further filled out the rifle companies. As a result, almost every company in the regiment was conducting some basic skills refresher training, but no two of the company-level programs were the same. In light of this, Colonel Lynch directed the regiment to begin a centrally directed eleven-week period of intensive training. Again, the focus was on bringing all members of the regiment up to a baseline standard from which units could progress to collective training. In addition to basic training the regiment emphasized physical training, including mandatory foot marches in conjunction with overnight bivouacs.[11]

The Chicks devoted almost the entire month of July to weapons training. Given the large number of replacement soldiers who had arrived since April as well as the high number of green lieutenants leading the platoons, weapons training made good sense. First, it dovetailed well with Colonel Lynch's desire to achieve a baseline level of readiness from which to begin collective training. Second, it completed the military socialization of the soldiers, disabusing new soldiers of the notion that service in the U.S. Army was similar to being in "the Boy Scouts [but] with pay."[12] Third, it provided both NCOs and junior officers with the opportunity to plan, resource, and execute training in a controlled environment. Practicing command and control of their units gave these leaders exactly the kind of training they needed to lead their men in combat.

Following a period of preliminary instruction at Camp Chickamauga and at Hijudai Maneuver Area, during which soldiers learned the fundamentals of marksmanship, the companies bivouacked at the Mori Maneuver Area under the supervision of their respective battalion headquarters. The firing ranges at Mori supported firing the field familiarization, known-distance, and qualification tables for the M1 rifle, M1 carbine, and .45-caliber pistol as well as the M1918A2 Browning Automatic Rifle. First Battalion reported 347 soldiers qualified as expert rifle marksmen (a remarkable 53 percent of those eligible), while 2nd Battalion reported 219 experts. In addition to qualifying on the rifle range, the Chicks executed a "routine" patrol through Oita Prefecture on Kyushu Island, and the rifle companies of 2nd Battalion completed familiarization training and qualification firing with the 2.36-inch rocket launcher. Even the regimental headquarters company became involved, bivouacking for four days and nights at the range while conducting weapons training from September 6 to 10.[13]

Bricks and Mortar: Focusing on Squad and Crew Proficiency

On September 1, 1949, the Chicks bade farewell to Colonel Lynch, who departed to take command of Kyoto Station. Commissioned in 1917, Lynch had served with the 352nd Infantry Regiment in combat in both world wars, as a platoon leader in 1917–18 and as regimental commander during the regiment's movement to North Africa in 1943. His replacement was Col. Guy S. Meloy. Unlike Lynch, Meloy had no experience leading troops in combat. For the remainder of September, as Meloy became familiar with his new command, both battalions focused on crew-served weapons training. After a week of instruction on crew drills, maintenance, and dry-fire techniques, the battalions returned to Oita Maneuver Area to conduct panel firing (firing at scaled silhouette targets painted on large wooden or canvas panels from a distance of ten yards) for both light and heavy .30-caliber machine guns (M1919A4 and M1917, respectively).[14] Because of the number of weapons in each battalion and how the Table of Organization and Equipment allocated them, machine gun training required the presence of considerably more personnel than just the crews. In addition to the rifle platoons' single .30-caliber M1919A4/6 light machine gun the battalions trained with their .30-caliber M1917A1 heavy machine guns. A water-cooled, tripod-mounted system dating from World War I, the M1917A1 was the standard U.S. Army machine gun at company and battalion level well into the Korean War. The crews for these weapons were organized into platoons in the heavy weapons companies of each battalion (Companies D, H, and M, respectively.) Since these weapons were normally apportioned to the rifle companies during combat operations it made sense to train them alongside the soldiers they would support in combat. The first iteration of machine gun firing lasted from September 26 to 29, with all crews completing their familiarization firing requirements. After transitioning from panel to field firing from October 3 to 7, both battalions' crews fired for record at Ishigaki Maneuver Area from October 16 to 18, 1949.[15]

After completing their weapons training and qualification, most of the rifle companies devoted the remaining days of September to introductory squad training. Second Battalion led the regiment in this transition by conducting a night approach march to Ishigaki Maneuver Area on the night of September 22–23. The next five days were devoted to squad-level tactics, some of which were new even to the veterans in the ranks. Changes made to the 1944 edition of FM 7-10, *The Infantry Rifle Company*, included alteration of squad and platoon formations for movement and assault. Practicing these maneuvers to build "muscle memory" would have required several days, but learning them was critical to success in upcoming squad and platoon training certification tests as well as for survival in combat. First Battalion rotated through Ishigaki beginning the morning of September 28, training there through October 4, 1949, while 2nd Battalion took advantage of the proximity of the rifle ranges to run the squads through another iteration of field firing with rifles and carbines before returning to Camp Chickamauga.[16]

After returning to garrison, both rifle squads and weapons crews continued training. The rifle companies executed squad-level problems in the vicinity of Camp Chickamauga, while the regiment's mortar crews finalized their preparations for live fire. Under the direction of 1st Lt. Byron D. Greene, commander of the Heavy Mortar Company, all mortar crews in the regiment took written gunnery exams for their respective systems (60-mm in the rifle companies, 81-mm in battalion heavy weapons companies, and 4.2-inch in the Heavy Mortar Company.) This exam was followed by live fires at Jumomji Maneuver Area from October 3 to 7, night training in occupation and establishment of firing positions at Ishigaki Maneuver Area on the night of October 11–12, and more live-fire training for 2nd Battalion's 81-mm crews at Jumomji on October 17. The regimental staff completed its certification of all rifle squads at Hijudai Maneuver Area on October 20, 1949. Training immediately began on platoon-level tactics.[17]

As platoon training began, Col. F. M Harris's inspection team from OCAFF arrived on Kyushu to observe and evaluate the general quality and efficiency of training. Although they rated the professionalism, bearing, and discipline of the soldiers of the regiment as "excellent to superior," other aspects of training drew harsher assessments. Observing training by 1st Battalion, the inspectors faulted two rifle company commanders and the battalion S-3 for failing to provide adequate guidance on terrain management. In both Company A and Company C, three platoons were simultaneously using maneuver space hardly adequate for a single platoon. Company D's heavy weapons training program earned an overall rating of very satisfactory, although some deficiencies noted should have been corrected during the previous months' emphasis on individual and crew proficiency. Despite these deficiencies and a general reluctance among NCOs and junior officers to make on-the-spot corrections, the inspection team rated 1st Battalion as very satisfactory. Finally, the battalion earned an excellent rating for the condition of barracks, mess hall, and kitchens.[18]

Second Battalion earned similar ratings. Although platoon training in this battalion emphasized techniques over doctrine, the inspectors judged that this did not detract from the overall effectiveness of the program. Moreover, the enthusiasm of the platoon leaders, most of them only recently assigned to the battalion, also energized the soldiers, who "were interested and trying hard." Company H, the heavy weapons company, earned an excellent rating for its training program, especially that conducted with the heavy machine gun platoon and subcaliber qualification firing by the 75-mm recoilless rifle section. Barracks, mess halls, and other facilities received "excellent" ratings as well, although both Companies F and G earned sharp rebukes from the inspectors. In both cases the company commanders had detailed long-term latrine orderlies (à la Andy Griffith in *No Time For Sergeants*), who consequently received no benefit from the training program.[19]

The pace of training increased in November as Colonel Meloy, Lt. Col. Walden J. Alexander (1st Battalion), and Lt. Col. Gilbert M. O'Neil (2nd Battalion) sought to complete all training and certification at company level and below before the end of the year. As the platoons deployed for ten-day exercises at Hijudai and Jumomji Maneuver Areas, the regimental staff and battalion staffs conducted a command post exercise at a field location just north of Camp Chickamauga.[20] First Battalion completed its rehearsals for AFF Training Test 7–2 on November 7 and moved directly to Mori Maneuver Area for evaluation by personnel from the division G-3 staff. Second Battalion's platoons followed on November 12. By November 17 all eighteen rifle platoons in the regiment had earned satisfactory scores, although several platoons of 2nd Battalion received low satisfactory scores, necessitating additional retraining. Moreover, the regimental I&R platoon passed its own evaluation. Colonel Meloy then directed the platoon to become proficient in aggressor tactics in order to act as the opposing force for the two battalions during their training and testing in 1950.[21]

Moving directly to company training, 1st Battalion conducted a week of company training at Camp Chickamauga after Thanksgiving Day, while 2nd Battalion's platoons completed their retraining. On December 6 the entire regiment deployed to Jumomji Maneuver Area in order to observe a combined arms firepower demonstration conducted by units of 2nd Battalion, the Heavy Mortar Company, and the 63rd Field Artillery Battalion. Second Battalion remained at Jumomji for another four days of company-level training. The Heavy Mortar Company, manned and operating only since March 20, 1949, had progressed far enough in its training to undergo certification by I Corps evaluators on December 14, the first company-sized unit in the 19th Infantry Regiment to do so. By December 15 all six rifle companies completed their certification, along with selected platoons from the heavy weapons companies.[22]

Training continued despite the proximity of the Christmas holiday. First Battalion spent seven days at Jumomji Maneuver Area conducting both tactical movement and firing exercises from December 15 to 22, then joined 2nd Battalion for a round of refresher weapons training in the days after Christmas. For the holidays, the various wives' groups at Camp Chickamauga hosted a regimental Christmas party on the evening of December 23 in front of the post exchange building. On Christmas Day the officers and their families joined the NCOs and soldiers for a noontime meal in the various companies' mess halls, as "every attempt was made to give the men of the Regiment as enjoyable a Christmas as possible."[23]

The Chicks ended 1949 on a high note. Rightly proud of what they had accomplished, the regimental S-1, Maj. Milton A. Sewell, attributed the regiment's progress to "an all-out effort by all personnel of the command."[24] The training forecast for 1950 appeared equally ambitious. In addition to certifying the battalions as combat ready, leaders at division, corps, and Eighth Army level expected that some portion of the regiment would also become proficient in amphibious operations and air transportability. Doing so required that every available training day be used. Accordingly, both battalions deployed in Kyushu's wintry drizzle to Jumomji (1st Battalion) and Ishigaki (2nd Battalion) for four days of battalion-level training from January 2 to 6, 1950. Prevented from remaining at their training areas by the need to rotate other divisional units into them, the Chicks spent the next week refitting their equipment and preparing for another week of field work. Both battalions conducted training at Jumomji from January 16 to 27, using the I&R platoon as an opposing force to replicate a thinking enemy. This pattern continued for the next ten weeks. The soldiers in the fighting elements of the 19th Infantry Regiment saw little of their barracks between New Year's Day and Easter of 1950. First Battalion spent forty days actually bivouacked in the field and approximately twelve days traveling to and from distant training areas in that period. Second Battalion's totals of thirty-eight and twelve days indicate that both battalion commanders felt equally strongly about the training program. In addition to battalion training, 2nd Battalion conducted squad and platoon refresher training at the end of February, an extra effort that proved well worth the additional investment in time and resources.[25]

Assessments and Perspectives

By mid-March the two battalions had progressed far enough along in their training for the division G-3 to schedule them for certification. Before executing the battalion tests, the regiment submitted its combat effectiveness report for the first quarter of 1950, dated March 20. Colonel Meloy's summary of training obstacles included the lack of authorized weapons, the relatively small size of available training areas, and the continuing high personnel turbulence. Meloy rated his regiment at 655.88 points of a possible 1000, or 66 percent combat ready. One of the principal reasons for such a low rating was the fact that reinforced battalion combat firing tests, previously scheduled for March 6–12, 1950, had been postponed because of heavy rains until March 20–27.[26]

Lieutenant Colonel Otho T. Winstead, commanding 1st Battalion since December 3, 1949, listed just one significant obstacle to training: "the large turnover of personnel," which required extensive "review[s] of squad and platoon training in order to continue with battalion and higher level training."[27] He could have listed a great many other items but opted to let the report speak for itself. First Battalion's first combat effectiveness report for 1950 highlighted many of the conditions that later were ascribed to the Eighth Army as a whole. For example, Colonel Winstead reported an individual weapon operational readiness rate of just 48 percent and a crew-served weapons rate of 76 percent. Clearly, the rigors of the previous months' training had taken a severe toll on the maintenance and operability of the battalion's weaponry. Though short just 22 rifles, the battalion reported an astonishing 287 M1 rifles as unserviceable—a deadline rate exponentially higher than that of any unit previously discussed. The high percentage of broken weapons significantly affected the battalion's ability to sustain its marksmanship training program. Only sixty soldiers qualified as expert marksmen with the rifle in January and February, and sixty-nine failed to meet even the minimal standards required for rating as marksman.[28] Similar results occurred with crew-served weapons proficiency and even vehicle readiness. Nor were conditions markedly better in 2nd Battalion.

Second Battalion's commander, Lt. Col. Thomas M. McGrail, cited a lack of crew-served weapons and inadequate training areas as the principal obstacles impeding his battalion's progress. However, his battalion also faced a major crisis. A total of 259 M1 rifles, eighty-one M1 carbines, and seventy-four M1911A1 pistols were unavailable for use as a result of maintenance problems. One-third of his battalion's authorized Browning Automatic Rifles were likewise broken or otherwise incapable of firing. As in 1st Battalion, only fifty-seven soldiers qualified as experts with their individual weapons for this report. Undoubtedly there was much sharing of rifles as squads, platoons, and companies sought to requalify all of their men. Unfortunately, such overuse no doubt only increased the number of broken weapons as individual rifles remained on the firing lines for hundreds of rounds between cleanings and inspections. McGrail rated his battalion's morale at 80 percent, though he offered no indication of how he arrived at this score.[29]

Both battalions as well as the Heavy Mortar Company reported significant shortages of communications equipment. Second Battalion possessed almost no capability to lay wire communications, and with six tactical radio sets unserviceable it is unlikely that battalion exercises would have gone smoothly. First Battalion was in marginally better shape. Although Colonel Winstead reported no broken radios, he did point out that he lacked more than twelve miles of communications wire. Of greater concern for the dismounted infantrymen of the regiment was the fact that 1st Lt. Elliot Cutler of the Heavy Mortar Company could not communicate by either wire or radio because of equipment shortages. Even had he been able to receive requests for fire support, however, he would have been constrained by the fact that he was still missing one of his authorized 4.2-inch mortars, and two others could not be fired.[30] All in all, the Chicks were in a deplorable state of readiness in terms of equipment and armament, and the fast-paced training schedule on which Colonel Meloy kept the regiment focused only exacerbated the problem. With limited repair capabilities to begin with, repeated deferrals of needed maintenance for lack of spare parts, and certification of weapons and equipment as safe for training only, the battalion's readiness rating should have decreased from the previous December. In fact, because commanders saw a continued flurry of tactical activity, logistics issues such as scheduled maintenance and inspections tended to be relegated to the background and appear to have had less impact than the situation warranted.

The 24th Infantry Division's other regiments submitted reports that both corroborated and contradicted the maintenance situation in the 19th Infantry, suggesting either a communication or a discipline problem in that division. It is unlikely that General McAuliffe's and later General Dean's subordinates failed to understand the importance of the training program or the role that proper maintenance played in achieving combat readiness. Therefore, the tone and substance of other battalions' combat effectiveness reports for this same time period indicate a haphazard emphasis on maintenance, supply discipline, and basic soldier proficiency with weapons and equipment that would prevent damage of items through ignorance. This last point leads back into a discussion of training. Individual soldier training is an NCO responsibility. But the general shortage of qualified, competent, and dedicated NCOs throughout the maneuver units of the U.S. Army in the late 1940s ensured that individual training, the all-important foundation for collective training, never produced the necessary results. Col. Jay B. Lovless, commanding the 34th Infantry Regiment, listed NCO shortages (29 of 59 authorized master sergeants, 89 of 158 sergeants first class, 152 of 258 staff sergeants, and an unbelievable 359 of 572 sergeants) as one of the four most significant obstacles to the success of the training program. Lt. Col. Lawrence G. Paulus reported a total of 474 unserviceable individual weapons on hand, including 333 M1 rifles. Twenty-one of his battalion's twenty-seven Browning Automatic Rifles were also broken. Lt. Col. David H. Smith of 3rd Battalion painted a starkly different picture, however. Evidently he believed that his battalion had sufficient NCOs to conduct meaningful training, for he didn't mention personnel turbulence or shortages at all. Moreover, his equipment deadline report contained a grand total of fourteen weapons: nine pistols, three mortars, one rocket launcher, and a single M1 rifle.[31]

In the 21st Infantry Regiment, the maintenance situation appeared somewhat better than in the 34th Infantry. The "Gimlets'" reports make clear that tactical training in basic infantry skills at the individual and small-unit level received the bulk of Col. R. W. Stephens's attention. For example, the hapless Lieutenant Colonel Smith smugly reported "No Obstacles to Training" less than four months before his soldiers discovered just how severe was the maintenance shortfall in the 24th Infantry Division. His counterpart, Lt. Col. Carl C. Jensen of 3rd Battalion, 21st Infantry, gave a more realistic assessment. In his view, the extended time requirement for weapons repairs, particularly of crew-served weapons, endangered the readiness of the entire battalion because of the "danger of overcrowding [those remaining] weapons that are available." Colonel Lovless did acknowledge a maintenance problem but was most concerned with what he perceived as an inordinately high number of broken vehicles, about one-half of which resulted from broken suspension parts. These diagnoses supported another obstacle Lovless cited: the long road distances between cantonment areas and training areas and the poorly developed Japanese road infrastructure.[32]

Pressing On

The Chicks continued on their trajectory to complete battalion training and testing through the months of February and March 1950. Deploying to Ishigaki and Jumomji Maneuver Areas in early March, the two battalion commanders focused their respective units on those tasks most likely to be tested by Eighth Army. From March 6–10, 1st Battalion executed a battalion defense of key terrain, a withdrawal under pressure, and a battalion attack as part of a regimental counterattack. Second Battalion's training program emphasized defensive operations. The battalion conducted two deliberate defenses followed by a battalion attack. Both battalions were supported by the regimental heavy mortar company, the regimental I&R platoon acting as the enemy, and one battery from the 13th Field Artillery Battalion. The following week both battalions remained at Camp Chickamauga to refit as much of their equipment as possible and prepare for testing. Lieutenant Colonel John H. Michaelis's team of umpire evaluators from the training branch of the Eighth Army G-3 staff oversaw both battalions' reinforced battalion combat firing tests from March 20 to March 24 at Hijudai Maneuver Area. Second Battalion passed both the offense and defense missions with satisfactory ratings. First Battalion, however, failed to earn a satisfactory rating for its defensive operations and therefore had to reschedule its certification for April.[33] Reviewing 1st Battalion's performance, General Walker directed his operations officer, Brig. Gen. Ward Maris, to inform General Dean that "in view of the relatively poor showing made by this battalion . . . the Commanding General has directed that the test be considered as an exercise only."[34] Maris offered no justification for Walker's tolerant approach, but it may have resulted from simple sentimentality: General Walker's first assignment upon graduation from West Point had been with the 19th Infantry, guarding the Texas-Mexico border, and his son Sam also served as a junior officer in the 19th Infantry at the time. Whatever the reason, giving them this break allowed the 19th Infantry Regiment to escape the ignominy of having a subordinate unit's failing grade posted to documents that would circulate among I Corps and Eighth Army units.

Following the conclusion of the March tests, both battalions returned to Camp Chickamauga. First Battalion spent the next two weeks reviewing leader tasks during the defense while squad and platoon training took place in and around the camp. Second Battalion spent several days coordinating their upcoming training program, then deployed to Ishigaki to conduct additional small-unit training focused on shortcomings identified during the battalion test. Returning to the camp at the end of April, 2nd Battalion then embarked on marksmanship training and qualification firing. First Battalion returned to Hijudai Maneuver Area on April 18 and again executed the offense and defense tasks of the certification test. This time the battalion received a satisfactory rating on both missions and returned to their camp before beginning the next phase of training.[35]

While 2nd Battalion continued their marksmanship program, 1st Battalion altered its focus somewhat from basic infantry training. Beginning in late May, elements of the battalion began conducting rehearsals for amphibious training. General MacArthur's guidance to General Walker in early 1949 included the admonition that at least one battalion from each infantry regiment should achieve familiarity (if not proficiency) in amphibious assault techniques. The designated unit for the Chicks, 1st Battalion traveled to the Japanese port of Shimonoseki and thence to Camp McGill on the island of Honshu for six weeks of training and practice in amphibious operations. Reflecting Walker's imperative to incorporate combined arms training whenever possible, elements of several other units accompanied 1st Battalion. These included a small detachment of the regimental headquarters, detachments from service and heavy mortar companies, the headquarters of the 13th Field Artillery Battalion plus a composite battery, a platoon from Company A, 78th Tank Battalion, a platoon of engineers from the division's 3rd Engineer Battalion, a detachment from the 24th Medical Battalion, and a platoon from Battery A, 26th Anti-Aircraft Artillery

(Automatic Weapons) Battalion.[36] The North Koreans invaded South Korea while the 19th Infantry Regiment was split between Kyushu and Honshu. To reassemble the regiment for deployment to Korea would have required several days plus the diversion of air or sea transport urgently needed elsewhere. This situation ensured that General Dean, when ordered to choose an element of his division to send to Korea, would not pick the Chicks despite their demonstrably superior readiness compared to that of the 21st Infantry Regiment.

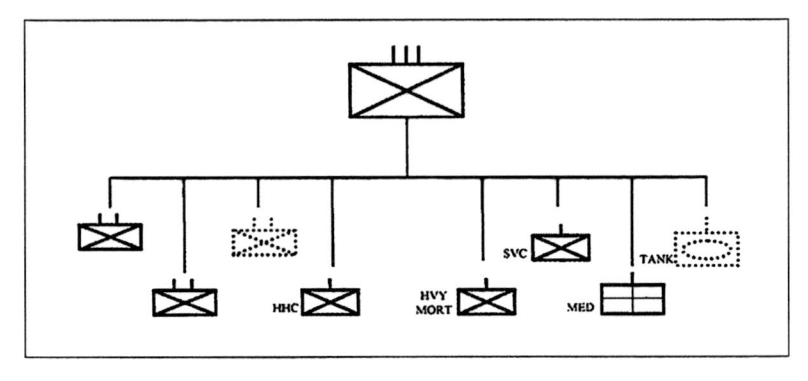

Standard U.S. Army infantry regiment organization, post-1948. During the lean years of the Occupation, the highest level of manning that a regimental commander could hope to achieve was two maneuver battalions, a heavy mortar company, a medical company, and a service company. Except for the segregated 24th Infantry Regiment, all regiments had one inactive battalion, and no regiment operated its own tank company.

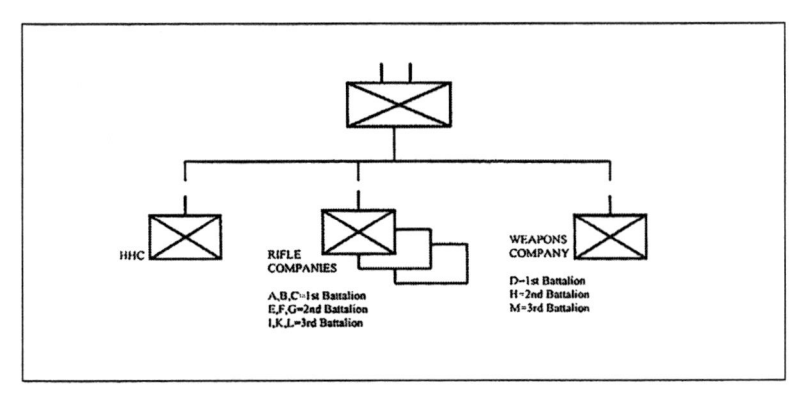

Standard U.S. Army infantry battalion organization, post-1948. In addition to the rifle companies, each battalion possessed an organic heavy weapons company equipped with 81-mm mortars, rocket launcher–armed antiarmor teams, and teams with water-cooled .30-caliber machine guns.

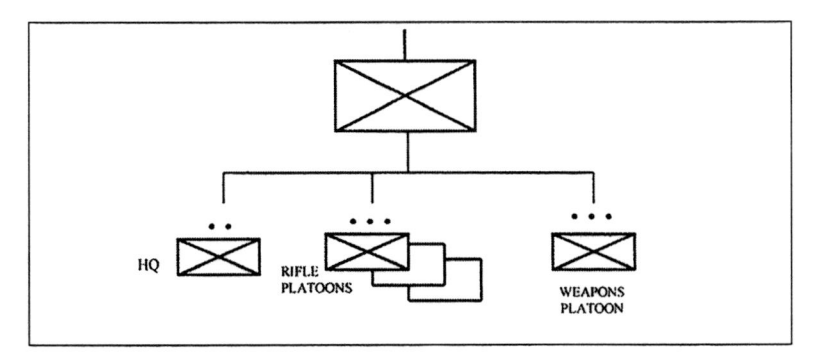

Standard U.S. Army infantry rifle company organization, post-1948. The weapons platoon included 60-mm mortars, rocket launchers, and air-cooled .30-caliber machine guns.

▲ Secretary of Defense Louis A. Johnson. His relationship with the service chiefs was perhaps worse even than those between Robert S. McNamara or Donald Rumsfeld and their respective uniformed subordinates. (Truman Library)

▲▶ Pres. Harry S. Truman. A National Guard officer in the Great War and unsuccessful applicant to West Point, Truman harbored an irrational hatred for professional officers that led him to distrust their advice on budgets and force structure in the years between V-J Day and the North Korean invasion of South Korea. (Truman Library)

▶ Lt. Gen. Walton Walker, Commanding General, Eighth U.S. Army. Walker commanded XX Corps during World War II under Gen. George S. Patton. In contrast to his relationship with MacArthur and Lt. Gen. Edward Almond, MacArthur's chief of staff, Walker got along quite well with Patton and Eisenhower. (U.S. Army Photo/National Archives)

General of the Army Omar N. Bradley, chairman of the Joint Chiefs of Staff (l), and Gen. J. Lawton Collins, army chief of staff. Having commanded VII Corps in World War II, MacArthur dismissed Collins as a "European" officer although he had previously commanded the 25th Infantry Division on Guadalcanal in 1942–43. (Truman Library)

General Collins aboard an M8 scout car as he prepares to review troops of the 1st Cavalry Division (Infantry) during his first visit to the Far East since 1943. To his right is his escort, Maj. Gen. Hobart R. Gay, Commanding General of the 1st Cavalry Division and Gen. George S. Patton Jr.'s chief of staff at Third U.S. Army during World War II. (U.S. Army Photo/National Archives)

▶ Pvt. Frank B. Hill (Temple, Texas), a member of the 1st Cavalry Division Military Police Battalion, stands guard at one of the gates of the emperor's palace in Tokyo, Japan. Behind him stand an unarmed member of the Tokyo Police and an Australian member of the British Commonwealth Occupation Forces. (U.S. Army Photo/National Archives)

Members of the 25th Armored Reconnaissance Company participate in a training program at Osaka, Japan. (U.S. Army Photo/National Archives)

Troops of the 1st Cavalry Division assist Japanese police in their efforts to control disorders caused by striking employees of the Toho Motion Picture Studio near Chofu, Japan. The disorders resulted when a group of employees refused to accept dismissal, barricaded the grounds, and resisted efforts to expel them. (U.S. Army Photo/National Archives)

Maj. Gen. Louis A. Craig (center), Department of the Army inspector general, talks with Pvt. Sidney McCoy (New Orleans, La.) (right), A Battery, 159th Field Artillery Battalion, 25th Infantry Division, during his inspection tour. (U.S. Army Photo/National Archives)

▲ Students at Shinodayama Maneuver Area use a field radio as part of their training at radio school (25th Infantry Division Specialists' School). L–R: Pvt. Alfred T. Tribble, Pvt. Andrew R. Matranga, Pvt. Frank Olweiler. (U.S. Army Photo/National Archives)

◀ Linemen from Company B, 394th Signal Operations Battalion, support one of the monthly Eighth Army command post exercises. (U.S. Army Photo/National Archives)

Pfc. Matthew F. Bazzano (Rome, N.Y.), assigned to Headquarters and Headquarters Company, 21st Infantry Regiment, 24th Infantry Division, operates a radio from his camouflaged jeep during a command post exercise (CPX) held at Shingu CPX Area, Kyushu, Japan. (U.S. Army Photo/National Archives)

An aerial view, looking south from over the Sea of Japan, at the Maizuru Maneuver Area. The close proximity of Japanese civilians to the training area exemplifies Eighth Army's constant need to balance readiness with community relations. (U.S. Army Photo/National Archives)

▲ With Mount Fuji in the background, members of the 95th Light Tank Company use the beach at Chigasaki, Japan, for training grounds. (U.S. Army Photo/National Archives)

◀ Lieutenant Jackson, Heavy Mortar Company, 35th Infantry Regiment, demonstrates installation of a subcaliber adapter into the tube of a 4.2-inch mortar. Use of subcaliber devices allowed for realistic training without using the more expensive full-caliber rounds. (U.S. Army Photo/National Archives)

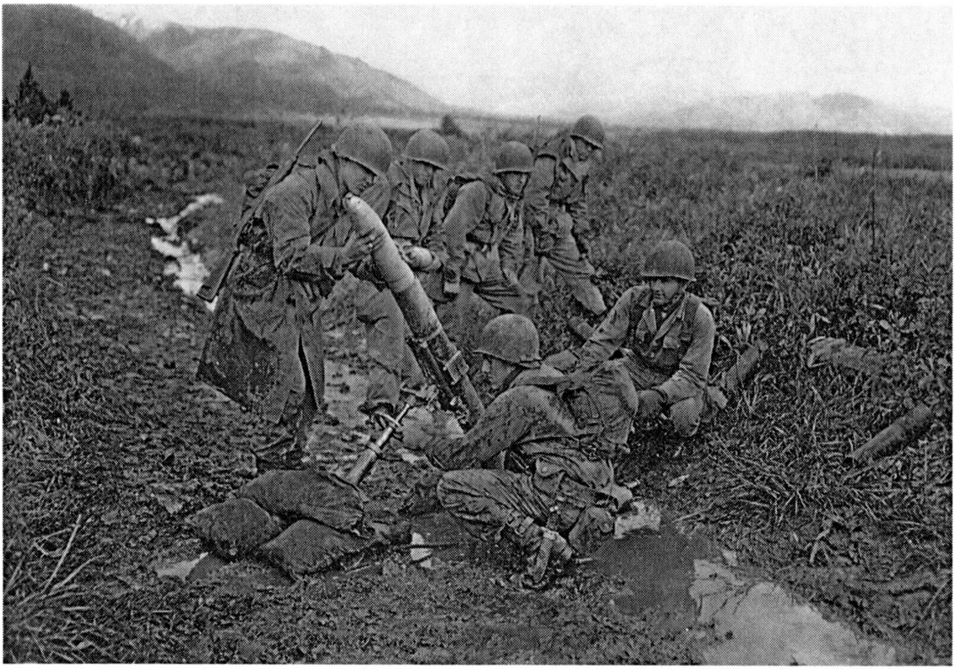

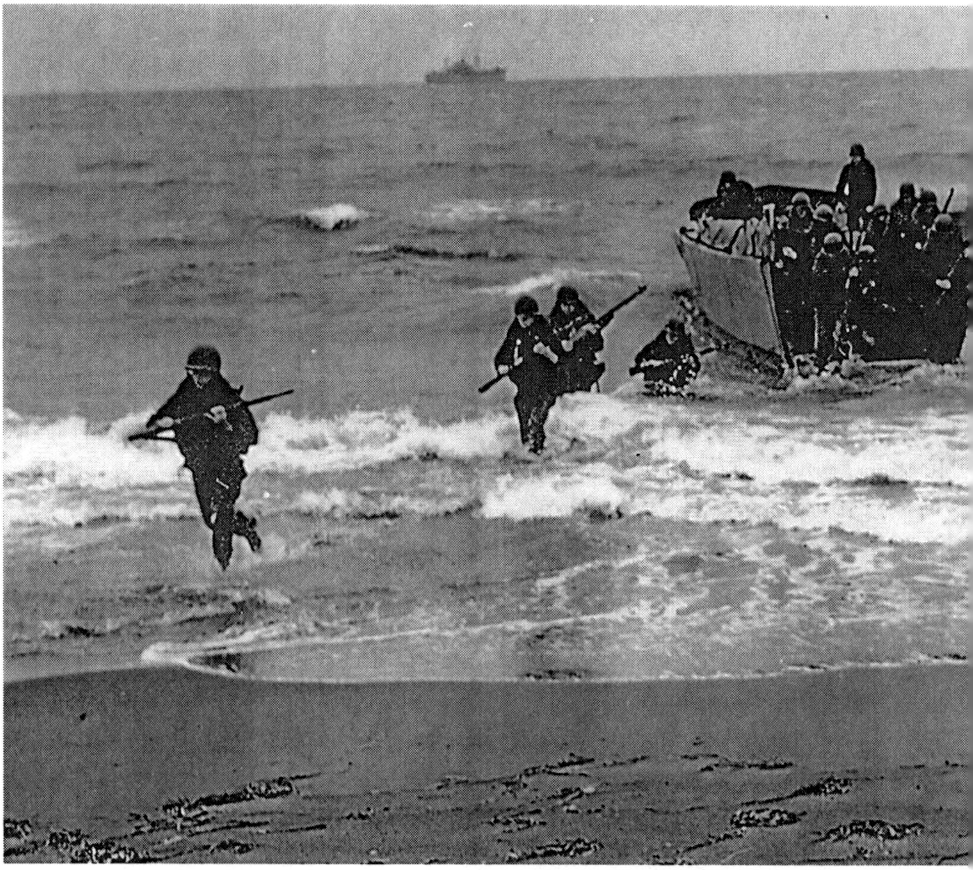

◀◀ Members of the Heavy Mortar Company, 35th Infantry Regiment, set and fire their mortar while on maneuvers. The choice of firing position leaves much to be desired. (U.S. Army Photo/National Archives)

◀ Lightly dressed and soaked to the skin, an unidentified Eighth Army soldier awaits instruction on where to move inland after landing on the beach at Chigasaki, Japan, as part of his battalion's practice assault. (U.S. Army Photo/National Archives)

◀ Members of the 25th Infantry Division and the 1st Cavalry Division hit the shore at Chigasaki Beach during amphibious training. Despite the U.S. Army's extensive experience with amphibious assaults during World War II, training for such missions returned to the U.S. Marine Corps. These soldiers were trained by Marines loaned to FECOM from the USMC Troop Training Center, Coronado, California. (U.S. Army Photo/National Archives)

The 1948 Far East Command Small Arms Tournament. In this photo, competitors engage targets at the three-hundred-yard line using the M1 Garand service rifle. (U.S. Army Photo/National Archives)

For many Eighth Army soldiers, marksmanship training marked their true initiation into the profession of arms. Here, members of the 65th Engineer Combat Battalion, 25th Infantry Division, engage targets from the seated position at Shinodayama Firing Range. The soldier on the far right, Pvt. Charles L. Caler, Baltimore, Md., is wearing low-quarter shoes instead of combat boots, demonstrating the depth of scarcity concerning even basic uniform equipment that affected the U.S. Army in the late 1940s. (U.S. Army Photo/National Archives)

◀ Focusing on marksmanship using more realistic firing positions, soldiers of the 31st Infantry Regiment used an array of nonstandard rifle marksmanship training stations from which soldiers were required to engage a succession of targets. In this photo, the soldier fires from an inclined prone position. (U.S. Army Photo/National Archives)

◀ Here, a Polar Bears soldier fires from around a tree trunk. The sawn-off stump offers the additional capability of being repositioned so that multiple angles of fire may be trained. (U.S. Army Photo/National Archives)

In an advanced marksmanship technique, a soldier of the 31st Infantry fires his weapon through a simulated window. The soldier has incorrectly allowed his rifle to protrude from the window, allowing any observer to identify his position. This deficiency should have been corrected prior to Colonel Ovenshine's forwarding of his report to Eighth Army. (U.S. Army Photo/National Archives)

In this photo the rifleman uses a mound of dirt to simulate natural relief as he engages targets. The soldier behind him will grade his shots before he moves to the next station. (U.S. Army Photo/National Archives)

Bazooka team training: Pvt. Walter D. Dusoblom (Northbridge, Mass.) inserts a round as Pvt. Hal Ethridge (Sterling, Ill.) holds the weapon on its target during the testing of 1st Battalion, 19th Infantry Regiment, at Hijudai Maneuver Area in March 1950. (U.S. Army Photo/National Archives)

Aerial view of the cantonment area of Camp Fuji, the Far East Command's only large-scale maneuvering area. The permanent buildings on the right housed the camp's administrative offices and personnel. Units at the camp for training were housed in the tent city regardless of the season. (U.S. Army Photo/National Archives)

A two-man 60-mm mortar crew from Company F, 2d Battalion, 19th Infantry, simulates firing their mortar during battalion tests at Mori Maneuver Area. By May 1950, when this photo was taken, ammunition shortages prohibited the use of most munitions for training. (U.S. Army Photo/National Archives)

Two Wolfhounds soldiers man an M1919A6 light machine gun during company-level training at Shinodayama Maneuver Area in November 1949. (U.S. Army Photo/National Archives)

Two 24th Infantry Division soldiers engage targets with their water-cooled .30-caliber machine gun at Camp Mower near Sasebo, Japan, less than a month before the North Korean invasion of South Korea. (U.S. Army Photo/National Archives)

Men of Company B, 27th Infantry, attack a line position during platoon training at Shinodayama. (U.S. Army Photo/National Archives)

Wolfhounds infantrymen maneuver against the "aggressor" force during battalion-level tests at Fuji-Susono Maneuver Area, March 1950. (U.S. Army Photo/National Archives)

Forward observers Lt. E. K. Andreasen and Pfc. Bobby L. Mayton work with Battery A, 8th Field Artillery Battalion, during firing tests at Fuji-Susono in April 1950. (U.S. Army Photo/National Archives)

Members of Battery B, 82nd Field Artillery Battalion, 1st Cavalry Division, observe and adjust fire for their battery from an observation post during exercises held at Aebano Maneuver Area. (U.S. Army Photo/National Archives)

▶ A rebuilt engine is being installed on a truck chassis in the motor pool at the Fuchu Ordnance Center, Fuchu, Japan. This is one of several photos used as a feature story about Operation Roll-Up by Pacific Stars & Stripes. (U.S. Army Photo/National Archives)

▶▶ Japanese workers repair jeeps at the Nissan Automobile Factory. Rebuilt American sedans, used for nontactical transportation, stand in the background ready for reissue. (U.S. Army Photo/National Archives)

Vehicles and equipment collected from the Philippines and Korea await refurbishment at the Fuchu Ordnanc

Plant as part of Operation Roll-Up. (U.S. Army Photo/National Archives)

Morning physical training became a daily requirement for all units in Eighth Army after publication of Training Directive Number Four in April 1949. (U.S. Army Photo/National Archives)

Men of Company H, 31st Infantry Regiment, celebrate the arrival of 1950 with a softball game played on snowshoes at Camp Crawford, January 3, 1950. (U.S. Army Photo/National Archives)

Members of the 1st Cavalry Division maintain their equipment at a company-level repair shop, February 1949. (U.S. Army Photo/National Archives)

The "gunboggan," created by Capt. Richard Hertel's Company E, 31st Infantry Regiment. (U.S. Army Photo/ National Archives)

7

The 8th Cavalry Regiment (Infantry), 1st Cavalry Division (Infantry)

THE 8th Cavalry Regiment ("Rocking Horse") began its service in 1866 as one of four new cavalry regiments authorized by Congress to protect westward expansion of the country.[1] Scattered across almost every western state in the final decades of the nineteenth century, the regiment participated in eight major campaigns against the Kiowa, Comanche, Apache, and Sioux tribes. At the outbreak of the Spanish-American War in 1898 the unit shipped out to Cuba. Arriving too late for combat, they nevertheless spent three years on occupation duty. Returning to the United States in 1902, the regiment made its headquarters at Fort Riley, Kansas, until the requirements of counterinsurgency in the Philippines compelled the War Department to transfer the regiment overseas again in 1905. For the next three years the 8th Cavalry operated as a mounted security force on the islands of Luzon and Jolo, safeguarding roads and freshwater supplies. With the end of the insurgent activities in 1907 the need for regular forces diminished considerably. The regiment returned to the United States in 1908 and was once again scattered among isolated posts in Arizona, Wyoming, and Montana.

The return to the routines of garrison life in the West proved short-lived, however. In 1910 the 7th and 8th Cavalry Regiments returned to the Philippines to help quell the rebellion in the southern islands of Jolo, Mindanao, and the Sulu Archipelago. For five years Rocking Horse troopers fought against the Muslim Moro tribesmen. Some fifty members of H Troop participated in the 1913 battle of Baksan, perhaps the most decisive battle of the insurgency, in which U.S. soldiers killed more than three hundred Moro rebels while suffering few casualties of their own.

In September 1915 the 8th Cavalry returned to the United States in response to a growing threat to the nation's southern border. Posted to Fort Bliss, Texas, the regiment arrived too late to become part of General John J. Pershing's Punitive Expedition and instead reverted to its decades-old mission of border security. Although assigned to the 15th Cavalry Division in December 1917, the regiment remained in the United States during World War I, actively engaged in interdicting both smugglers and raiders from Mexico from 1915 until well into the 1930s. The incorporation of the regiment into the newly activated 1st Cavalry Division on September 13, 1921, changed nothing. Joining the 8th Cavalry as organic regiments of this new formation were the 1st, 7th, and 10th Cavalry Regiments, in two brigades of two regiments each. Subsequent changes saw the substitution of the 5th Cavalry Regiment for the 1st Regiment and the 12th Cavalry Regiment for the 10th. During breaks in constabulary duty along the border, officers of the regiment engaged in polo matches, both intramural as well as with military and civilian teams from throughout the United States and Mexico. In March 1937 Lt. Charles P. Walker of the 8th Cavalry bested all other contenders in a 150-mile endurance race from Fort Bliss, Texas, through New Mexico and back to Fort Bliss. Polo and feats of equestrian skill proved of little value in preparing the regiment for war, however. In February 1943 the War Department dismounted the division, making it an infantry division in all but name.

The 8th Cavalry's World War II baptism of fire took place on March 8, 1944, at Manus Island in the Bismarck Archipelago. Operations on Samar, Leyte, and Luzon in 1944 and 1945 marked the regiment's third combat tour in the Philippines in less than forty years. As part of Brig. Gen. William Chase's Flying Column, men of the 8th Cavalry would proudly claim the title "First in Manila" when U.S. forces liberated that city beginning February 3, 1945. With Japan's surrender on September 2, 1945, the men of Rocking Horse quickly shifted their focus from training for the planned invasion of Japan to Occupation duties. The 1st Cavalry Division received metropolitan Tokyo as its area of responsibility for the Occupation. The 8th Cavalry's headquarters and 2nd Battalion found quarters in the former Third Imperial Guard regiment barracks in downtown Tokyo, close to both its parent headquarters, the 2nd Cavalry Brigade, and the Imperial Palace. The 1st Battalion was stationed at Camp King near Omiya, on the outskirts of Tokyo. The regiment underwent the same slow diminution of ranks as every other unit in the U.S. Army in the months and years following V-J Day.[2]

In its Occupation duties in Tokyo, much of the 8th Cavalry's responsibilities revolved around providing security to key industries and infrastructure needed to ensure the daily functions of GHQ in its role as the military government of

Occupied Japan. Accordingly, in case of an emergency or civil disturbance, the 8th's troopers would secure Route 11 where it passed through Toda-Bashi, a suburb of Tokyo; radio transmitter and station locations throughout greater Tokyo; and the U.S.-used airfield at Irumagawa. In addition, one-half of one squadron would pass to the control of the 2nd Cavalry Brigade as a reserve force, and the remainder of the squadron would secure the brigade command post in Tokyo and be prepared to augment security forces at both Yokota and Tachikawa airfields. Finally, individual troops were assigned patrol areas in case of the declaration of an emergency. These objectives were all infrastructure-related sites on whose continued function both GHQ and the Japanese economy depended.[3]

The daily Occupation routine for Rocking Horse appeared almost as strenuous as the emergency measures described above. The density of Tokyo's population ensured that Allied personnel would be busy monitoring a host of activities. In March 1948 the regiment conducted 1,010 mounted and dismounted patrols within Tokyo and monitored thirty-one meetings of the Japanese Communist Party as well as ten meetings held by expatriate Korean groups. Other duties included the demilitarization of Japanese industrial facilities and the removal and destruction of war material, including over two hundred kilograms of phosgene and lewisite gas discovered by 8th Cavalry soldiers at the site of the former 6th Japanese Military Laboratory. Other Occupation missions conducted by members of the unit included food supply surveillance and control, election monitoring, suppression of black market activities, and deployment of military government (civil affairs) teams.[4]

Although Major General Chase, the division commander since 1945, sought to reemphasize combat readiness in early 1948, the continued requirements of the Occupation and pending personnel shortfalls prevented him from carrying out his plans. Aside from on-the-job training for new replacements in their Occupation tasks, the only meaningful training accomplished during this time was the completion of a "command and staff course" in air transportability planning by forty-one officers of the division and the creation of a cadre of six officers and thirty-seven enlisted men for a division-sponsored air transportability school. With the imposition of peacetime personnel ceilings on all divisions in Japan, almost no collective training was possible. Moreover, the Far East Command had to brace itself for an increased shortage of personnel beginning in early 1948. This resulted from cutbacks in enlistments in order to allow the newly reauthorized Selective Service System to forecast draft calls properly. Another byproduct of this policy was the early release of recruits in the training centers to their gaining units, some with as little as three or four weeks' training.[5]

Preparatory Actions

The number of impediments to training remained virtually unchanged for the remainder of 1948 and into early 1949, when two important changes occurred. First, General Walker published his new Training Directive Number Four, reorienting all units of Eighth Army toward building combat effectiveness. Second, the 1st Cavalry Division shed its obsolete "square" organization and became a triangular division like the other divisions in Japan. The transition from Occupation to training required this update to the division's organization. Shedding one regiment, even one as reduced in strength as the 12th Cavalry in 1949, provided badly needed manpower infusions to the other units in Eighth Army. By making all four divisions alike in number and type of subordinate units, Eighth Army and GHQ FEC could more easily track the progress of each division toward the goals stipulated by General MacArthur. The inactivation of the two cavalry brigade headquarters shortly afterward offered a smaller number of replacements, but the greater proportion of mid-level and senior NCOs thus freed for line duties made them much more valuable than their numbers would indicate.

As in other units, NCOs of any ability were in short supply within the 8th Cavalry Regiment in 1949. And like other units, the 1st Cavalry Division opted to train its own promising young soldiers in the rudiments of combat leadership in an attempt to overcome this institutional shortage. The division leadership school opened in mid-1949 with a capacity of sixty students per class. Although officers in the division rated the school's output as satisfactory, Lt. Col. John H. Dilley, the division G-3, acknowledged that the school's capacity was much less than what was needed by the several units of the 1st Cavalry Division.[6] The shortage of experienced leaders was exacerbated by the implementation of the Eighth Army's Constant Flow personnel management program. In order to distribute losses equally across all divisions, as the most overstrength division in Japan the 1st Cavalry Division received orders to send three thousand of its personnel to the other divisions. This levy was in addition to the wholesale transfer of the personnel of the old 12th Cavalry Regiment to the 7th Infantry Division. As a division G-1 information paper explained, the additional levies would exchange "men whose departure dates [from Japan] are after November 1951 to other divisions [in return for] men whose departure dates are prior to November 1951 [thus ensuring] that no particular unit will suffer in effectiveness because of a large number of its personnel returning to the United States at any one time." The first iteration of the exchange program involved a swap of four hundred enlisted men with the 24th Infantry Division in March 1949. As almost none of the new arrivals were NCOs, the division historian acknowledged that the burden for supplying NCOs to subordinate units within the division would continue to fall on the shoulders of the units themselves.[7]

The shortage of high-quality leaders at the company level precipitated a general decline in discipline within the 8th Cavalry Regiment. Col. Alexander McNabb, commanding the 8th Cavalry, instituted several policies in early 1949 designed to tighten up his regiment. First, to halt widespread flaunting of a SCAP directive prohibiting the use of indigenous laundry establishments by soldiers, the 2nd Cavalry Brigade's military police company raided several downtown Tokyo laundries and confiscated all U.S. military clothing. Offending soldiers who wished to reclaim their laundry were required to report to the regimental S-2 for retraining on the appropriate Occupation regulations. Second, a decline in motor vehicle maintenance and readiness led McNabb to institute thirty minutes of "motor stables" every day. During this period McNabb expected to see his subordinate officers supervising the NCOs and soldiers conducting their maintenance inspections in order to instill in them an understanding that their responsibilities extended to all facets of army life. Third, a similar decline in the care and appearance of personal and organizational equipment forced McNabb to require each company-level unit to spend thirty minutes per day training soldiers on proper procedures to clean, maintain, and care for their equipment. Finally, McNabb detailed a lieutenant from the regimental staff to conduct a four-week program of instruction for corporals and sergeants on the fundamentals of conducting training in basic military subjects. In addition, beginning in March, McNabb ordered formal refresher training for both officers and NCOs to be held every Monday, Tuesday, and Thursday nights for two hours to stress supply discipline, principles of leadership, and training methods. The fact that Colonel McNabb felt compelled to direct the attention of his regiment to tasks that are universally understood to be the purview of noncommissioned officers speaks volumes about the overall quality of leadership within his regiment at the time.[8]

During this period the 8th Cavalry's location in downtown Tokyo guaranteed that it would retain significantly greater Occupation responsibilities than infantry regiments from outlying divisions. The most noteworthy of these tasks was providing guards and escorts for suspected war criminals from the former Imperial Japanese Army during their transit to and from Sugamo Prison in Tokyo and the International Military Tribunal in Yokohama. Less visible but just as great a distraction in terms of personnel requirements were guard posts at the Tokyo Quartermaster Depot and the Tokyo Ordnance Center. The implementation of the training program did not relieve the regiment from these responsibilities. Indeed, as the Eighth Army's organization became more streamlined throughout 1949, the metropolitan regiments received additional short-term Occupation missions. For example, in August the regiment raided a commercial warehouse in Tokyo, seizing 266,294 grams of silver. As a reward for this successful action the 8th Cavalry received the mission of providing a company to guard the Bank of Japan, where the silver was stored until FEC received instructions for its disposition. These guard requirements affected training in several ways. First and most obvious, companies detailed to Occupation missions found it difficult to sustain proficiency in combat-related tasks. Second, numerous instances of ill-trained or badly informed interior guards led Colonel McNabb's replacement, Col. Raymond Palmer, to direct that all soldiers posted to guard duties must pass a written examination with at least a 70 percent score. Those that did not could not be detailed as guards.[9] Any commander who wished to have the widest pool of men available for guard duty was thus required to expend extra time and effort retraining soldiers to pass this exam instead of preparing them for combat training.

The dilution of the 8th Cavalry's efforts in the second quarter of 1949 resulted in abysmally low readiness ratings. The entire regiment underwent Mobilization Training Plan (MTP) testing in April 1949 to assess the level of knowledge and ability of individual soldiers. If the battalion and regimental commanders and staff expected to be able to progress rapidly to collective training, they were sorely disappointed. Capt. Hugh Queenin, the regimental S-3, conservatively rated the regiment's overall effectiveness at 40 percent. The loss of 802 officers and men under the personnel exchange program reduced this figure even more.[10] It is important to remember that MTP testing did not test an individual soldier's MOS competency. Rather, MTP testing measured how well a soldier had mastered the common core tasks associated with basic training. Unit training programs were expected to provide necessary MOS training. In the 8th Cavalry's case, however, considerable effort would be required before the several elements of the regiment would be ready to progress to collective training. Colonel McNabb had focused his subordinates on MTP training beginning in January, but the program was quickly overcome by continued Occupation missions. Hence, the chance to escape from Tokyo and concentrate fully on tactical proficiency afforded the regiment a golden opportunity to build a solid foundation of tactical proficiency at the individual and small-unit level.

Scratching the Surface

On May 18, 1949, Colonel McNabb relinquished command of the 8th Cavalry Regiment. As his replacement was not yet in theater, Lt. Col. William Grunert of 1st Battalion assumed temporary command of the regiment. The next day the men of Rocking Horse boarded trucks and trains, bound for a four-week stay at Camp McNair on the slopes of Mount Fuji. Before leaving the regiment, McNabb envisioned this training deployment as a chance for the rifle companies to complete MTP training and introduce the rifle squads to collective training. In his parting guidance he had stressed that deficiencies in individual training needed to be fixed before progressing to any collective training event. In light of the results of the previous months' MTP tests, Captain Queenin recommended the establishment of a provisional battalion at Camp King to conduct refresher training for both new replacements and intratheater transfers while the remainder of the regiment trained at Camp McNair. This would have freed squad leaders to concentrate on training those men who had already passed the tests but would have further dissipated the already overstretched NCO cadre of the regiment. Colonel McNabb opted to leave the integration of new soldiers to unit commanders, perhaps in hopes of more quickly building cohesion and esprit de corps within the squads and platoons of the line companies. It may also have resulted from McNabb's realization that his subordinate commanders needed all the experience they could get in maneuvering their units in light of the test schedule published by the 1st Cavalry Division G-3 section. Owing to scheduling constraints the 8th Cavalry Regiment could expect to undergo company and battalion testing during midsummer 1949, relatively early in the overall training program.[11]

To achieve success under "the present unusual circumstance," Lieutenant Colonel Grunert inaugurated a seventeen-week training cycle for the regiment. Each training week would last a minimum of forty hours and extend across five and one-half days per week. This training was progressive; the first thirty-six hours of training (from May 2 to 16) would cover squad tactics, focused on seven critical tasks: squad acting as lead element of a larger formation, flank security, night approach march to an objective, day and night attacks, night combat patrols, and defense of a key terrain feature. The next seventy-two hours, from May 23 through June 6, concentrated on platoon operations and led directly to an introduction to company-level operations. In addition to emphasizing training to develop the competence of specialists such as radiotelephone operators, drivers, and intelligence analysts, Grunert's program dedicated five training hours per week to physical fitness and mandatory organized athletics on Wednesday afternoons in accordance with established army traditions. This training was to complement the training that infantrymen would undergo as they developed their proficiency as members of squads and platoons. Most important, Grunert emphasized that the target audience of the training program would be "those individuals whose retention within the Battalion as key personnel is reasonably assured."[12] In other words, Colonel Grunert acknowledged that he would not be able to retain fully manned squads. Instead, he sought to develop NCO proficiency by training them on tasks that stressed the leader's actions. This emphasis made the most of the resources available, especially time, and provided a greater benefit to the battalion (in the form of more competent squad leaders) than time devoted solely to passing MTP tests.

This does not mean that individual skills were neglected during this phase. As surviving documents make clear, some of the collective exercises were vehicles to harden the newer soldiers to the rigors of infantry campaigning. For example, the training task "operate as lead element of an advanced guard" became the scenario upon which a foot march to an overnight bivouac was built. Of the nine training objectives listed, only two could be considered collective training. The others all focused on the individual soldier. In particular, Lieutenant Lepski, the battalion assistant S-3, emphasized that the number one training objective was "preparation" by individuals. In other words, how much critical thought a soldier or especially a junior leader put into preparing for this training event outweighed how quickly the unit completed the march.[13]

Training records of this initial period at Camp McNair from 2nd Battalion, 8th Cavalry, indicate a similar desire to focus on junior leader development. In the directive for the rifle platoon exercise "approach march, attack, assault, and reorganization," squad and platoon leaders constituted the primary training audience; individual squad members' knowledge of their MOS-related tasks was a secondary consideration. Actions assessed by umpires included the planning and issuing of combat orders, control of tactical movements from the point of departure to the objective area, leaders' control and distribution of rifle and machine gun fire, and leader actions taken after seizure of the objective. Following execution of this training event, leader training remained the primary objective during 2nd Battalion's foot march and overnight bivouac exercise, held on the night of June 6–7, 1949.[14]

Colonel Raymond D. Palmer took command of the 8th Cavalry Regiment in a simple ceremony at Camp McNair on June 8. He immediately began a series of visits to the various companies of the regiment, of which the lettered companies were engaged in squad combat firing tests. Squad testing ended on June 16, signifying 8th Cavalry's completion of Phase II MTP training. Tabulated scores indicate a slightly higher level of training proficiency among the soldiers of 2nd Battalion, of which Company F posted the highest overall squad average of 84.5 percent.[15]

The 8th Cavalry's training cycle at Camp McNair ended on June 17; battalion tests had been postponed on Colonel Palmer's request. The final training event was a demonstration of a company-level attack against a prepared objective in conjunction with tanks. The inclusion of tanks resulted from the insistence by Lt. Col. D. P. Frazier of the GHQ FEC G-3 Section that the maneuver area at Mount Fuji would support limited use of armored vehicles in a tactical role. The 1st Cavalry Division's 8th Engineer Battalion had recently completed improvements to the road infrastructure and fixed facilities at Camp McNair, and doubtless Frazier felt that units in training there should be given every opportunity to develop their proficiency in combined arms tactics.[16] Soldiers from 1st Battalion constructed the objective, while 2nd Battalion received the mission to conduct the demonstration. The tank "company" actually consisted of officers and soldiers from all four divisions in Japan. For them the exercise was the culminating event of their attendance at the 1st Cavalry Division's Armored Cadre School. Colonel Frazier observed the demonstration and found the exercise "well planned and executed by the participating troops. The attack to the 1st objective by Co F, 8th Cav, and Co A, 71st Hv Tk Bn was excellent. . . . The control of the infantry squads was excellent. The mortar and 75mm rifle fire of H Co adequately covered the objective prior to H Hour." From this experience Frazier concluded that "participating and observing troops both received some good training."[17]

Except for the Heavy Mortar Company, which remained at Camp McNair for live fire gunnery, the regiment returned to Tokyo on June 23. Five days later Colonel Palmer published a new training memorandum based in part on his observations of training at Camp McNair. Recognizing that the disparity of training proficiency within units of the regiment stemmed from the previous program's decentralized execution, Palmer now sought to standardize the training program across the regiment. Doing so would allow the regiment to make better use of limited training facilities, sustain the proficiency achieved during the field training cycle at Camp McNair, and also better prepare units for scheduled platoon and battalion tests later in 1949. As part of this standardization, Palmer removed the authority of individual units to schedule range firing; henceforth, marksmanship training would be controlled by the regiment and executed by battalions in order to facilitate scheduling. The following weeks would constitute an "interim training period" during which all soldiers would fire their weapons for record and any soldier not yet certified as having passed AFF TT MTP 21–1 would do so. As a result, both battalions dedicated all of July and most of August to marksmanship training in addition to Occupation-driven guard requirements and special tasks. To foster *esprit de corps* and encourage soldier performance, Colonel Palmer announced that he would award a marksmanship trophy to the company achieving the highest overall rifle qualification scores during this marksmanship training period. By the end of August both battalions reported qualification rates above 90 percent for individual small arms and at 100 percent for crew-served weapons. In addition, all soldiers present for duty as of September 2, 1949, were certified as having passed the MTP 21-1 tests. During this period 2nd Battalion received a new commander when Lt. Col. Eugene J. Field replaced Lt. Col. Wherlen F. Cheney on July 16, 1949. The regimental and battalion staffs participated in a two-day command post exercise at the end of July.[18]

The Collective Training Cycle, September–December 1949

During the first week of September, elements of the 7th Cavalry Regiment relieved the 8th Cavalry of its guard posts in Tokyo as part of the normal rotation of Occupation responsibilities. With external training distracters reduced to the minimum, Colonel Palmer now targeted internal personnel overhead requirements in an effort to maximize participation in the upcoming field training cycle at Camp McNair. Company barracks guards were abolished, and daily maintenance tasks and housekeeping duties were turned over to Japanese laborers whenever possible. To combat soldier absenteeism because of venereal disease, Palmer ordered Capt. Lawrence W. Biggs, the Medical Company commander, to conduct personal hygiene training for each company of the regiment. Evidently, Palmer's implementation of the Regimental Commander's Streamer, a monthly award to the company with the lowest composite score of disciplinary actions, had not had the desired effect. The regiment's overall infection rate for 1949 was approximately 18 percent, hardly a statistic that Palmer would have wanted to share with his superiors.[19]

The remainder of September was devoted to additional marksmanship training and small unit maneuver training at Camp Palmer at Chiba on the northeast shore of Tokyo Bay. In addition, 2nd Battalion's H Company conducted training in techniques of fire to improve marksmanship and improve the machine gun crews' skill proficiency. According to 1st Battalion's plan for range use, this period of training would allow every soldier in the battalion to fire at least two weapons: his assigned weapon for qualification record and one other shoulder-fired weapon for familiarization. This was a modest attempt to familiarize the average rifleman with every U.S. weapon he might encounter in training or in combat. The problem with such limited programs was that they didn't impart enough knowledge. As soldiers repeatedly stressed after enduring months of combat in Korea, one of the keys to survival in battle was soldier proficiency with weapons.[20] Hence, the repetition of such a fundamental skill was in fact one of the three or four most critical areas on which the U.S. Army needed to focus in 1949–50.

Both battalions devoted the first week of October to squad and platoon training. A surviving example of 2nd Battalion's plan to maximize training time indicates a heavy emphasis on the fundamentals of movement for the rifle companies and on crew drills, fire commands, and integration of heavy weapons into the rifle companies' formations. At the conclusion of each training day, Colonel Field directed that all personnel conduct ninety minutes of operator-level maintenance on their weapons and equipment in order to minimize equipment losses due to breakage.[21] Training was interrupted, however, by the need to conduct a parade in honor of visiting Army Chief of Staff Gen. J. Lawton Collins. The parade was conducted at the Imperial Plaza in Tokyo on October 11, and the following day General Collins inspected 8th Cavalry's facilities at the former Imperial Guard barracks. According to the regimental history, General Collins made Colonel Palmer aware of "certain deficiencies in training practice," though no details are included.[22] Since Collins observed no training activities, it is difficult to avoid concluding that his comments had more to do with the appearance of the interior guards he observed than with any tactical training.

First Battalion arrived at Camp McNair on October 21 and prepared the camp for the remainder of the regiment. Morale appears to have suffered somewhat, owing to the low quality of life most soldiers experienced there. Despite the onset of winter weather, soldiers slept in squad tents both in the cantonment area and on bivouac. Rain, snow, and subfreezing temperatures soon led to a dearth of firewood. Since the only means of heating the squad tents was by means of wood-burning stoves, and because nightly temperatures routinely dipped below freezing, soldiers naturally tended to use as much firewood as possible. By the end of the four-week training period "it became necessary to institute rigid fuel consumption controls," since resupply operations from outside the camp were severely hampered by poor road conditions. As a result the soldiers soon took advantage of the services of local Japanese farmers. Obligingly, these farmers appeared at the camp gate each evening, offering to rent their horses to soldiers on an hourly basis. "It became evident, however, that some of these horsemen were selling whiskey of a dubious quality and (or) were soliciting for women." Moreover, when given passes from the camp to the local villages, some of the soldiers became involved in "disturbances" with the local population, necessitating the establishment of a courtesy patrol. In an attempt to bolster sagging morale, Colonel Palmer declared November 17 a training holiday. Unfortunately for the soldiers of the regiment, the holiday became a parade in honor of Brig. Gen. Henry I. Hodes, the assistant division commander, whom Palmer had invited to address the regiment. Unsurprisingly, the regiment's AWOL rate increased upon its return to Tokyo, as did other incidences of indiscipline. As a result, the regiment ended 1949 having conducted 412 courts-martial in the preceding twelve months.[23]

The AWOL rate remained low while the regiment was at Camp McNair for two principal reasons. First, the remoteness of the location and the harshness of the weather meant that few soldiers were motivated to live off the land for several days while avoiding apprehension. Second, the training schedule was full, and the soldiers would have been quite exhausted by the physical efforts of completing the training. After the regiment devoted the initial days to establishment of the camp and basic living conditions, evaluators from the division G-3 section arrived to test the platoons. 1st Battalion completed its platoon tests on November 4, 2nd Battalion having finished them the week before.[24] Second Battalion achieved an overall score of 82.8 percent; 1st Battalion lagged far behind at 74.1 percent. Moreover, of the ten highest-ranking platoons, nine were from companies in 2nd Battalion. Significantly, the two highest-rated platoons, both weapons platoons from rifle companies, were led by sergeants, not lieutenants. First Battalion's lower overall achievement can perhaps be attributed to Company B for having lagged behind in completing the required preparatory training. The men of that company completed only up to week 9 of the Phase II collective training plan because of additional guard requirements in Tokyo in August and September; the rest of the battalion had reached week 18. As a result, none of Company B's four platoons scored higher than 80 percent, while one earned a dismal 65 percent rating. There was some consolation for B Company, however. The "goat" of platoons was Lt. Paul K. Thompson's 1st Platoon of Company C, which earned a negligible 35 percent. Even the hand-picked battalion I&R platoon failed to shine, however, earning only a 76 percent score when it completely failed the evaluated task "motor patrolling" despite this being a critical Occupation task as well as a combat mission. Second Battalion's superior performance apparently resulted from a greater attention to detail and focus on the fundamentals than in 1st Battalion. For example, during the train-up period in early October, Col. F. M. Harris's observer team from OCAFF found the battalion engaged in a demonstration of the battle task "platoon in the attack." All rifle platoons were present, as well as all company commanders. Although the task was "conducted on flat, open terrain and . . . not too realistic," the evaluators lauded it as a training technique, especially the detailed critique of the demonstration platoon's performance afterward.[25]

Following a four-day period of retraining and refocusing of leaders' attention, both battalions underwent certification by the division G-3 section. This additional check on progress allowed the division commander to protect both his own and his subordinates' reputations as well as identify critical training deficiencies. Both battalions passed, however, and the day after the training holiday they marched into the maneuver area to be tested by evaluators from the IX Corps G-3 staff. The test, Army Field Forces Training Test 7–12 (Reinforced Infantry Battalion Combat Firing Test) evaluated the battalion on both offensive and defensive missions. The 99th Field Artillery Battalion fired its 105-mm howitzers in support of each battalion's attack missions. Each test lasted forty-eight hours and included nighttime, limited-visibility tasks. In addition to battling the regimental I&R platoon, which served as the aggressor force, both battalions fought the elements. Heavy rains hampered 1st Battalion's execution of the defense, while five inches of snow nearly led to the cancellation of 2nd Battalion's deliberate attack.[26] Despite this, both battalions received satisfactory ratings from IX Corps and departed for Tokyo on November 23 on a high note. The regiment observed a delayed Thanksgiving Day, feasting on November 29 instead of November 22 so that a proper meal could be prepared and served. Thus, by the beginning of December 1949 the 8th Cavalry Regiment had achieved the training goals established for infantry battalions in General Walker's Training Directive Number Four. Colonel Palmer and his subordinates could anticipate the arrival of the new year as an opportunity to build on "a valuable training period which [would] permit the Regiment to assemble to its fullest strength and operate as a unified team."

Training in December focused on limited collective training, marksmanship training for new replacements, command post exercises for headquarters elements, and a significant attempt to reduce the number of soldiers absent from training in order to take remedial education classes. Although division headquarters acted in November to curtail this problem by requiring new replacements to pass a basic skills test or be processed for separation, the solution did nothing for those soldiers already in regimental assignments. Within the 8th Cavalry Regiment thirty-four soldiers were enrolled in special classes designed to improve the reading and writing skills of soldiers who did not possess the equivalent of a fifth-grade education and/or an AGCT score of 71 or higher. This program only addressed the most severe cases, however. The bulk of the regiment's enlisted strength resided in AGCT categories III (769 soldiers) or IV (888 soldiers). One college-educated lieutenant complained that he could hardly communicate with his men; their vocabularies were so different from his that in order to make himself understood he had to resort to "comic book English." To counter this negative impression, however, the regimental historian was quick to point out that 360 soldiers had voluntarily subscribed to various correspondence courses for personal improvement, the most popular being English grammar and automotive repair. Moreover, other factors also acted to hinder the attainment of combat readiness, including high officer turbulence, limited training areas, and the volume of administrative overhead required to keep higher headquarters abreast of training, Occupation, and administrative issues.[27]

On November 29, 1949, Maj. Gen. Hobart Gay issued his training guidance for the coming calendar year to all units of the 1st Cavalry Division. The new year's training plan specifically emphasized the creation of an offensive combat capability within the division, a focus absent from other divisions' training plans. Continuing the progressive nature of the previous year's training plan, General Gay envisioned completion of testing and certification at the regimental combat team level by July 15, 1950, and completion of a division exercise by September 1, 1950. In addition, specialty training such as air transportability, air-to-ground training and coordination of close air support, and certification of battalion amphibious assault teams would also be conducted during the spring and summer of 1950. Acknowledging the reality that the division's presence in Tokyo necessitated a continued Occupation role, Gay nevertheless directed his regimental commanders to ensure that "no tactical unit will be assigned, other than temporarily, missions incompatible with its final objective of becoming an effective part of the next higher combat echelon." Gay considered the training mission, and specifically collective training of battalions and regiments, so important that he ordered his subordinates to minimize the time and resources devoted to small-unit and basic training. In order to correct a trend that he discussed with subordinate commanders at a conference in November, Training Memorandum 18 emphasized the importance of trainer preparation to the success of any training event: "Attention to detail, combined with 'Knowledge of the Subject' and 'Knowledge of the Methods of Instruction' will increase the quality of instruction." The number of hours per week allocated to training increased modestly and remained spread across five and one-half days. Finally, Gay encouraged his subordinates to be creative in the ways they resourced their training programs. Limited training and exercise budgets would require improvisation on the part of leaders to provide that "quality instruction" that Gay demanded of his subordinates.[28]

Remarkably, General Gay implicitly directed his subordinates to ignore Training Memorandum 18 just days after it was published. After expressing his satisfaction with the progress of unit training over the course of 1949, Gay outlined his vision for the first quarter of calendar year 1950:

During the first three months of next year, our training program calls for what we might term, a review of individual and specialist training. Really, this is garrison training. During this three-month period I want you to emphasize:

a. The position of the soldier at attention. The posture of too many of our men is improper.

b. The proper fitting and wearing of the uniform. Many of our uniforms indicate that the wearer has never been to the Quartermaster fitting room.

c. Proper fitting and repair of shoes.

d. Discipline and courtesy.

e. Manual of arms.

f. Maintenance and care of vehicles.

g. Improvement of messes and barracks, particularly the messes, bathing and toilet facilities.

In other words, this is a period of sprucing up, and I want everybody to go after it.[29]

Thus, despite his earlier admonition to commanders to "start at the top and, through the chain of command, to the bottom demand and get a higher standard of leadership," Gay's remarks indicate the continued intrusion of peacetime and "chickenshit" mindsets into the realm of Cold War readiness.

Acceleration: January to June 1950

General Gay's focus on individual soldier discipline and appearance may have resulted from reports by his staff of the detrimental effects that the previous year's training cycle had had on unit commanders' abilities to ensure that all soldiers met the army's minimum individual training requirements. As reiterated at the January conference, the 1st Cavalry Division's policy was that "no man will be sent from the Division Replacement Company to his unit until his records (Form 20) show that he is MTP qualified. . . . Qualification consists in general of a man's taking and passing the physical fitness test and taking and passing the general military subjects examination. . . . [MTP qualification] should be completed prior to the first day of February 1950."[30] Anticipating this focus, company commanders in the 8th Cavalry had already identified, trained, and scheduled the certification of their soldiers. On January 8 and January 24, 1950, a total of forty-three replacements from the regiment earned their MTP certification. While this went on, commanders focused the bulk of their training effort on marksmanship, squad and platoon problems, communications training, and fire direction training for members of mortar platoons and sections. Also, the regiment detailed selected personnel from each unit for training on the basics of air transportability. This training continued into February, interrupted by the requirement to field a parade unit of approximately seventy-five soldiers in honor of a visit by the Joint Chiefs of Staff to Tokyo. As the G-3 recorded, "All division units continued intensive training during February pointed toward final preparation for the Camp McNair training period."[31]

The 8th Cavalry's planned share of available time at Camp McNair amounted to four three-week periods between mid-April and late September 1950. The first event, scheduled for April 22 to May 9, focused on refresher training at squad, platoon, and company level as well as recertification of squads and platoons. Recertification was a necessary prerequisite before proceeding to company and battalion tests because of the continued high turnover of personnel within maneuver battalions. Training Memorandum Number 18 directed subordinate commanders to manage personnel losses in order to preserve certification as long as possible, but even this was only a stop-gap measure. Average personnel turbulence meant that a rifle squad would have lost its certification after only sixty days. This fact highlights the difficulty of meeting the training and certification prerequisites of a progressive training program without a coherent manpower policy for the U.S. Army. As it was, the division historian acknowledged that the coming summer months would see a drop in combat effectiveness across the division resulting from continued high turbulence within its ranks. As a result, both the schedule and objectives for collective training at Camp McNair changed in late March. Under the new guidance, the 8th Cavalry's scheduled training periods shifted to May 6–27 and June 3–24, 1950. During this time the battalions were expected to complete all Phase II training and certification up to platoon-level proficiency.[32]

Both battalions easily met this goal, having spent much of March completing refresher training on the training tasks "platoon in the attack" and "platoon defense" as well as familiarization and qualification firing with individual weapons at close ranges. In addition, the regiment's allocation of seats at the division air transportability course remained fully subscribed, and the regimental headquarters participated in the monthly Eighth Army command post exercise. Also during March the 8th Cavalry participated in the 1st Cavalry Division Small Arms Tournament; Rocking Horse's pistol team lost to the 5th Cavalry Regiment by just three-tenths of a point.[33]

Training came to a sudden halt in April, however. The transfer of authority and relaxation of Occupation controls led some Japanese to complain about the continued heavy presence of American soldiers in metropolitan Tokyo. As a result, GHQ FEC directed Eighth Army to relocate nonessential units. For the 8th Cavalry Regiment, their staggered battalion deployment schedule allowed 2nd Battalion and the "provisional battalion" of the regiment (medical, support, and heavy mortar companies along with the regimental headquarters company) to move from the Third Imperial Guard Barracks to Camp Zama, Japan, while 1st Battalion completed platoon testing in mid-May 1950. The new location, approximately 75 miles northwest of Tokyo, removed a significant number of American soldiers from the metropolitan area while keeping them close enough to respond to civil unrest or a military emergency. This move was completed between May 4 and June 1, 1950. Plans to move 1st Battalion from Camp King at Omiya to Camp Zama in July were also published during this month. Second Battalion soldiers underwent limited training during their move, including techniques of fire and landscape target firing (dry fires) for machine gun crews and domestic disturbance exercises for the rifle squads.[34]

Certification of 1st Battalion's rifle platoons and specialty platoons ended on May 24. During the division-administered tests, each rifle platoon executed an assault on a fixed fortification site and a defense of key terrain. In addition to testing the platoon leader's mastery of his own unit's fires, General Gay stipulated that each rifle platoon also have a 60-mm mortar section and a medium machine gun section attached to it. The regimental heavy mortar company, a platoon of tanks from Company A, 71st Tank Battalion, and a firing battery from the 82nd Field Artillery Battalion were also at Camp McNair to conduct their own tests in conjunction with 1st Battalion.[35] Besides forcing the sergeant or lieutenant platoon leader to think in terms of combined arms, employing a common exercise for multiple units allowed for concurrent evaluations, thus helping to reduce scheduling conflicts.

During June the 1st Battalion conducted its own relocation to Camp Zama, while 2nd Battalion finished refresher training for squads and platoons and completed its own platoon certifications on June 23. Consolidating the regiment at their new home, Colonel Palmer anticipated a full summer of training activities. The 1st Cavalry Division's Training Memorandum Number 13, issued in early May, laid out an ambitious schedule of higher-unit exercises and certification. Breaking the remainder of the calendar year into two blocks, General Gay expected his subordinates to complete training and testing at the battalion and regimental level in time to allow division-level exercises for each regimental combat team to be completed by November 4. The remaining weeks of 1950 would then be devoted to retraining on deficiencies noted during testing and certification. Palmer's 8th Cavalry Regiment would conduct battalion training and certification by August 19 and earn regimental certification by representatives of Eighth Army G-3 during the period September 30 to October 7. During battalion testing, commanders could plan for additional mortars, tanks, engineers, and artillery to be attached to their units as well as the opportunity to employ close air support sorties flown by elements of the Far East Air Force. Both battalion and regimental tests focused on unit movements, execution of a deliberate attack, unit reorganization and defense of seized terrain, and a withdrawal at night.[36]

CHAPTER 7

The outbreak of war in Korea two days after the 8th Cavalry consolidated at Camp Zama initially caused no change to planned training beyond a heightened alert status for air defense units. However, on July 2, Eighth Army asserted control of all subordinate units. Training was suspended, and the 1st Cavalry Division began planning for movement of some or all of the division to Korea for combat. All division schools were closed, and replacements were hurried to their gaining units. On July 4 the division G-3 notified Eighth Army that the sudden transfer of NCOs to fill out the 24th and 25th Divisions had significantly lowered the combat effectiveness of the division. Although he requested an additional authorization of ammunition to conduct at least familiarization fires by squads, operational requirements soon rendered his question moot. The 8th Cavalry's 1st Battalion departed Camp Zama for seaports on the west coast of Honshu on July 10. The remainder of the regiment joined it two days later. On July 18, 1950, Rocking Horse landed in Korea; a week later they were in combat near Yongdong.[37]

8

Conclusions

THE preceding chapters present a detailed picture of Eighth Army's readiness. Although it would be incorrect to state that units in Japan were fully prepared for combat in 1950, the descriptions of soft Occupation soldiers offered by most of the authors discussed in chapter 1 simply do not stand up to scrutiny. It is a fact that the U.S. Army in 1950 suffered from a multitude of internal and external problems, and the cumulative effects of these problems made success in combat problematic. Three other facts must be borne in mind, however, in making any assessment of Eighth Army's training program. First, most of these problems did not originate in Eighth Army. Instead, they resulted from decisions made by officials of the Truman administration with the active assistance of senior U.S. Army officers. Second, these problems did not deter commanders at every level from seeking to enhance the combat readiness of their units. The variety of solutions pursued by combat, combat support, and even combat service support units described above indicates that the shift in outlook was not restricted to infantry regiments or artillery battalions. Instead, there was a force-wide attempt to instill a warrior ethos in the soldiers of the Eighth Army. As incomplete and uneven as this process was on June 25, 1950, it is not difficult to imagine Eighth Army's fate had it not begun at all. Third, it is incorrect to lay the bulk of the blame for the reverses suffered in the summer and fall of 1950 at the feet of the officers and men of Eighth Army. The elimination of critical components of infantry and artillery organizations, the promulgation of personnel policies that retarded the development of unit cohesion, and a willful disregard for the importance of maintaining a basic training program of instruction that produced fully qualified soldiers were deliberate decisions made by the Army Staff in Washington, D.C., without consideration for the tactical and operational impact such decisions would have on combat operations. Moreover, the Truman administration's chronic inability to articulate a force structure requirement that it could live with for more than a few months generated unsustainable personnel turbulence on the entire U.S. Army. Therefore, critics of the army's performance in the Korean War must cast a wider net for clues as to why the nation that defeated Germany and Japan left its army hardly capable of retaining a lodgment in southeastern Korea only five years later.

Some basic themes emerge from this study that will help in the search for those clues. First, many if not most Americans viewed a large army with ambivalence in 1950. Second, the postwar demobilization and the U.S. Army's own personnel policies resulted from President Truman's failure to articulate a feasible and acceptable national military policy following the Japanese surrender. Third, no one in the War/Defense Department in the late 1940s seems to have understood the national security implications inherent in the unregulated disposal of war material and an almost nonexistent procurement budget. Fourth, and related to the second theme, the army's training doctrine had not changed significantly from what had sufficed to defeat the Axis powers. Little agitation for change existed because of wide acceptance of the alert-train-deploy model regarding use of ground forces. Finally, the influence battlefield experience or lack thereof played in coloring the perceptions and priorities of officers and noncommissioned officers cannot be quantified but must be considered as a factor bearing on individual units' achieving the desired readiness goals.

The use of the atomic bomb to end World War II changed the paradigm of national defense for the United States. Contemporary observers both in and outside the Defense Department began to believe that conventional ground and even naval forces were henceforth not just useless but dangerous if by their existence they encouraged leaders to contemplate war. Acknowledging the need for an Occupation force to maintain order in the defeated Axis nations by no means equated to an open-ended commitment to the maintenance of a large standing army. Indeed, such a force was believed to be antithetical to the economic interests of the republic and a break with tradition. The rapid demobilization of the U.S. Army in 1945–47 resulted directly from congressional demands that American citizens be released from service with the passing of the emergency—as had happened after every conflict since 1783. By this reasoning the army should have been told to anticipate manpower authorizations somewhat higher than pre-1940 levels in order to execute Occupation duties but to be prepared to shrink further immediately upon ratification of peace treaties with the former Axis powers. Thus, in the crucial years between V-J Day and the Soviet announcement of a successful atomic weapon test, when the West explicitly sought to prevent the spread of Communism into vulnerable areas of the world, the dominant factor in defense planning in both the executive and legislative branches was fiscal, not strategic. Few officials believed that the nation could afford to maintain a ground combat force large enough to meet all potential contingencies, and fewer still spoke their minds. As we have seen, even Omar Bradley believed that the FY 1950 budget appropriation could not have been significantly increased without threatening the health of the national economy. Others gravitated to the view that air forces had supplanted other services in terms of value for money and voted accordingly.

The continuation of Selective Service in 1946, its lapse in 1947, and its resuscitation in 1948 reflected the conflicts raging in Congress and the Truman administration between officials who desired a return to prewar practices and those who sought to gird the nation against an ill-defined but emerging threat. This conflict had not resolved itself when Kim Il-sung's army crossed the 38th Parallel on June 25, 1950. Even among those who recognized the threat posed to the West by Communism, many doubted that a large ground force was the proper solution. The Truman administration's support for a collective security arrangement in Europe resulted in part from its understanding that the principal military contribution expected of the United States would be atomic weapons and strategic air forces. The Europeans themselves were originally expected to provide the land armies to contain and then defeat a Soviet invasion. Thus, the United States would not bankrupt itself by raising and maintaining a multimillion-soldier army but instead invest in areas where it believed it already possessed a commanding lead over the Soviets: aerospace engineering, aircraft manufacturing, and atomic weapons.

This conception dovetailed well with bipartisan legislative and executive policies on demobilization in the first two years after 1945 and with prevalent expectations of how a future war would develop. The clamor to "bring the boys home" became so loud that even General of the Army Dwight D. Eisenhower could not staunch the flow of personnel. It was simply inconceivable to most American leaders that the postwar era would require a large standing army. The reestablishment of a coherent and effective Reserve component in the wake of demobilization assumed greater importance than the manning of the Regular Army precisely because experience in 1917 and in 1940 had supposedly demonstrated the validity of maintaining a skeletal Regular force to be augmented in an emergency by Reserves. Even in the atomic age it was assumed that after the initial exchange of atomic weapons a lengthy stalemate would ensue. During this time both sides would bind their wounds, mobilize their populations and resources, and only then begin ground combat operations in an attempt to win decisively. No one anticipated that the obsolescence of traditional Great Power diplomacy after 1945 would not diminish but amplify the need for the two leading powers to demonstrate their commitment and their credibility to ally and enemy alike in order to sustain their positions. This need, executed in the Cold War context of potential atomic/nuclear warfare, made it imperative for both sides to react quickly to any provocation. Gone were the days when either side could exchange face and space for time, because to do so in the atomic age theoretically invited an enemy to conduct a first strike to settle the question once and for all. The Eighth Army in 1949–50 was not organized, trained, or equipped to act as a strategic containment force. Rather, its leaders envisioned deployments in Japan that were substantially the same as were actually executed in Korea: tactical and operational delays to allow employment of a strategic reserve. Thus, the Truman administration's inability to develop and communicate a viable national security policy led directly to the deployment of the Eighth Army for a mission that the rest of America's military establishment could not support.

Even if it had not been so tasked, however, the U.S. Army's own personnel policies in the late 1940s threatened the coherence and efficiency of all units. Unable to convince the Truman administration of the strategic necessity to impose a floor on personnel reductions, the U.S. Army shrank in size every year from 1945 to 1950. Moreover, these reductions occurred in fits and starts, not according to a timetable or master plan. There was no program to retain technical specialists or mid-grade noncommissioned officers in the aftermath of World War II and no attempt to field a regular army of the size and capability recommended by General Eisenhower in 1945. The army that emerged from the dust of demobilization in the summer of 1947 was hardly worthy of the name. The vast majority of the soldiers had entered service after September 1945. The officer corps was riven by strife between officers with Regular Army (US) commissions and those commissioned into the Army of the United States (AUS). Both groups sought to limit the other's perceived advantages for promotion, retention on active duty, and assignments. Then, too, in the aftermath of the war the army conducted an officer drawdown similar to what had occurred in the period 1919–20. Many officers with combat experience, US as well as AUS, saw themselves reduced in rank for no apparent or logical reason. As John Michaelis put it, combat-proven officers were reduced in rank because "someone in Washington thought we were too young to be colonels."

Just as insidious was the emergence of a supposedly scientifically deduced career path for officers and noncommissioned officers. The idea that officers of the Regular Army should not possess expertise in a single field but should be superficially acquainted with a variety of different specialties could only have had merit within the confines of an out-of-touch bureaucracy. This emphasis on "universal" officers and NCOs who could be placed in leadership positions in units of any type in an emergency diluted what little institutional memory of combat remained in the U.S. Army after 1947. Again because few people and no leaders in the army recognized that the paradigm for national security had changed as a result of the Cold War and atomic weapons, the field army was forced to accept abbreviated command tours and tours of duty away from soldiers in order to allow officers and NCOs to "punch their tickets." Extending this concept to its logical conclusions resulted in situations that were inimical to the interests and security of the United States. The assignment of noninfantry officers to command infantry battalions, either as a reward for past performance, as a tombstone assignment, or to gain command experiences unavailable in the officer's basic branch, offered no benefit to the army and can only be described as the exacting of revenge by bureaucratic agents uncomfortable with their own contributions to national defense during World War II.

The majority's acceptance of the mobilization paradigm for national defense also allowed both Congress and the Truman administration to deny the necessity of either maintaining war stocks already on hand or of placing new orders in the years after 1945 to maintain a go-to-war capability. As in other areas the dominant consideration appears to have been financial. To receive, catalog, store, and maintain several billion dollars' worth of military equipment with no apparent threat appeared to be an extravagance that the U.S. Army could ill afford in the lean years of 1946–50. In all theaters hundreds of tons of material were left in place, sold to enterprising locals for pennies on the dollar, or given away as reconstruction aid grants to foreign governments. The scattering of equipment across the Pacific exacerbated the problem for the Eighth Army. Consolidation of equipment from several geographically isolated depots established to support the island-hopping campaigns would have required an enormous investment in time, money, and manpower. Stocks of munitions, vehicles, spare parts, aircraft, and even uniforms and web gear rotted away in the tropical weather as ships and airplanes were diverted to demobilization until those platforms were themselves sold as surplus. Such material as remained by the late 1940s was in dire need of refurbishing. Complete overhauls using reclaimed parts offered only a partial solution, however, and retooling the Japanese industrial base to accommodate the needs of the U.S. military occurred too late to prepare Eighth Army adequately for war. Even so, both in Europe and the Far East the efforts made to reclaim equipment procured before 1945 allowed the U.S. Army to enhance its readiness at a fraction of the cost of new procurement. That this process did not yield materials comparable to newly manufactured items is hardly the fault of the soldiers and civilians of

Base Industrial Group 5, who did the best job they could with what was given them.

The creation of an independent command to develop and implement training for both individual soldiers and units marked a break with the past for the U.S. Army. Before World War II the mobilization of units occurred as a result of both national and state efforts, and the army left training up to unit commanders. It provided printed doctrine and little else in the way of support. However, General Marshall recognized in the wake of the 1941 Louisiana Maneuvers that the War Department staff was simply unable to simultaneously mobilize, train, and employ the mass army anticipated for war against Germany and Japan. Henceforth, Army Ground Forces would execute the mobilization and training. The concept of centralized basic training survived postwar demobilization but not in the form desired by General Devers and his subordinates. Driven by personnel turbulence caused by demobilization and by constantly shifting personnel requirements, AGF watched as the institutional advantages of the training centers fell victim to expediency. For long periods between 1945 and 1950 the training centers were little more than way stations between the recruiter's office and the gaining unit, with only cursory attention devoted to imparting soldier skills or socialization into the army. As a result many officers and senior NCOs mistakenly viewed the training centers as the problem. Hence, General Walker decided to require every unit in Eighth Army to begin their unit training programs with individual basic training for all soldiers with less than twelve months' service in the Far East. However, even had every replacement received in the Far East after April 15, 1949, been fully trained under the fourteen-week program, the fact that overseas tours were arbitrarily shortened in late 1949 in order to reduce end strength would have rendered such a qualitative increase moot. As regimental records unanimously indicate, readiness levels actually dropped in the first quarter of 1950 because of the rotation of so many soldiers to the Zone of the Interior. Walker's decision to conduct basic training within the parent unit at least allowed Eighth Army to benefit from the team-building aspects of such a program, but that advantage paled in comparison to the superior skill training that a fully resourced training center could have provided. Moreover, such intangible benefits evaporated in the rush of body-snatching that characterized Eighth Army's attempt to fill out the 24th and 25th Infantry Divisions in June and July of 1950.

Unit commanders correctly diagnosed this problem and attempted to alleviate it through iterative training. The continued emphasis on fundamental skill mastery that occurred between major training events such as battalion or regimental exercises demonstrates that commanders at those levels recognized the importance of integrating newly arrived soldiers into the training program as quickly as possible. Only if the replacement soldier fully understood his role as an individual rifleman and a member of a fire team and squad could the unit hope to progress in its collective training program. With turbulence as high as 50 percent every sixty days for a nine-man rifle squad, the challenge for commanders remained one of maintaining basic competency, not of progressing to full mastery of every tactical task that might need to be performed in combat.

Several problems existed that were either specific to Eighth Army or more prevalent in Japan than in other areas. These included a general lack of maneuver training areas large enough to accommodate units above a reinforced infantry battalion; a poorly developed road network that required any large-scale unit move to be accomplished using the Japanese rail system, itself heavily damaged during the war; the continued requirement to execute Occupation-related missions during the training cycle; and a lack of funds to maintain equipment damaged during training. Each of these problems affected Eighth Army's ability to build combat readiness among the infantry divisions. Their combined effects amplified the challenges imposed on commanders by the personnel and force structure decisions made at the national level.

The most frequent complaint by veterans of the 1949–50 period in Japan concerns the lack of suitable training areas. As was the case in Europe, American units made extensive use of former enemy facilities. Because of the necessity not to interfere with the rehabilitation of the Japanese economy, however, and the vast differences between Imperial Japanese Army and U.S. Army tactical doctrine, many of these facilities proved less than adequate. Time and again commanders highlighted this issue in their combat effectiveness reports. The dictates of Japanese geography prevented Eighth Army or FEC from doing much to alleviate the problem, however. The maneuver area at Mount Fuji was expanded in 1949 to allow regimental combat team exercises, but this came at the cost of returning smaller training areas to Japanese control. Those maneuver areas that remained under U.S. control became highly sought-after commodities whose use was regulated by divisions and even Eighth Army. The problem with the local training areas was that they were too small to conduct more than company-level training. Consequently, repeated use for battalion exercises or even multiple company training lanes ensured that soldiers became quite familiar with the terrain in the area and reduced many training exercises to rote execution of tasks.

The size and layout of these training areas also conspired to limit them to one or two locations suitable for the establishment of command posts, usually chosen with greater emphasis on radio reception than security or other tactical considerations. As a result, communications platoons seldom trained to the maximum effective range of their equipment, and command post personnel seldom learned how to relocate the command post at frequent intervals and still maintain situational awareness. Moreover, the directed nature of the training program naturally led units to conduct the same missions on the same ground over the course of several iterations. Doing so doubtless robbed the exercises of some of their realism and adversely affected the attitudes of soldiers. And yet this type of repetition could have served a better purpose had the training been conducted in the units' planned defensive positions. Under those conditions the repetitive nature could have been tied to war plans and contingencies. The evolving nature of the U.S.-Japanese relationship, however, prohibited conducting exercises outside of designated maneuver areas. Consequently, commanders did the best they could with the resources they had.

These limited resources were spread very thinly in an attempt to provide some training benefit to all four divisions. The divisions had to balance achievement of the training goals with the residual Occupation tasks they retained even after April 1949. At times these requirements diverted units from the training program, as happened to the 8th Cavalry Regiment in August 1949. It would have been better for everyone involved had General Walker taken the initial division of his staff's Occupation and training responsibilities to its logical conclusion. For example, given the geographic dispersion of units in Japan, he could have designated one division in each of the two former corps areas as a constabulary force while focusing the other division on the defense of Japan. This had been done with some success with U.S. forces in the American Occupation Zone in Germany. Alternately, with the demise of the corps headquarters in March 1950 General Walker could have tasked the 1st Cavalry Division with the Occupation mission. This did not occur in Japan, however, for the same reasons that the U.S. Constabulary in Europe reorganized as a composite infantry-armored division in 1948. The growing tensions arising from the Cold War demanded that what limited military capability the U.S. possessed must be devoted to defense and security. Hence OCAFF's exhortation in 1949 that "*every soldier,* regardless of assignment, has as his primary duty the obligation to fight or support the fight." A similar debate occurred in the U.S. Army in the mid-1990s as the Bush and Clinton administrations committed U.S. forces to stability operations on an unprecedented scale. The justification for not doing so remained unchanged from 1950: despite the end of the Cold War and the collapse of the Soviet Union, the strategic threats arrayed against the United States and its allies precluded the reorganization of the 10th Mountain Division as a constabulary-only force.

The fact that all four divisions embarked on the training mission placed an incredible strain on the logistics system. Operation Roll-Up and the creation of the Base Industrial Group in Japan had only begun to address the equipment

CONCLUSIONS

needs of the Occupation force. Expanding the requirement to include combat systems such as tanks and howitzers only added to the workload. Units in combat quickly exhausted the supply of refurbished or out-of-mothballs World War II–era equipment. The lack of a postwar procurement program prevented U.S. Army logisticians from preparing contingency stocks. One consequence of this situation was the extension of the service life of many items long past what the manufacturer had envisioned. Recapped tires, rebuilt engines and transmissions, and reconditioned weapons systems (all of which had seen extensive combat service) were the norm, not the exception. And although some units did report sufficient quantities of replacement and repair parts at the local level, at the theater level stocks of everything from ammunition to vehicles to uniforms remained below minimum wartime needs. The ammunition situation became so critical in early 1950 that the training program required modification. Had Eighth Army not imposed a prohibition on small arms live fires during battalion and regimental combat team certifications, the units deployed to Korea in June and July may have been unable to delay the Communists as long as they did.

Americans do not like to prepare for war. They have only grudgingly come to accept a large standing army and huge defense budgets as a result of experience in the Cold War and especially since the attacks of September 11, 2001. That many in both Congress and the Bush administration could, as late as the summer of 2001, contemplate a reduction of the Regular Army from ten to eight divisions indicates that the lessons that should have been learned in the summer of 1950 have yet to sink in. National security will always entail domestic political tradeoffs, but these should never occur at the expense of the soldiers whom the nation sends into harm's way as a result of national policy. The use of Task Force Smith as a metaphor for unreadiness has done incalculable harm to the reputation of the soldiers of the Eighth Army in 1950 and allows policy makers to shift blame away from themselves. It is my hope that the preceding chapters will renew the debate regarding the preparation and employment of U.S. ground troops in combat in 1950 and that the focus of the debate will shift from the assignment of blame to an understanding of the true pillars of combat readiness.

NOTES

Chapter 1

1. Doris M. Condit, *History of the Office of the Secretary of Defense*, vol. 2, *The Test of War, 1950–1953*, 53; General of the Army Douglas MacArthur, *Reminiscences*, 336.

2. Roy K. Flint, "Task Force Smith and the 24th Infantry Division: Delay and Withdrawal, 5–19 July 1950," in *America's First Battles 1776–1965*, ed. Charles E. Heller and William A. Stoft, 266–99. See also Clay Blair, *The Forgotten War: America in Korea, 1950–1953*, 101–103; Jonathan M. House, *Combined Arms Warfare in the Twentieth Century*, 185ff.

3. Roy E. Appleman, *South to the Naktong, North to the Yalu*, United States Army in the Korean War series, 73–74, 77–82, 92–100, 132–37; Blair, *Forgotten War*, 168; James L. Stokesbury, *A Short History of the Korean War*, 58ff.

4. Col. William J. Davies, "Task Force Smith: A Leadership Failure?" study project, U.S. Army War College, 66; "Why Are We Taking a Beating?" *Life* 29, no. 4 (July 24, 1950), 21.

5. Letter, Lt. Gen. (Ret.) W. W. Dick to Clay Blair, December 14, 1984, Folder "24th/25th Divisions," *Forgotten War* Papers, Clay and Joan Blair Collection, U.S. Army Military History Institute (USAMHI), Carlisle Barracks, Pennsylvania; Sam Boal, "New Soldiers for New Tasks," *New York Times Magazine*, July 23, 1950, 7–9, 40–42; Bill Davidson, "The New G.I. Joe: He Never Had It So Good," *Collier's* 126, no. 14 (September 30, 1950), 24–25, 71–75.

6. Compton Pakenham, "Green Men under Fire," *Newsweek* 36, no. 3 (July 17, 1950), 16–18; Carl Mydans, "It's One Ration. Save It, Boys," *Life* 29, no. 2 (July 17, 1950), 22–23; Frank Gibney, "Advance Patrol Pushes Up through Enemy Fire," *Life* 29, no. 2 (July 17, 1950), 36–37. Cf. Harold Levin, "Hell Country: Of Mud, Muck, and Human Excrement . . . ," *Newsweek* 36, no. 6 (August 7, 1950), 20–21; W. H. Lawrence, "A Day in the Life of a Platoon," *New York Times Magazine*, September 10, 1950, 13, 70.

7. Bevin Alexander, *Korea: The First War We Lost*, 46. Like Appleman, Alexander served as a U.S. Army historian in Korea in 1951 and 1952. Paul M. Edwards, *To Acknowledge a War*, 28ff.

8. Matthew B. Ridgway interview, Senior Officer Oral History Program, Combat Leadership in Korea series, U.S. Army Military History Institute; Col. John T. Corley, "Lean and Hungry Soldiers," *Combat Forces Journal* 1, no. 12 (July 1951), 16–18; Eugene Kinkead, *In Every War but One*, 211ff; Edwards, *To Acknowledge a War*, 59. The army's own research showed that fewer than 20 percent of nonveteran volunteers named "travel, adventure, or new experiences" as their primary motivation for enlisting in the late 1940s. Thirty percent named the opportunity for vocational experience as the dominant factor (thus validating Corley's criticism to a certain degree). Veterans overwhelmingly attributed their return to the army to a

desire for economic and employment security. Data from Maj. Paul D. Guernsey, "New Army, New Soldiers," *Army Information Digest* 3, no. 5 (May 1948), 26–30.

9. Russell F. Weigley, *A History of the United States Army*, provides the most concise summary, 502–504. See also James F. Schnabel, *Policy and Direction: The First Year*, United States Army in the Korean War series, 42–62; D. Clayton James, *Refighting the Last War: Command and Crisis in Korea, 1950–1953*, 1–8; Donald A. Carter, "From G.I. to Atomic Soldier: The Development of U.S. Army Tactical Doctrine, 1945–1956," Ph.D. diss., The Ohio State University, 1987, 14–53.

10. Keith D. McFarland and David L. Roll, *Louis Johnson and the Arming of America: The Roosevelt and Truman Years*, 188ff., 204 (chapter 12, "Like a Meatchopper on Roundsteak," provides the most concise synopsis of Johnson's impact on the Defense Department budget); "Why Are We Taking a Beating?" *Life* 29, no. 4 (July 24, 1950), 21.

11. Matthew B. Ridgway and Harold H. Martin, *Soldier: The Memoirs of Matthew B. Ridgway*, 165, 190. Ridgway knew better than to cast stones at Walker. In his final report to the secretary of the army in 1948, Eisenhower warned that the army as then constituted could not conduct wartime operations. See Carter, "From G.I. to Atomic Soldier," 16.

The Doolittle Board, convened in 1945, was charged with "ironing out the iniquities [sic] that were alleged to exist at the time between the officer and the enlisted men." The board interviewed just forty-two witnesses and admitted as evidence fewer than one thousand letters, many written by demobilized soldiers "who manifestly hated regimentation and resented the loss of their personal identity" when inducted into the army for World War II. The board recommended several changes in the manner by which a commander enforced discipline and also greatly expanded the role of the Inspector General, which henceforth "permits a soldier to appeal from his superior's authority to a third person who was not present when that authority was exercised." Numerous letter writers in the service journals describe the period of adjustment to the new system in 1945–46 as "The Great Wailing and Gnashing." For an example, see Capt. Mark M. Boatner III, "Martinets or Mollycoddlers," *Combat Forces Journal* 1, no. 5 (August 1950), 11.

12. J. Lawton Collins, *War in Peacetime: The History and Lessons of Korea*, 5–6, 74. Collins evidently needed the twenty-year gap between an observation trip to Japan in 1949 and publication of his book in order to understand what he had seen; his initial report of his observations of training in Japan concluded that EUSA units "are making excellent progress with realistic field training. . . . In another six months the division I inspected [the 25th on Honshu Island] should be in excellent shape" (Collins to Secretary of the Army Royall, October 20, 1949, cited in Schnabel, *Policy and Direction*, 57).

Omar N. Bradley and Clay Blair, *A General's Life: An Autobiography by General of the Army Omar N. Bradley*, 487 (presumably Bradley was still alive to give this statement to ghostwriter Blair); Testimony by Army Chief of Staff Bradley before the Senate Armed Services Committee, 25 March 1948, as recorded in "Our Military Requirements," *Army Digest* 3, no. 5 (May 1948), 61–63.

13. Edwards, *To Acknowledge a War*, 32; William Manchester, *The Glory and the Dream: A Narrative History of America, 1932–1972* (Boston: Little, Brown & Company, 1973), 778–79; T. R. Fehrenbach, *This Kind of War: A Study in Unpreparedness*, 90–92, 100, 123, 124, 162.

Fehrenbach arrived in Korea in 1952 and served in the 72nd Tank Battalion, 2nd Infantry Division, as well as in staff assignments.

See also Olivier Zunz, *Why the American Century?* (Chicago: University of Chicago Press, 1998), chaps. 4–7; James R. Kerin, "The Korean War and American Memory," Ph.D. diss., University of Pennsylvania, 1994; and Henry Berry, *Hey Mac, Where 'Ya Been? Living Memories of the U.S. Marines in the Korean War* (New York: St. Martin's, 1988).

Many veterans contacted regarding this project agreed that they had buried their memories for years before confronting them. See, for example, Robert H. Brothers, speech written for the Tell America program, copy provided to the author, January 1, 2002.

14. Appleman, *South to the Naktong*, 180; Charles W. McCarthy, "Lessons for All Ranks," *Army* 14, no. 2 (September 1963), 82. Nothing found in the Appleman Collection at the U.S. Army Military History Institute indicates that he relied on more than hearsay to determine the training status of the units he described.

Fehrenbach himself stated that his principal source material for *This Kind of War* came from stories he heard in 1952 and 1953, by which time everyone involved in the 1950 campaigns would have left Korea. Appleman's three subsequent books that discuss the Chosin Reservoir campaign, *Disaster in Korea: The Chinese Confront MacArthur* (College Station: Texas A&M University Press, 1989); *Escaping the Trap: The U.S. Army X Corps in Northeast Korea, 1950* (College Station: Texas A&M University Press, 1990); and *East of Chosin: Entrapment and Breakout in Korea, 1950* (College Station: Texas A&M University Press, 1993) all painted a poor picture of U.S. Army leadership at the regimental, division, and corps level, further eroding the army's credibility.

15. Weigley, *History of the United States Army*, 519; Blair, *Forgotten War*, 28–29; William M. Donnelly, "Army Readiness in 1950," unpublished Center of Military History paper, 2002, copy in author's possession, 9; Report of the Department of the Army Board on Educational System for Officers [the Eddy Board], Annex 4, "Assignment of the Newly Commissioned Officer," online document, U.S. Army Military History Institute, http://www.carlisle.army.mil/cgi-bin/usamhi/DL/showdoc.pl?docnum=120), 23–28.

16. Letter, Douglas MacArthur to Maj. Gen. R. W. Stephens, Chief, U.S. Army Center of Military History, November 15, 1957, subject: Comments on *South to Naktong, North to Yalu*, Roy E. Appleman Collection, U.S. Army Military History Institute.

17. L. James Binder, "No More Task Force Smiths," *Army* 42, no. 1 (January 1992), 18–26; Major Michael Cannon, "Task Force Smith: A Study in (Un)Preparedness and (Ir)Responsibility," *Military Review* 67, no. 11 (February 1988), 63–73.

18. Bruce Cumings, *The Origins of the Korean War*, vol. 2, *The Roaring of the Cataract, 1947–1950*, 665. Cumings dates the end of the "War for Containment" as October 1, 1950—the date ROK Army patrols crossed the 38th Parallel into North Korea. See also Allan R. Millett's three books *Mao's Generals Remember Korea* (Washington, D.C.: Brassey's, 2000); *Their War for Korea: American, Asian, and European Combatants and Civilians, 1945–1953* (Washington, D.C.: Brassey's, 2002); and *The War for Korea: A House Burning, 1945–1950*.

19. Lt. Col. (Ret.) Charles M. Bussey, *Firefight at Yechon: Courage and Racism in the Korean War* (Washington, D.C.: Brassey's, 1991); Lyle Rishell, *With a Black Platoon in Combat: A Year in Korea* (College Station: Texas A&M University Press, 1993); William T. Bowers, William M.

Hammond, and George L. McGarigle, *Black Soldier, White Army: The 24th Infantry Regiment in Korea*, 61–62. Many veterans offered up their own personal observations of the 24th's poor performance, including two who remembered threatening to shoot members of that regiment for deserting under fire.

20. Maj. Richard Wiersema, "No More Bad Force Myths," tactical monograph, U.S. Army Command and General Staff College School for Advanced Military Studies, Fort Leavenworth, Kansas, 1996; Interview, Col. (Ret.) Wilson Heefner, November 29, 2001. MacArthur made the comparison to then-Captain Samuel Walker when the latter returned to Japan from Korea to escort his father's body to the United States for burial in December 1950.

21. S. L. A. Marshall, *Bringing Up the Rear: A Memoir*, 183; S. L. A. Marshall, "Our Army in Korea—The Best Yet," *Harper's Magazine* 203 (August 1951), 21–27; F. D. G. Williams, *SLAM: The Influence of S. L. A. Marshall on the United States Army*, 82ff.

22. Davies, "Task Force Smith"; Robert L. Bateman, "GI Life in Postwar Japan," *MHQ: The Quarterly Journal of Military History* 15, no. 1 (Autumn 2002), 60–63. *This Kind of War* is the only book covering the Korean War on the Army Chief of Staff's Professional Reading List (www.army.mil/cmh-pg/CSAList/CSAList.htm).

Chapter 2

1. *Semiannual Report of the Secretary of the Army, January 1 to June 30 1950*, chap. 4, "Personnel," 86; *Annual Report of the Secretary of the Army for Fiscal Year 1949*, chap. 6, "Disposition of Troops," 143, and chap. 5, "Composition of the Army," 140. In these years the U.S. Army's fiscal year ran from July 1 to the following June 30.

2. Steven L. Rearden, *History of the Office of the Secretary of Defense*, vol. 1, *The Formative Years, 1947–1950*, 325ff; Kenneth W. Condit, *History of the Joint Chiefs of Staff*, vol. 2, *The Joint Chiefs of Staff and National Policy, 1947–1949*, 210; Paul Y. Hammond, "Super Carriers and B-36 Bombers: Appropriations, Strategy, and Politics," in *American Civil-Military Decisions*, ed. Harold Stein, 476ff.; Walter Millis, ed., *The Forrestal Diaries*, 435; *Military Organization of the United States*, 12ff.

3. Omar N. Bradley and Clay Blair, *A General's Life: An Autobiography by General of the Army Omar N. Bradley*, 482.

4. Robert A. Doughty, *The Evolution of U.S. Army Tactical Doctrine, 1946–1976*, Leavenworth Paper Number 1, 7; William Glenn Robertson, *Counterattack on the Naktong, 1950*, Leavenworth Paper Number 13, 3; Roy K. Flint, "Task Force Smith and the 24th Infantry Division: Delay and Withdrawal, 5–19 July 1950," in *America's First Battles 1776–1965*, ed. Charles E. Heller and William A. Stoft 269; James F. Schnabel, *Policy and Direction: The First Year*, 53. The only exception to these reductions was the 82nd Airborne Division.

5. Schnabel, *Policy and Direction*, 47; Secretary of the Army Kenneth C. Royall, "Civil Functions of the Army in the Occupied Areas," *Military Review* 29, no. 5 (August 1949), 37–43; Lt. Col. H. L. Hille, "The Eighth Army's Role in the Military Government of Japan," *Military Review* 27, no. 11 (February 1948), 10, 14.

6. "27th Infantry," *History of the Occupation of Japan*, 20, 23; Interview, Gen. (Ret.) John H. Michaelis, Senior Officer Oral History Program, Combat Leadership in Korea series, U.S. Army Military History Institute, 38; Flint, "Task Force Smith," 271. According to General

Dick, a private's pay "allowed him to live off base for ten dollars a month, with a girl to do the cleaning" (letter, Lt. Gen. (Ret.) W. W. Dick to Roy Appleman, Roy E. Appleman Collection, U.S. Army Military History Institute.

7. Ambassador William J. Sebald with Russell Brines, *With MacArthur in Japan: A Personal History of the Occupation* (New York: W. W. Norton, 1965), 95; Robert A. Fearey, *The Occupation of Japan: Second Phase, 1948–1950*, 11; Steven T. Ross, *American War Plans, 1945–1950*, 110–11; Annual Historical Report, 1949, 2, Headquarters Eighth U.S. Army Historical Section, RG 407, NARA II.

8. *Annual Historical Report, 1949*, 3. For an enlisted man's perspective on the early Occupation, see Edward Chaze, *Stainless Steel Kimono*. Chaze, a private in the 11th Airborne Division, served in Japan in 1945 and 1946. His experience typifies the "stability" phase of the U.S. Occupation. See Dudley C. Gould, *Follow Me Up Fool's Mountain: Korea 1951* (Middletown, Conn.: Southfarm Press, 2002); and William H. Funchess, *Korea POW: A Thousand Days of Torment* (privately published, 1997).

9. Robert L. Eichelberger and Milton Mackaye, *Our Jungle Road to Tokyo*, 270ff.; Eiji Takemae, *Inside GHQ: The Allied Occupation of Japan and Its Legacy*, trans. Robert Ricketts and Sebastian Swann, 120, 468ff.; Staff Memorandum no. 26, 21 June 1949, "Changes in Designation of Military Government Sections and Teams," Folder: Staff Memorandums, 1949, Subject File, Office of the Chief of Staff, Supreme Commander for the Allied Powers, RG 331, NARA II.

10. Condit, *Joint Chiefs of Staff*, 9–12, 271ff.; Ross, *American War Plans*, 110; GHQ FEC G-3 Section, "A Study of the Current Situation in the Far East Command," 7, Adjutant Generals Top Secret Correspondence Files, G-3 Section, RG 554, NARA II; Walter S. Poole, *History of the Joint Chiefs of Staff*, vol. 4, *The Joint Chiefs of Staff and National Policy, 1950–1952*, 87.

11. Operations Division Narrative, "Changes No. 7 to Occupation Instruction No. 5," Office of the Assistant Chief of Staff, G-3, GHQ FEC Historical Report 1 January–31 December 1949, vol. 1, 13, RG 554, NARA II; GHQ FEC G-3 Section, "A Study of the Current Situation in the Far East Command," 7; GHQ FEC Training Memorandum Number 1, 1 June 1947, specified that the first mission priority for Eighth Army was to maintain combat readiness "in the event of civil disorder" (Decimal File 333.2, G-3 Section, 1945–1948, RG 554, NARA II).

12. Eighth U.S. Army OPLAN 5–50, 010800 May 1950, paragraph 3, "Tasks for Subordinate Units," Adjutant Generals Section, Top Secret Correspondence, 1945–1952, Folder "May 1950," RG 338.9.9, NARA II.

13. Ent, *Fighting on the Brink: Defending the Pusan Perimeter* (Paducah, Ky.: Turner Publishing Co., 1996). 10.

14. Eighth Army Training Directive Number Four, 15 April 1949, Section I (General Plan), 1 (original emphasis), and Paragraph 6, "Training Phases and Objectives," Decimal File 353, RG 338.9.9, NARA II; Schnabel, *Policy and Direction*, 55; HQ, I Corps, Eighth Army, Training Directive 2, 15 May 1949, Decimal File 333, Folder January–June 1949, RG 338.9.9, NARA II; Interview, Gen. (Ret.) Peter D. Clainos, Senior Officers Oral History Program, Combat Leadership in Korea series, U.S. Army Military History Institute, Carlisle Barracks, Pa.

15. Hanson W. Baldwin, "The Condition of the Army," *New York Times*, June 22, 1950, sect. 1, p. 5. Concurrent readiness programs of the European Constabulary had considerably more flexibility in terms of ammunition available, scheduling of units for live-fire facilities,

and the number and variety of training areas open to use. See Paul Burckhardt, *The Major Training Areas of Germany: Grafenwöhr/Vilseck, Hohenfels, Wildflecken*, 4th ed.; Interview, Col. (Ret.) John Stratis (C Troop 72nd Constabulary Squadron, 1946–49), 24 July 2001. "Walker Creates Dual Deputies" *Stars and Stripes*, October 17, 1948, 3.

16. "Biography of Lt. General Walton Harris Walker (O-3405), Commanding General, Eighth Army," folder 211K, Adjutant General's Files, RG 338.9.9, NARA II.

17. Headquarters, 7th Infantry Division, Training Memorandum Number 1, 17 January 1949, 7th Infantry Division Annual History for 1949, RG 407, NARA II. For a brief overview of U.S. Army training in 1948 and 1949, see Gen. Mark Clark, "The Payoff in Training," *Army Information Digest* 5, no. 1 (January 1950), 3–8.

18. Gen. Jacob L. Devers, Chief, Army Field Forces, "Training the Army of Today," *Army Information Digest* 4, no. 4 (April 1949), 3–8; Annual Historical Report, 25th Infantry Division, 1949, dated "20 October 1950, Master," 3, Folder 325, vol. 1, "Historical Report, 25th Infantry Division 1949," RG 407, NARA II.

19. Peter Bates, *Japan and the British Commonwealth Occupation Force, 1946–1952* (New York: Brassey's, 1993), 105.

20. William T. Bowers, William M. Hammond, and George L. McGarigle, *Black Soldier, White Army: The 24th Infantry Regiment in Korea*, Table 4 ("GCT Breakdown, 25th Infantry Division Units [As of 19 September 1950])," 62; Telephone interview, William H. Trotter, USMA '46, 29 January 2004 (Trotter served in the division artillery of the 6th Infantry Division in Korea until U.S. forces were withdrawn in 1949); E-mail, Maj. (Ret.) Arthur L. Dorie (C/32nd Infantry Regiment, 7th Infantry Division, 1944–47), 28 February 2005; *History of the Occupation of Japan*, 4–7.

21. Interview, Gen. John H. Michaelis, Senior Officer Oral History Program, U.S. Army Military History Institute. See also memorandum, Chief of Staff U.S. Army to Vice-Chief of Staff U.S. Army, June 3, 2003, "Implementing Warrior Ethos for the Army," copy in author's possession.

22. G-3 Monthly Narrative for January 1950 (Annex 3 to 1st Cavalry Division Narrative History Summary for January 1950), and G-3 Monthly Narrative for March 1950 (Annex 3 to 1st Cavalry Division Narrative History Summary for March 1950), both in Eighth U.S. Army Military History Section, Monthly Summaries, 1946–1950, RG 554, NARA II (hereafter cited as G-3 Monthly Narrative and date).

23. Robert R. Palmer, Bell I. Wiley, and William R. Keast, *The Army Ground Forces: The Procurement and Training of Ground Combat Troops*, United States Army in World War II (Washington, D.C.: U.S. Army Center of Military History, 1948), 369, 372ff.; Kent Roberts Greenfield, Robert R. Palmer, and Bell I. Wiley, *The Army Ground Forces: The Organization of Ground Combat Troops*, United States Army in World War II (Washington, D.C.: U.S. Army Center of Military History, 1947), 30–39; Leonard L. Lerwill, *The Personnel Replacement System in the United States Army* (Washington, D.C.: U.S. Army Center of Military History, 1954), 357.

24. John C. Sparrow, *A History of Personnel Demobilization in the U.S. Army*, 143ff., 165–67, 202–17; J. Lawton Collins, *Lightning Joe: An Autobiography*, 333; Michael Sherry, *Planning for the Next War: America Plans for Postwar Defense, 1941–1945* (New Haven: Yale University Press, 1977), 36–38.

25. U.S. Congress, Senate, Committee on Military Affairs, *Hearings before the Senate Committee on Military Affairs on S. 1355, "A Bill to Provide for the Speedy Return of Veterans to Civilian Life, for the Immediate Military Needs of the United States, and for Other Purposes,"* 79th Cong., 1st and 2d sessions, 15 January 1946, 339ff.; William Epley, *America's First Cold War Army, 1945–1950*, 6.

26. G-1 Annex, 1st Cavalry Division Operations Report for May 1947, RG 407, NARA II.

27. Sparrow, *History of Personnel Demobilization*, 217ff.; Col. Harvey C. Jones, USMA '45, to author, 25 January 2004.

28. Roger R. Trask and Alfred Goldberg, *The Department of Defense, 1947–1997* (Washington, D.C.: Historical Office, Office of the Secretary of Defense, 1997), 59; B. C. Mossman, "Peace Becomes Cold War," in *American Military History*, ed. Maurice Matloff (Washington, D.C.: U.S. Army Center of Military History, 1969), 530–31; Edward A. Kolodziej, *The Uncommon Defense and Congress, 1945–1963* (Columbus: The Ohio State University Press, 1966), 60–61; S. Arthur Devan and Bernard Brodie, *Universal Military Training*, Public Affairs Bulletin 54 (Washington, D.C.: The Library of Congress Legislative Reference Service, June 1947), 2; Allan R. Millett and Peter Maslowski, *For the Common Defense: A Military History of the United States of America*, rev. ed. (New York: Free Press, 1994), 505–506; General of the Army Dwight D. Eisenhower, *Final Report of the Chief of Staff United States Army to the Secretary of the Army* (Washington, D.C.: U.S. Government Printing Office, 1948), 4–5.

29. Epley, *America's First Cold War Army*, 12; CG 60390, CINCFE to Subordinate Commands, 4 May 1948, AC of S, G-3, Training Division, GHQ/FEC/SCAP/UNC, NARA II; Col. (Ret.) Harvey C. Jones to author, 25 January 2004.

30. *Annual Report of the Secretary of the Army for Fiscal Year 1949*, 138–140; William M. Donnelly, "The Best Army That Can Be Put in the Field in the Circumstances: The U.S. Army, July 1951–July 1953," paper produced for the U.S. Army Center of Military History, 9, copy in author's possession.

31. "PIO Release on Division Change from Square to Triangular Division," 25 March 1949, Enclosure 1 to 1st Cavalry Division Command and Unit Historical Report, 1949; and Headquarters Eighth U.S. Army Historical Section, Annual Historical Report, 1949, Folder #1 (G-1 Section), 7, 12–14, paragraphs 5, 17, both in RG 407, NARA II.

32. Army Ground Forces lost its status as a separate command with the retirement of Gen. Jacob Devers on 30 September 1949. Lieutenant General Mark Clark became Chief, Army Field Forces, on 1 October 1949. Office of the Chief, Army Field Forces, *Annual History for 1949*, chap. 6 ("Troop Training"), 4–5, Headquarters, Army Field Forces, Special Staff, Historical Section, Annual Reports, 1949–1950, RG 337.6.1, NARA II; *Basic Military Training Program (14 Weeks) for Newly Enlisted Men*, Army Training Program 21–1, 4.

33. *Basic Military Training Program*, 1; Epley, *America's First Cold War Army*, 13.

34. "Report of Training Inspection of the United States Army, FECOM, by Col. F. M. Harris and Party" (hereafter cited as Harris Report), 2, and Enclosure 1 ("A Study of Types and Quality of Replacements Received in EUCOM") to "Report of Training Inspection of the European Command by Col. E. M. Starr and Party," both in Report Number 85, General Staff, United States Army, Copy 23, Decimal File 333.11, RG 337.6.1, NARA II; "Percentage Distribution of AGCT Groups by Grade," G-1 Annex, 76, Eighth Army Command Report, 1 January–30 June 1950, RG 407, NARA II.

Chapter 3

1. Memorandum, A.P.F. [unidentifed FECOM staff officer] to Chief of Staff [Maj. Gen. Edward Almond], 7 June 1949, Decimal File 319, RG 554, NARA II. See also Col. Henry C. Newton, "The Officer Problem," *Infantry Journal* 44, no. 12 (December 1948), 19–21, for a fuller discussion of tensions between Regular and non-Regular officers.

2. Almond to Bull ["Dear Pinky"], 21 June 1949, Decimal File 319, RG 554, NARA II.

3. Memorandum for Assistant Chief of Staff G-3 [FECOM], 20 June 1949, "Report of Staff Visit to 1st Cavalry Division" and related papers, Decimal File 333, RG 554, NARA II.

4. Office of the Chief, Army Field Forces, Annual History for 1949, chap. 6, "Troop Training," 7, RG 337, NARA II; "AFF Makes Its Postwar Report," *Army Information Digest* 4, no. 12 (December 1949), 23–33, quote from 23; *Basic Military Training Program (14 Weeks) for Newly Enlisted Men*, Army Training Program 21–1.

5. Annual History, Office of the Chief, Army Field Forces (1949), vol. 1, paragraph 9d, chap. 6, "Troop Training," Army Field Forces Special Staff Historical Section Annual Reports, 1949–1950, RG 337, NARA II.

6. *Army Training*, Training Circular Number 7, 28 July 1948, paragraph 3a, paragraph 10; Army Field Forces Training Memorandum Number 1, 9 August 1949, paragraph 5, Decimal File 353, Adjutant General's Correspondence Files, RG 337, NARA II; Office of the Chief of Staff, U.S. Army, memorandum dated 29 September 1949, subject: "Change in Responsibilities of Chief, Army Field Forces," Decimal File 333, Adjutant General's Correspondence Files, RG 337, NARA II; Report of Training Inspection of the European Command by COL E. M. Starr and Party, 23 May 1949, Report of Training Inspection of United States Army, Pacific, by COL P. R. Dwyer and Party, 22 October 1949, RG 337, NARA II.

7. Training Directive Number Four, 4.

8. Peter R. Mansoor, *The GI Offensive in Europe: The Triumph of American Infantry Divisions in World War II*, 24; Training Directive Number Four, 5.

9. G-3 Summary, Eighth Army Annual Historical Report for 1949, 13–14, and paragraph 4f, "Conduct of Training," 2, Historical Section, Eighth United States Army, Japan, RG 338, NARA II; Staff Conference Summary, 29 March 1949, Tab 33, Folder 3, Historical Report, G-3, 1949, RG 407, NARA II; Eighth Army Training Memorandum Number 1, 18 July 1949, Paragraph 4b, "Training Policy," 2, Tab 45, Decimal File 353, RG 338, NARA II.

10. GHQ FEC Training Memorandum Number 1, 10 June 1949, paragraph 5, "Training Policy," 3, Decimal File 353, RG 554, NARA II.

11. Army Field Forces Annual History, 1949, 7–8, and Annual History, 1950, Volume I, Office of the Chief, Army Field Forces, chap. 4, "Reporting Operational Readiness," 4–6, both in Army Field Forces Special Staff Historical Section Annual Reports, 1949–1950, RG 337.6.1, NARA II.

12. Memorandum, CG, Eighth Army, to CG, I Corps; CG, IX Corps; CG, 40th AAA Brigade, subj: Combat Effectiveness Reports, dated 22 June 1949, Eighth Army Historical Reports, Tab 43, Decimal File 322, RG 407, NARA II.

13. Army Field Forces Annual History, 1950, 6, Army Field Forces Special Staff Historical Section Annual Reports, 1949–1950, RG 337.6.1, NARA II.

14. J. Lawton Collins, *Lightning Joe: An Autobiography*, 350. For a revealing look at the lure

held by systems analysis for army personnel officers, see Lt. Col. C. D. Coleman, "Observing Personnel Management at Work," *Military Review* 28, no. 19 (January 1949), 56–62. See also discussion of the Johnston Plan for U.S. Army reorganization in James E. Hewes Jr., *From Root to McNamara: Army Organization and Administration, 1900–1963*, 182–205, for a short discussion of the migration of business management to the army staff.

15. Maj. Gen. Edward F. Witsell, "Administration and the New Army," *Army Information Digest* 4, no. 2 (February 1949), 4; Maj. Gen. Willard S. Paul, "Guiding Army Careers," *Army Information Digest* 2, no. 8 (August 1947), 3, 4. Witsell was the army G-1 in 1949. His characterization "New Army" underscores his desire to break with past practices. Paul was the director of the Personnel and Administrative Division of the War Department General Staff, and as such one of the principal architects of the Career Guidance Program in the 1947–48 period.

16. Col. C. W. Van Way, "Career Guidance—A New Army Function," *Military Review* 27, no. 2 (December 1947), 9, 11; Col. Reuben Horchow, "Careers for Infantrymen," *Army Information Digest* 2, no. 9 (September 1947), 27. As an example of technical specialists' rank reduction, Joseph Marlett arrived in Japan as a technician fifth grade (nominally a corporal). After conversion, he was a single-stripe private first class (Marlett interview, 8 June 2001). Others were reduced to the new rank of "recruit," despite having in some cases several years of service behind them. The practice of applying the "recruit" rank beyond training units ended in late 1950 amid popular outcry over next-of-kin notifications about "Recruit So-and-so being KIA" (Lloyd Pittman, F Company 17th Infantry, telephone conversation, 17 December 2001).

17. Lt. Gen. Willard S. Paul, "Putting the Personal into Personnel," *Military Review* 29, no. 2 (May 1949), 28–30; Horchow, "Careers for Infantrymen," 26; Col. Reuben Horchow, "Ladder to the Top," *Infantry Journal* 61, no. 3 (September 1947), 4–10; "No Place for the Unfit," *Infantry Journal* 61, no. 9 (February 1948), 60.

18. First Sgt. Wayne A. Jendro, "What's Happened to the NONCOM?" *Infantry Journal* 60, no. 9 (March 1947), 20; Col. Reuben Horchow, "Classification Didn't Kill the NONCOM," *Infantry Journal* 60, no. 12 (June 1947), 21.

19. Lt. Col. George E. Baya, "New Promotion Law for Officers," *Army Information Digest* 2, no. 9 (September 1947), 15.

20. Chap. 14, "Career Planning," *The Officers' Guide*, October 1950 ed. (Harrisburg: Military Service Publishing Company, 1950), 269; Ira H. Cushin, "Officers' Attitudes toward Their Careers," *Army Information Digest* 4, no. 9 (September 1949), 55–59; Col. James C. Fry, "Career Planning for Officers," *Army Information Digest* 2, no. 8 (August 1948), 11, 9.

21. Paul, "Putting the Personal into Personnel," 30; Interview, Col. (Ret.) Wilson Heefner, 29 November 2001; Harris Report, 8.

22. Harris Report, 'Obstacles to Training,' subparagraph j.

23. "Report of the 1st OCAFF Observer Team with Comments," Section II, 'Conclusions,' subparagraph 1d, and Section III, 'Recommendations," 30, Book I, Case 8, Decimal File 333, G-3, Plans and Operations Division, RG 319, NARA II.

24. Memorandum, Col. E. A. Chazal to G-3, 4 December 1950, Case 8, Book I, Decimal File 333, RG 319, NARA II (emphasis added). Chazal wrote the memorandum in his capacity as

acting chief, Manning Division. Chazal's attitude is somewhat puzzling, since he commanded an infantry regiment in the 63rd Infantry Division in World War II. His defense of the program as executed in FECOM became much more understandable after I discovered that until early 1950 Colonel Chazal had served as Walker's G-1 in Japan and thus had overseen the placement of many unqualified officers into command positions. For example, the officer commanding the 64th Field Artillery Battalion until early 1950 had no troop experience at all; though a veteran of the European Theater, he had spent all of his time then as an aerial observer, not working in artillery battalions (interview, Lt. Col. [Ret.] Joseph Bell, 10 December 2001). Bell initially served as survey officer for Battery A, 64th Field Artillery Battalion. He eventually commanded the battery in Korea.

25. "News and Comment," *Infantry Journal* 46, no. 3 (March 1950), 27. "Reblue" is modern army slang that nevertheless accurately encompasses the intent of this course.

26. James F. Schnabel, *Policy and Direction: The First Year*, 59; Clay Blair, *The Forgotten War: America in Korea, 1950–1953*, 92.

27. Public Law 457, chap. 479, stat. 765, 78th Cong., 3 October 1944. Section 12 of this law required all government agencies first to seek surplus equipment to meet their needs before submitting a request for appropriations for new materials. Section 13b authorized owning agencies to "destroy or otherwise dispose of" surplus property of "no commercial value or [whose] cost of its care and handling exceeds the estimated proceeds" of its sale.

28. Schnabel, *Policy and Direction*, 58; Sasha Archibald, "Million Dollar Point," *Cabinet Magazine Online* 10 (Spring 2003), 1.

29. *Operation Roll-Up: The History of Surplus Property Disposal in the Pacific Ocean*, 4:32.

30. Public Law 584, chap. 723, stat 754, 79th Cong., 1 August 1946.

31. Capt. Robert D. Connolly, "Men and Machines in Occupied Japan," *Army Information Digest* 5, no. 6 (June 1950), 17–22. In 1949 alone, over 200,000 metric tons of surplus equipment were shipped to Japan (Schnabel, *Policy and Direction*, 59).

32. Brig. Gen. Urban Niblo, "Notes for Use in the Presentation of FY 1952 Budget Requirements for Ordnance Funds, 1 May 1950," Annex XIV, Ordnance Section, GHQ FEC Command Report, 1 January–31 October 1949, Staff Section Reports, Annexes XVIII–XXI, RG 407, NARA II.

33. Bernard J. Quinn, "Triple R Helps EUCOM Pay Its Way," *Army Information Digest* 4, no. 10 (October 1949), 24.

34. Schnabel, *Policy and Direction*, 59; Letter, Douglas C. Ellis, 142nd Ordnance Battalion, 12 November 2001.

35. Ordnance Section, Monthly Summary #23, June 1948, paragraphs 3 and 4, Monthly Summaries #23–30, May–December 1948, Eighth U.S. Army Military History Section Monthly Summaries, 1946–1950, RG 338, NARA II; Interview, Lt. Col. (Ret.) Joseph Bell, 10 December 2001. As a battery executive officer from January to August 1950, Bell would have been intimately familiar with the maintenance status of everything assigned to the battery. On the preserved howitzers, cf. "Canned Guns Inspected," *Infantry Journal* 62, no. 6 (June 1948), 55: "The canning system is relatively expensive initially but the huge, recurring expense of periodic overhaul and regreasing is eliminated."

36. Letter, Jack Goodwin, Company C, 21st Infantry, 29 November 2001. Goodwin was captured on 6 July 1950 and held by the communists until 29 August 1953. Interview, Carl F. Bernard, 1 March 2000, owner-KOREAN-WAR-L@listproc.cc.ukans.edu.

37. Statement by Jim Trumble, Company E, 27th Infantry, quoted in Cressie Johnson, *Korea, 1950–1951: A Wolfhound Story*, 7; Letter, Lloyd Pittman, Company F, 17th Infantry, 17 December 2001; Bill McWilliams, *On Hallowed Ground: The Last Battle for Pork Chop Hill* (Annapolis: Naval Institute Press, 2003), 133.

38. 21st Ordnance Company (MM), Annual Report for 1949, 5, and 5th Ordnance Medium Maintenance Company Annual History, 13 January 1950, 2, both in I Corps Occupational Histories, 1950–1951, Subordinate Units, 1949, to I Corps History, 1949–1950, RG 338, NARA II.

39. Command Report, GHQ-FEC/SCAP/UNC G-4, 1 January–31 October 1950, GHQ FEC Command Report, 1 January–31 October 1949, RG 407, NARA II.

40. George D. Jeffcoat, *United States Army Dental Service in World War II*, 203; Selective Service System, *Physical Examination of Selected Service Registrants*, Special Monograph Number 15, 1:173.

41. Mabel Lee, *A History of Physical Education and Sports in the U.S.A.*, 228–29.

42. S. Arthur Devan and Bernard Brodie, *Universal Military Training*, Public Affairs Bulletin 54 (Washington, D.C.: The Library of Congress Legislative Reference Service, June 1947), 34; Haydn S. Pearson, "An Argument for Military Training," *New York Times Magazine*, 27 August 1944.

43. Schnabel, *Policy and Direction*, 56. See also Robert M. Malina and G. Lawrence Rarick, "Growth, Physique, and Motor Performance," *Physical Activity: Human Growth and Development*, ed. G. Lawrence Rarick, 141, and Lee, *History of Physical Education*, 61.

44. *Physical Training*, Field Manual 21–20, 3ff.; Lt. Col. F. M. Greene, "PT," *Infantry Journal* 41, no. 4 (October 1947), 68; Gen. Maxwell D. Taylor, *Swords and Ploughshares* (New York: W. W. Norton, 1972), 47.

45. *Physical Training*, FM 21–20, 332, 347–49; Lee, *History of Physical Education*, 231.

Chapter 4

1. Robert J. Maddox, *The Unknown War with Russia: Wilson's Siberian Intervention*, 61–73; John Albert White, *The Siberian Intervention*, 137; Jack Pearl, "The Saga of the Wolfhounds," *Saga Magazine*, August 1963, 69. Since 1919 the regiment has kept wolfhounds as regimental mascots; all are named Kolchak.

2. *The Bark of the Wolfhounds, 27th Infantry Regiment: Organization Day, 2 May 1950*; "27th Infantry Regiment, The Wolfhounds," lineage and honors statement, U.S. Army Center of Military History, 25 July 1996 (http://www.history.army.mil/html/forcestruc/lineages/branches/inf/0027in.htm).

3. Unit History, Twenty-Seventh United States Infantry, Nineteen Forty-Nine, 5, Folder 325, Unit Reports—25th Infantry Division, 1949, RG 407, NARA II; *Table of Organization and Equipment 7–17N, Infantry Rifle Company*, with Change 1. Experience in Korea quickly proved the value of increasing the number of light machine guns to two per platoon.

4. *Table of Organization and Equipment 7–17N, Infantry Rifle Company*, 9 December 1947, with Change 1, 6.

5. Interview, M. Sgt. (Ret.) Joseph E. Marlett, B Company, 27th Infantry Regiment, 8 June 2001. Training Directive Number Four, Annex No. 9, specified that "all rifle squads and platoons will be given training in the combat formations outlined in War Department *Training Circular 5*, 28 June 1948" pending a revision of Field Manual 7–10, *Rifle Company, Infantry Regiment*, dated 18 March 1944. This document specifically directs preliminary training to occur "on open terrain, such as a parade ground" (Paragraph I-3a, p. 1, *Combat Formations, Training Circular Number 5*).

6. It was not always possible for NCOs at the training divisions to allot sufficient time to individual soldiers to impart more than enough knowledge to pass with a minimum qualification. Some soldiers remarked that they owed their proficiency with their weapons to the marksmanship training they received from their sergeants' "superior advice and example" during service in the 27th Infantry Regiment. E-mail message, Jack L. Borden (HQ Company, 27th Infantry Regiment), 14 February 2001.

7. *Qualification Scores*, Training Circular Number 9; *Weapons Familiarization Courses*, Training Circular 10, 2–3, 6. All time estimates are based on personal experience with soldiers of varied proficiency levels firing a progressive program of grouping/zero-field fire/known distance–qualification firing with standard military small arms on both manually and electronically scored firing ranges.

8. Army Field Forces Training Test 7–1, *Rifle Squad, Rifle Company, Table of Organization and Equipment 7–17N*, 27 September 1948.

9. Unit History, Twenty-Seventh United States Infantry, 1949, 6; Interview, M. Sgt. (Ret.) Joseph E. Marlett.

10. Unit History, Twenty-Seventh United States Infantry, 1949, 6.

11. Harris Report, Tab R, "25th Infantry Division."

12. Ibid., "27th Infantry Regiment." For example, C Company's most egregious errors involved platoon leader misorientation during movement, lack of employment of fire support assets to cover an approach, and poor route selection. D Company (heavy weapons) received a "very satisfactory" assessment of platoon defensive positions but committed errors in alternate position selection and crew-served weapons emplacement. Uzal W. Ent, *Fighting on the Brink: Defending the Pusan Perimeter*, 11; Interview, M. Sgt. (Ret.) Joseph E. Marlett; Interview, Brig. Gen. (Ret.) Uzal W. Ent, 8 September 2001.

13. Unit History, Twenty-Seventh United States Infantry, 1949, 6; *Rifle Platoon, Rifle Company*, Army Field Forces Training Test 7–2, 27 September 1948 (Washington, D.C.: Department of the Army). The rocket launcher course comprised three hours of preliminary instruction, observation of a demonstration of both high explosive antitank and white phosphorus rounds, and three subcaliber training rounds per man fired at a stationary target from 150 yards (*Weapons Familiarization Courses*, Training Circular Number 10, 5). Unit History, Twenty-Seventh United States Infantry, 1949, 6.

14. Memorandum, CG, I Corps, to CG, Eighth Army, dated 15 September 1949, Decimal File 353, RG 338.9.9, NARA II. In this memo, the I Corps G-3 stated that shortages of serviceable 57-mm and 75-mm recoilless rifles, 37-mm antiaircraft guns, medium tanks, and both

high explosive and white phosphorus ammunition for 4.2-inch mortars significantly hampered unit training.

15. James F. Schnabel, *Policy and Direction: The First Year,* 55.

16. Eighth Army Annual Historical Report for 1949, 15; Historical Report—25th Infantry Division, 1949, 2–3.

17. The Infantry School, "Motti Tactics," *Infantry Journal* 46, no. 1 (January 1950), 8–14; Capt. Donald E. Rivette, "Stop That Tank," *Infantry Journal* 46, no. 3 (March 1950), 7–11; Col. John G. Van Houten, "Keep That Doughboy Lightly Loaded," *Infantry Journal* 46, no. 3 (March 1950), 12–13.

18. Unit History, Twenty-Seventh United States Infantry, 1949, 9; Memorandum, CG, Eighth Army, to CINCFE, 30 January 1950, subject: Schedule of Training Exercises, 2, Decimal File 352, G-3 Correspondence File, RG 338.9.9, NARA II.

19. HQ, 27th Infantry Regiment, Summary of Activities for January, 1950, paragraphs 6 and 7, Folder, 27th Infantry Regiment Historical Report, 1950, 27th Infantry Unit History 1949—27th Infantry Command Reports, September 1951, RG 338.8, NARA II.

20. "Spotlight on HQ 1st Bn," *The Newshound* 5, no. 20 (6 June 1950), 6; Folder, 27th Infantry Regiment History, 1950 (January–June), 27th Infantry Unit History 1949—27th Infantry Command Reports, September 1951, RG 338.8, NARA II; HQ, 27th Infantry Regiment, Summary of Activities for January 1950, paragraph 6. Check commanded 1st Battalion until 13 February 1951, when he succeeded Colonel Michaelis as regimental commander. See Clay Blair, *The Forgotten War: America in Korea, 1950–1953,* photo opposite p. 337.

21. HQ, 27th Infantry Regiment, Summary of Activities for February 1950, paragraphs 5, 7, 8.

22. HQ, 27th Infantry Regiment, Summary of Activities for March 1950, paragraphs 1, 4, 5; Annex 8, "Weapons," paragraph 2a, "Combat Firing," 4, Training Directive Number Four.

23. Eighth Army Training Memorandum Number 1, 18 July 1949, paragraph 4, "Training Policy," 2, Tab 45, Decimal File 353, RG 338.9.9, NARA II.

24. HQ, Eighth Army, Training Directive Number Five, 3 April 1949, paragraphs 4, 5a, "Policy," 2, Decimal File 353.01 (January–August 1950), RG 338.9.9, NARA II (emphasis added).

25. HQ, 27th Infantry Regiment, Combat Effectiveness Report, dated 20 March 1950, paragraphs 1, 2a, 3, and Enclosure 1, 25th Infantry Division Combat Effectiveness Reports, Book 2 (1st Quarter 1950, ending 20 March 1950), Tab "27th Inf," RG 338.9.9, NARA II.

26. HQ, 1st Battalion 27th Infantry Regiment, Combat Effectiveness Report, dated 20 March 1950, ibid.; Ent, *Fighting on the Brink,* 11. An FPL, final protective line, is a direction of fire closely parallel to a friendly defensive line. A call to fire the FPL requires machine gun crews to fire their weapons at the maximum rate of fire until ammunition is exhausted or ordered to cease fire and is only fired in order to prevent a unit from being overrun by an enemy force.

27. Air transportability training loomed large in the Eighth Army's overall training program, for the obvious reason that in order to respond rapidly to a crisis in the Far East, an infantry battalion would need to fly its personnel and equipment into the area of operations.

See HQ, Eighth Army Training Memorandum Number 1, dated 19 May 1950, subj: Air Transportability Training, Decimal File 353.01, RG 338.9.9, NARA II; HQ, 2nd Battalion 27th Infantry Regiment, Combat Effectiveness Report, 20 March 1950.

28. HQ, 27th Infantry Regiment, Summary of Activities for April 1950. In the division's annual history for 1949, Lieutenant Colonel Hardman, 25th Infantry Division G-3, had complained that "a continuous stream of VIP's for whom large formations had to be held were annoying." Hardeman evidently failed to see the equally deleterious effect of self-inflicted ceremonies on unit preparations for testing.

29. Eighth United States Army Operations Report 266, Period Ending 17 April 1950, and G-3, Eighth United States Army, G-3 Journals, Book 1, Historical Summary, April 1950 (dated 25 May 1950), 5, "Tests and Inspections," both in RG 338.9.9, NARA II; HQ, 27th Infantry Regiment, Summary of Activities for April 1950, paragraphs 2, 4, 5.

30. G-3, EUSA, Historical Summary, April 1950, 5.

31. HQ, 27th Infantry Regiment, Summary of Activities for April 1950, paragraphs 4, 5; Summary of Activities for May 1950, paragraph 2; Eighth United States Army Operations Reports 269, period ending 8 May 1950, and 272, period ending 29 May 1950; G-3, EUSA, Historical Summary, May 1950 (dated 20 June 1950), 3. During this make-up, 2nd Battalion's supporting artillery fires came from Battery B, 159th Field Artillery Battalion, not their habitual supporting unit. Unit identification from Memorandum, Summary of Field Artillery Performance, dated 1 June 1950, Decimal File 353 (January–August 1950), RG 338.9.9, NARA II.

32. HQ, 27th Infantry Regiment, Summary of Activities for June 1950, paragraphs 1, 2. This document, the last in the folder for 1950, is the only handwritten summary in the collection and was clearly produced in haste while the regiment prepared to move to Korea in early July 1950.

33. Interviews, M. Sgt. (Ret.) Joseph E. Marlett and Brig. Gen. (Ret.) Uzal W. Ent; Electronic mail message from Col. (Ret.) Robert W. Hill, 29 August 2001. See also, for example, Harry J. Maihafer, *From the Hudson to the Yalu: West Point '49 in the Korean War*, 5–9; Robert Roy, M Company 21st Infantry Regiment, cited in Rudy Tomedi, *No Bugles, No Drums: An Oral History of the Korean War*, 1–2. Maj. Gen. William F. Dean and William L. Worden, *General Dean's Story*, 14. Cressie Johnson, *Korea, 1950–1951: A Wolfhound Story*, 5; Addison Terry, *The Battle for Pusan: A Korean War Memoir*, 3–4. Terry, originally assigned to Battery B, 49th Field Artillery Battalion, 7th Infantry Division, served as an 8th Field Artillery Battalion forward observer for the 27th Infantry Regiment in Korea. He is no relation to Lt. Col. Augustus Terry, commander of the 8th Field Artillery Battalion.

Chapter 5

1. Donald A. Jordan, *China's Trial by Fire: The Shanghai War of 1932* (Ann Arbor: University of Michigan Press, 2001), 205ff.

2. E-mail, Col. (Ret.) Karl H. Lowe to author, 10 January 2005.

3. James A. Sawicki, *Infantry Regiments of the U.S. Army*, (Dumfries, Va.: Wyvern Publications, 1981), 112–13; *31st Infantry Regiment: History, Lineage, Honors, Decorations, and*

Seventy-Third Anniversary Yearbook (Fort Sill, Okla.: 4th Battalion (Mechanized) 31st Infantry Regiment, 1989), chapters 1–5. Unit crest from Global Security (http://www.globalsecurity.org/military/agency/army/4-31in.htm), accessed 26 November 2004.

4. Unit History, 31st Infantry, Japan, Jan–Dec. 1949, 2; RG 338.8: Records of U.S. Army Commands in the Pacific, Post World War II, 1944–72, Unit Records (A): Infantry Divisions 1940–67, Seventh Infantry Division, NARA II (hereafter cited as Unit History, 31st Infantry).

5. Ibid., 3, 5.

6. Annex Number 2, *Personnel*, to Operations Instructions Number 7, 11 August 1948, Operation TWIN BORN, Evacuation of U.S. Personnel from Korea; ACofS, G-3, Narrative Historical Report of the G-3 Section, 1 January 1947 thru 31 December 1948, Volume II; Military History Section, Command and Staff Section Reports 1947–52, Secret 1947–48; RG 554: Records of GHQ FEC/SCAP/UNC, NARA II; 7th Infantry Division, Annual Unit History, 1 JAN 1949–31 DEC 1949, 1; Folder 307, Organizational & Unit Historical Report, 7th Infantry Division, 1949; RG 338.8: Records of U.S. Army Commands in the Pacific, Post World War II, 1944–72,Unit History, 31st Infantry, NARA II.

7. Unit History, 31st Infantry, Japan, Jan-Dec. 1949, 3.

8. Operations Narrative, 7th Division Historical Report, February 1949, "31st Infantry Regiment;" 7th Infantry Division Historical Reports; RG 338.8: Records of U.S. Army Commands in the Pacific, Post World War II, 1944–72, Unit History, 31st Infantry, NARA II.

9. 31st Infantry Regiment Monthly Historic Report, March 1949; 7th Infantry Division Historical Reports; RG 338.8: Records of U.S. Army Commands in the Pacific, Post World War II, 1944–72, Unit History, 31st Infantry, NARA II.

10. Unit History, 31st Infantry Regiment, 1–30 April 1949.

11. Unit History, 31st Infantry Regiment, Jan–Dec 1949, 7.

12. Headquarters, Eighth U.S. Army, Circular 178, "Literacy Training and Standards," 28 October 1947; Chief of Staff's General Correspondence Files; RG 554: Records of GHQ FEC/SCAP/UNC, NARA II.

13. Headquarters, 7th Infantry Division, Training Memorandum Number 1, "17 January 1949–30 April 1949," 11 January 1949; Decimal File 353.1, G-3 Correspondence Files; RG 407: Records of the Adjutant General, 1917–: Seventh Infantry Division, NARA II.

14. Unit History, 31st Infantry Regiment, 1–30 April 1949.

15. Headquarters, 7th Infantry Division, Training Memorandum Number 13, "Training of Replacements," 21 March 1949; Decimal File 353.1, G-3 Correspondence Files; RG 407: Records of the Adjutant General, 1917–: Seventh Infantry Division, NARA II. Paragraph 3c of this memo specifically forbade the formation of "separate or provisional companies."

16. Unit History, 31st Infantry Regiment, 1 May–31 May 1949.

17. Unit History, 31st Infantry Regiment, Jan–Dec 1949, 6.

18. Major General Dean to All Officers and Non-Commissioned Officers, 7th Infantry Division, "Letter of Transmittal, Training Memorandum Number 1," 11 January 1949, 1; Decimal File 353, G-3 Correspondence Files; RG 407: Army-AG Command Reports, 1949–54: Seventh Infantry Division, NARA II.

19. Unit History, 31st Infantry Regiment, 1–28 February 1949, and "Division Historical

Report, March 1949;" RG 338.8: Records of U.S. Army Commands in the Pacific, Post World War II, 1944–72, Unit History, 31st Infantry, NARA II.

20. Unit History, 31st Infantry Regiment, 1st Battalion July 1949.

21. Ibid.

22. Unit History, 31st Infantry Regiment, 1–30 June 1949.

23. Headquarters, 7th Infantry Division, Training Memorandum Number 9, 15 February 1949; Decimal File 353, G-3 General Correspondence Files; RG 407: Records of the Adjutant General, 1917–: Seventh Division; NARA II.

24. Chapter VII, "Military Personnel Division," Annex I (Assistant Chief of Staff, G-1), GHQ FEC Command Report, 1 January 1949–31 December 1950, Vol. II; RG 554: Records of GHQ FEC/SCAP/UNC, NARA II.

25. General Headquarters, Supreme Commander for the Allied Powers and Far East Command, Staff Memorandum Number 7, "Enlisted Replacements," 6 February 1950; Decimal File 220.3, Chief of Staff's Correspondence Files; RG 554: Records of GHQ FEC/SCAP/UNC, NARA II.

26. Headquarters, 7th Infantry Division, Training Memorandum Number 15, "1 May–30 September 1949," 19 April 1949; Decimal File 353, G-3 Correspondence Files; RG 407: Records of the Adjutant General, 1917–: Seventh Division; NARA II.

27. Unit History, 31st Infantry Regiment, 1st Battalion August 1949.

28. "Foreign Legion," *Regimental Day* (Camp Crawford, Japan: August 13, 1949); Unit History File, 31st Infantry Regiment; Unit Reports—7th Infantry Division, 1949; RG 407: Records of the Adjutant General, 1917–: 7th Infantry Division; NARA II.

29. Unit History, 31st Infantry Regiment, Jan–Dec 1949, 8.

30. Unit History, 31st Infantry Regiment, 1st Battalion July 1949.

31. Unit History, 31st Infantry Regiment, Jan–Dec 1949, 8; Division Artillery Annual Unit History 1949, 2; RG 338.8: Records of U.S. Army Commands in the Pacific, Post World War II, 1944–72,Unit History, 31st Infantry, NARA II.

32. Unit History, 31st Infantry Regiment, 1–30 August 1949.

33. Training Memorandum Number 15,4, paragraph i(2).

34. Headquarters, IX Corps, Training Memorandum Number 12, 23 August 1949; copy in Decimal File 333.5, G3 Correspondence Files, 7th Infantry Division; RG 407: Records of the Adjutant General, 1917–: Seventh Infantry Division, NARA II.

35. Unit History, 31st Infantry Regiment, Jan-Dec 1949, 9–10.

36. Annual Historical Report of the 31st Field Artillery Battalion, 1949, 4; RG 338.8: Records of U.S. Army Commands in the Pacific, Post World War II, 1944–72, Unit History, 31st Infantry, NARA II.

37. Unit History, 31st Infantry Regiment, Month of September 1949.

38. Army Field Forces Training Test 7–2, 27 September 1948, and Army Field Forces Training Test 7–25, 18 December 1951, Decimal File 352, General Correspondence Files, Office of the Chief, Army Field Forces; RG 337.6.1: Records of Administrative Sections, Headquarters Army Ground Forces/Army Field Forces, NARA II.

39. Unit History, 31st Infantry Regiment, Jan-Dec 1949, 10; Unit History, 31st Infantry Regiment, Month of September 1949.

40. Unit History, 31st Infantry Regiment, Month of September 1949.

41. Unit History Narrative, 31st Infantry Regiment, October 1949.

42. Annual Historical Report of the 31st Field Artillery Battalion, 1949, 4; 7th Division Artillery Monthly History, September 1949; RG 338.8: Records of U.S. Army Commands in the Pacific, Post World War II, 1944–72,Unit History, 31st Infantry, NARA II.

43. Unit History, 31st Infantry Regiment, Month of September 1949.

44. Unit History, 31st Infantry Regiment, Jan–Dec 1949, 11.

45. Unit History Narrative, 31st Infantry Regiment, October 1949.

46. Report of Training Inspection of the United States Army, FECOM, by Col. F.M. Harris and Party, Tab P, 7th Infantry Division, 5; Decimal File 333.11, Army Field Forces Headquarters, Adjutant General's Section, Communications & Records Division, Secret Decimal File 1949–50; RG 337.6.1: Records of Administrative Sections, Headquarters Army Ground Forces/Army Field Forces, NARA II.

47. Ibid., 7.s

48. 7th Division Monthly Historical Report, November 1949; Unit History, 31st Infantry Regiment, Jan-Dec 1949, 12; Unit History, 31st Infantry, Month of November 1949; Unit History, 31st Infantry, Month of December, 1.

49. 31st Infantry Regiment, Monthly Historical Summary for January 1950.

50. Edmund G. Love, *The 27th Infantry Division in World War II* (Washington, D.C.: Infantry Journal Press, 1949), 651.

51. 31st Infantry Regiment, Monthly Historical Summary for February 1950.

52. 31st Infantry Regiment, Monthly Historical Summary for March 1950.

53. G-3 Monthly Historical Summary #44, March 1950, 31st Infantry; Eighth U.S. Army Military History Section, Section III (Historical Section) Monthly Summaries #43–46: February–May 1950; Historical Officers' Files, 1949–50, RG 338.8: Records of U.S. Army Commands in the Pacific, Post World War II, 1944–72,Unit History, 31st Infantry, NARA II.

54. 31st Infantry, Monthly Historical Summary for April, 1950; G-3 Monthly Historical Summary #45, April 1950, "31st Infantry;" Eighth U.S. Army Military History Section, Section III (Historical Section) Monthly Summaries #43–46: February–May 1950; Historical Officers' Files, 1949–50; RG 338.8: Records of U.S. Army Commands in the Pacific, Post World War II, 1944–72, Unit History, 31st Infantry, NARA II.

55. 31st Infantry, Monthly Historical Summary for April, 1950.

56. Ibid.; Monthly Historical Summary #45, April 1950; Eighth U.S. Army Military History Section, Section III (Historical Section) Monthly Summaries #43–46: February–May 1950; Historical Officers' Files, 1949–50; RG 338.8: Records of U.S. Army Commands in the Pacific, Post World War II, 1944–72,Unit History, 31st Infantry, NARA II.

57. Combat Effectiveness Reports, 2nd and 3rd Battalions 31st Infantry Regiment, 26 June 1950; Decimal File 322, G-3 Correspondence Files, 7th Infantry Division, 1949–50; RG 338.8: Records of U.S. Army Commands in the Pacific, Post World War II, 1944–72,Unit History, 31st Infantry, NARA II.

58. Ibid.

59. Appleman, *South to the Naktong*, 539–40. Lieutenant Colonel Summers and Lt. Col. Lester K. Olson, regimental S-3 (operations officer), were among those wounded in action.

Chapter 6

1. James A. Sawicki, *Infantry Regiments of the U.S. Army*, 90–91; *A Brief History of the 19th Infantry Regiment; The Nineteenth Infantry Regiment, 1861–1949*, Organization Day brochure.

2. Memorandum, Headquarters, 19th Infantry Regiment, to Adjutant General, ATTN: Chief, Historical Records Section, dated 24 January 1950, subject: Command and Unit Historical Report (hereafter cited as 19th Infantry History for 1949), 2, 24th Infantry Division Historical Reports, 1949, RG 338, NARA II; *The Rock of Chickamauga, 1861–1972*, 18.

3. History of the 24th Infantry Division, 1949, iii, 24th Infantry Division Historical Reports, 1949, RG 338, NARA II.

4. Tab G, "24th Infantry Division Potential Noncommissioned Officer School," to History of the 24th Infantry Division 1949, ibid.

5. Headquarters, 24th Infantry Division, Training Memorandum Number 8, 17 May 1949, Decimal File 353, G-3 Correspondence Files, 24th Infantry Division, RG 338, NARA II.

6. Headquarters, 24th Infantry Division, Training Memorandum Number 10, 17 July 1949, Decimal File 353, G-3 Correspondence Files, 24th Infantry Division, RG 338, NARA II; War Department Circular 271, 3 July 1944, U.S. Army Military History Institute, Carlisle Barracks, Pennsylvania.

7. Headquarters, 24th Infantry Division, Training Memorandum Number 12, 17 August 1949, Decimal File 353, G-3 Correspondence Files, 24th Infantry Division; RG 338, NARA II.

8. History of the 24th Infantry Division, 1949, iv–v, 24th Infantry Division Historical Reports, 1949, RG 338, NARA II; 19th Infantry History for 1949.

9. 24th Infantry Division History of the Occupation of Japan, January 1949, "G-3 Activities," 5, 24th Infantry Division Historical Reports, 1949, RG 338, NARA II; 19th Infantry History for 1949, 3–4.

10. 19th Infantry History for 1949, 7–8.

11. Ibid., 8.

12. "G3 Activities (Training)," 24th Infantry Division History of the Occupation of Japan for July 1949, 4, 24th Infantry Division Historical Reports, 1949, RG 338, NARA II; Allan R. Millett, *The War For Korea: A House Burning*.

13. "G3 Activities (Training)," 24th Infantry Division History of the Occupation of Japan for August 1949, 6, 24th Infantry Division Historical Reports, 1949, RG 338, NARA II; and 19th Infantry History for 1949, 9, 24th Infantry G-3, Operations Report 35 (121800 September to 091800 September 1949), paragraph 2(b)(1) (hereafter cited as 24th Infantry OPREP number and date), Decimal File 353.1, G-3 Correspondence Files, RG 338, NARA II.

14. Biographical information on Lynch and Meloy is from the 19th Infantry Regiment Organization Day publication, *The Rock of Chickamauga, 1861–1972*, 4–5; 24th Infantry OPREP 36, 091200 September to 161200 September 1949.

15. *Table of Organization and Equipment 7–17N, Infantry Rifle Company*; 24th Infantry OPREPs 37 (161200 September to 231200 September 1949); 38 (231200 September to 301200 September 1949); 39 (301200 September to 071200 October); and 41 (141200 October to 211200 October 1949).

16. 24th Infantry OPREPs 37 (161200 September to 231200 September 1949) and 38 (231200 September to 301200 September 1949).

17. 24th Infantry OPREPs 39 (301200 September to 071200 October); 40 (071200 October to 141200 October, 1949); and 41, (141200 October to 211200 October 1949); 19th Infantry History for 1949, 11.

18. Harris Report, "19th Infantry Regiment," 2.

19. Ibid., 3.

20. 19th Infantry History for 1949, 12; 24th Infantry OPREPs 43 (281200 October to 031200 November 1949) and 45 (101800 November to 181800 November 1949).

21. 24th Infantry OPREP 47 (251800 November to 021800 December 1949); "G3 Activities," 24th Infantry Division History of the Occupation of Japan, November 1949, 4, 24th Infantry Division Historical Reports, 1949, RG 338, NARA II.

22. 24th Infantry OPREPs 48 (021800 December to 091800 December 1949) and 49 (091800 December to 161800 December 1949); "G-3 Activities, 24th Infantry Division History of the Occupation of Japan, December 1949, 4, 24th Infantry Division Historical Reports, 1949, RG 338, NARA II; 19th Infantry History for 1949, 13.

23. 24th Infantry OPREPs 50 (151800 December to 231800 December) and 51 (231800 December to 31 1800 December); 19th Infantry History for 1949, 14.

24. 19th Infantry History for 1949, 15.

25. 24th Infantry OPREPs 1 (011800 January to 071800 January 1950), 3 (131800 January to 201800 January), 4 (201800 January to 271800 January), 5 (271800 January to 031800 February), 6 (031800 February to 101800 February), 7 (101800 February to 171800 February), 8 (171800 February to 241800 February), 9 (241800 February to 031800 March 1950), 10 (031800 March to 101800 March).

26. Headquarters, 19th Infantry Regiment, Combat Effectiveness Report, 1st Quarter, 1950, 1 April 1950, 1.

27. Headquarters, 1st Battalion, 19th Infantry Regiment, Combat Effectiveness Report, 20 March 1950, 1.

28. Item 3, "Authorized Individual Weapons on Hand in Serviceable Condition," Enclosure 17, "Infantry Battalion," 3, 1st Battalion Combat Effectiveness Report, 20 March 1950, and Item 8, "All Enlisted Men Qualified with Individual Weapons," Enclosure 17, "Infantry Battalion," 8, both in 1st Battalion Combat Effectiveness Report, 20 March 1950.

29. Headquarters, 2nd Battalion, 19th Infantry Regiment, Combat Effectiveness Report, 20 March 1950.

30. Headquarters, Heavy Mortar Company, 19th Infantry Regiment, Combat Effectiveness Report, 20 March 1950, Item 4, "Authorized Crew-Served Weapons, or Acceptable Substitutes, on Hand in Serviceable Condition."

31. Headquarters, 34th Infantry Regiment, Camp Mower, Kyushu, Japan, Combat Effectiveness Report, 31 March 1950; Headquarters, 1st Battalion, 34th Infantry Regiment, Camp Mower, Kyushu, Japan, Items 3 and 4, Combat Effectiveness Report, 27 March 1950; Headquarters, 3rd Battalion, 34th Infantry Regiment, Camp Mower, Kyushu, Japan, Items 3 and 4, Combat Effectiveness Report, 28 March 1950.

32. Headquarters, 1st Battalion, 21st Infantry Regiment, Combat Effectiveness Report, 24 March 1950; Headquarters, 3rd Battalion, 21st Infantry Regiment, Combat Effectiveness Report, 24 March 1950; Headquarters, 34th Infantry Regiment, Camp Mower, Kyushu, Japan, Combat Effectiveness Report, 31 March 1950.

33. 24th Infantry OPREP 10 (031800 March 1950 to 101800 March 1950) and 24th Infantry OPREP 12 (171800 March 1950 to 241800 March 1950).

34. G-3, Eighth U.S. Army, to Commanding General, 24th Infantry Division, 27 April 1950, subject: "Battalion Combat Firing Tests," Decimal File 322, G-3 Correspondence Files, 24th Infantry Division History Reports, RG 338, NARA II.

35. 24th Infantry OPREPs 15 (071800 April 1950 to 141800 April 1050), 16 (141800 April to 211800 April 1950), and 17 (211800 April to 281800 April 1950).

36. 24th Infantry OPREP 23 (021800 June to 091800 June 1950).

Chapter 7

1. Although the current 8th Cavalry nickname is "Mustangs," several veterans informed me that in the late 1940s the unit was known as "Rocking Horse" for its distinctive unit insignia. The most adamant correction was received in an e-mail from former intelligence officer Ed Parmenter, 10 April 2008.

2. *8th Cavalry Regiment: Honor and Courage* (http://www.first-team.us/journals/8th_rgmt/), Cavalry Outpost Publications (online journal of the 8th Cavalry Association), accessed 9 February 2005; James A. Sawicki, *Cavalry Regiments of the U.S. Army*, 166–68; Maj. Gen. John K. Herr and Edward S. Wallace, *The Story of the U.S. Cavalry 1775–1942*, 142–252 *passim*; Leon C. Metz, *Fort Bliss: An Illustrated History*, 134.

3. Headquarters, 8th Cavalry Regiment, Operational Memorandum Number 3, "Emergency Action—8th Cavalry," 20 November 1947, 1st Cavalry Regiment Historical Reports, Adjutant General's Correspondence Files, RG 338, NARA II.

4. *Occupation Diary: First Cavalry Division 1945–1950*, 30–31; G-3 Section, Annual Command and Unit Historical Report 1949, 1st Cavalry Division (Infantry), Camp Drake, Japan (hereafter cited as G-3 History for 1949), 1, 1st Cavalry Division Historical Reports, 1949–1950, RG 338, NARA II.

5. *Occupation Diary*, 31; Radio Message CG 60390, CINCFE to Subordinate Commanders, 4 May 1948, copy included in Narrative Historical Report of the G-3 Section 1 January 1947 through 31 December 1948, vol. 1, Office of the Chief of Staff, Chief of Staff Subject Files 1945–1952, RG 554, NARA II.

6. G-3 History for 1949, 4.

7. "Purpose of 8th [sic] Army Levy to Transfer Men," Enclosure 5 to G-3 History for 1949; Headquarters, IX Corps, Monthly Summary #33 (March 1949), Eighth U.S. Army Military History Section, Monthly Summaries 1946–1950, RG 554, NARA II; Headquarters 1st Cavalry Division, History of the 1st Cavalry Division for March 1949, 1st Cavalry Division Historical Reports, 1949–1950, RG 338, NARA II.

8. Headquarters, 8th Cavalry Regiment, 8th Cavalry Regiment (Infantry) Command and Unit Historical Report 1949 (hereafter cited as 8th Cavalry History for 1949), 1–3, 1st Cavalry Division Historical Reports, 1949–1950, RG 338, NARA II.

9. 8th Cavalry History for 1949, 1, 7; Headquarters, 1st Battalion, 8th Cavalry Regiment, S-3 Periodic Report 240 (9–16 August 1949), Adjutant General's Memoranda 1949–1953, Folder "1949," RG 550, NARA II (hereafter cited as 1st or 2nd Battalion Periodic Report with dates).

10. 1st Battalion Periodic Report 229, 26 April to 3 May 1949; Headquarters, IX Corps, Monthly Summary #34, April 1949, "1st Cavalry Division G-3," Eighth U.S. Army Military History Section, Monthly Summaries 1946–1950, RG 554, NARA II.

11. 8th Cavalry History for 1949, 4, 5; G-3 History for 1949, 4.

12. Headquarters, 1st Battalion, 8th Cavalry Regiment, Training Memorandum Number 1, 3 May 1949, subject: Training Program 2 May 1949 to 15 August 1949, and Annex 1 and Annex 2, Adjutant General's Memoranda 1949–1953, Folder "1949," RG 550, NARA II

13. Headquarters, 1st Battalion, 8th Cavalry Regiment, Special Training Memo dated 26 May 1949, subject: Overnight Bivouac, ibid.

14. Headquarters, 2nd Battalion, 8th Cavalry Regiment, Training Memorandum Number 12, dated 2 June 1949, subject: Field Exercise, Rifle Platoon in the Approach March, Attack, Assault, and Reorganization, and Training Memorandum Number 13, dated 4 June 1949, ibid.

15. 8th Cavalry History for 1949, 6, and Enclosure 2, Results of Testing At Camp McNair—June 1949.

16. 8th Cavalry History for 1949, 6; Col. A. M. Parsons, Memorandum for Record, dated 19 June 1949, subject: Field Tng [sic], Document 437-A, File 353, binder 15, General Correspondence Files, Assistant Chief of Staff, G-3, Administration Division, RG 554, NARA II; Headquarters, 8th Engineer Combat Battalion, Command and Historical Report for 1949, 3, 5, 1st Cavalry Division Historical Reports, 1949–1950, RG 338, NARA II.

17. Lt. Col. D. P. Frazier, Report of Staff Visit to 1st Cavalry Division (Infantry), dated 20 June 1949, Document 437-A, File 353, binder 15, General Correspondence Files, Assistant Chief of Staff, G-3, Administration Division, RG 554, NARA II.

18. 8th Cavalry History for 1949, 6–8; Headquarters, 8th Cavalry Regiment, Training Memorandum Number 22, dated 28 June 1949, subject: Training 28 June—31 December 1949; Adjutant General's Memoranda 1949–1953, Folder "1949," RG 550, NARA II; 2nd Battalion Periodic Reports 239 (5–12 July 1949) through 246 (26 August to 2 September 1949).

19. 8th Cavalry History for 1949, 6, 9, Enclosure 3, "V.D. Rate 1949."

20. 1st Battalion Periodic Reports 244 (06–13 September 1949) through 247 (30 September–7 October 1949); 2nd Battalion Periodic Reports 1 (09–16 September 1949) through 4 (30 September–7 October 1949); Headquarters 1st Battalion, 8th Cavalry Regiment, Special Training Memorandum, dated 2 September 1949, subject: Range Program, Adjutant General's Memoranda 1949–1953, Folder "1949," RG 550, NARA II; PRS Report 954, in *Strengths and Deficiencies of Precombat Training as Reported by Infantrymen in Korea* (Washington, D.C.: The Adjutant General's Office, Department of the Army, January 1952), Appendix B.

21. Headquarters, 2d Battalion, 8th Cavalry Regiment, Memorandum dated 27 September 1949, subject: Training Activities for 2d Battalion, 3–7 October 1949, Adjutant General's Memoranda 1949–1953, Folder "1949," RG 550, NARA II.

22. 8th Cavalry History for 1949, 10.

23. Ibid., 11, and Enclosure 7, Court Martial Rate 1949.

24. Enclosure 5, Schedule at Camp McNair Oct–Nov 1949, to 8th Cavalry History for 1949.

25. 8th Cavalry History for 1949, 11, and Enclosure 6, Standings on Platoon Tests, 31 October—5 November 1949, Paragraph c, "8th Cavalry Regiment," "1st Cavalry Division," 4, Report of Department of the Army Training Inspection of the Far East Command, 24 September to 29 October 1949, Decimal File 333.11, RG 338.8, NARA II.

26. Ibid., 12, and Enclosure 5, Schedule at Camp McNair Oct-Nov 1949; 1st Cavalry Division Command and Historical Report 1949, 3.

27. 8th Cavalry History for 1949, 12, 13–14; 1st Cavalry Division Command and Historical Report 1949, 8, Paragraph c, "8th Cavalry Regiment," "1st Cavalry Division," 1, Report of Department of the Army Training Inspection of the Far East Command, 24 September to 29 October 1949, Decimal File 333.11, RG 338.8, NARA II.

28. Headquarters, 1st Cavalry Division (Infantry), Training Memorandum Number 18, dated 29 November 1949, subject: Training for the Period 1 Jan–31 Dec 1950, 1–3, Decimal File 353, G-3 Correspondence Files; and Commanding General's Conference Memorandum Number 3, 7 November 1949, Conferences & Meetings 1949–1952, Adjutant's Files, both in RG 338, NARA II.

29. Commanding General's Conference Memorandum Number 5, 2 December 1949, Conferences & Meetings 1949–1952, Adjutant's Files, ibid.

30. Notes from Commanding General's Conference Number 6, 18 January 1950, 4, Conferences & Meetings 1949–1952, Adjutant's Files, ibid.

31. 1st Battalion Periodic Reports 261 (January 6–13, 1950) and 263 (January 20–27, 1950); G-3 Monthly Narrative for February 1950.

32. Paragraph 5, "Administrative Procedure," and Annex 5 (Maneuver Periods and Target Dates for Completion of Training) to Training Memorandum Number 18, dated 29 November 1949, subject: Training for the Period 1 Jan–31 Dec 1950, 1–3, Decimal File 353, G-3 Correspondence Files, RG 338, NARA II; G-3 Monthly Narrative for February 1950; Headquarters 1st Cavalry Division, Operations Order Number 1 (Training), dated 25 March 1950, subject: Field Training at Camp McNair, Period 15 April–1 July, Enclosure 7 to G-3 Monthly Narrative for March 1950.

33. Headquarters 1st Cavalry Division, G-3 Periodic Report (1800 17 March to 1800 24 March 1950), Enclosure 2 to G-3 Monthly Narrative for March 1950.

34. G-3 Monthly Narratives for March 1950 and May 1950; G-3 Periodic Reports 299 (1800 23 April 1950 to 1800 05 May 1950), 300 (1800 05 May 1950 to 1800 12 May 1950), 301 (1800 12 may 1950 to 1800 19 May 1950), 302 (1800 19 May 1950 to 1800 26 May 1950), and 303 (1800 26 May to 1800 02 June 1950); 1st Cavalry Division Monthly Narrative for May 1950.

35. Headquarters, 1st Cavalry Division, Operations Order Number 1 (Training), "Field Training—Camp McNair—Period 15 April—1 July 1950," dated 25 March 1950, Enclosure 7 to G-3 Monthly Narrative for March 1950.

36. Headquarters, 1st Cavalry Division, Training Memorandum Number 13, subject: Field Training and Testing for Period 1 July–31 December 1950, dated 9 May 1950, Decimal File 353, G-3 Correspondence Files, RG 338, NARA II.

37. G-3 Section, 1st Cavalry Division, Activities Report for the Month of July [1950], Eighth U.S. Army Military History Section, Monthly Summaries 1946–1950, RG 554, NARA II.

BIBLIOGRAPHY

Archives and Collections

National Archives and Records Administration, College Park, Maryland
Record Group 111, Signal Corps Photos (World War II).
Record Group 319, Records of the Army Staff.
Record Group 331, Records of Allied Operational and Occupation Headquarters, World War II.
Record Group 337, Records of Administrative Sections, Headquarters Army Ground Forces/Army Field Forces.
Record Group 338, Records of U.S. Army Commands, 1942–.
Record Group 407, Records of the Adjutant General's Office, 1917–.
Record Group 554, Records of General Headquarters, Far Eastern Command/Supreme Commander Allied Powers/United Nations Command.

United States Army Military History Institute, Carlisle Barracks, Pennsylvania
Roy E. Appleman Collection.
Clay and Joan Blair Collection.
Capt. Russell A. Gugeler Interviews (Papers pertaining to U.S. Army Center of Military History publication *Combat Actions in Korea*).
Korean War Veterans Questionnaires, 25th Infantry Division.
Miscellaneous Interview Folder, Korean War—OCMH Interviews.
Miscellaneous Korean War Documents Collection.
Brig. Gen. (Ret.) Charles B. Smith Interview (Papers pertaining to Col. William J. Davies's "Task Force Smith: A Leadership Failure?").
Senior Officer Oral History Program, Combat Leadership in Korea series.

Harry S. Truman Presidential Library
Still Photo Archive.
George M. Elsey Papers.

Official Army Publications

Annual Report of the Secretary of the Army for Fiscal Year 1949. Washington, D.C.: Department of the Army, 1949.
Army Training. Training Circular Number 7. Washington, D.C.: Department of the Army, July 28, 1948.

BIBLIOGRAPHY

Basic Military Training Program (14 Weeks) for Newly Enlisted Men. Army Training Program 21-1. Washington, D.C.: Department of the Army, April 6, 1949.

Combat Formations. Training Circular Number 5. Washington, D.C.: Department of the Army, June 28, 1948.

Combat Information Bulletin Number 1. Seoul[?], Korea: Headquarters, Eighth U.S. Army Korea, 1950.

Field Service Regulations. Field Manual 100-5. Washington, D.C.: Department of the Army, October 1949.

The Fighting Heart. Department of the Army Pamphlet 20-137. Washington, D.C.: Department of the Army, August 1951.

Individual Training: The First Step. Department of the Army Pamphlet 20-131. Washington, D.C.: Department of the Army, October 1950.

Leadership. Training Circular Number 6. Washington, D.C.: Department of the Army, July 19, 1948.

Military Organization of the United States. Fort Leavenworth, Kans.: U.S. Army Command and General Staff College, 1926.

More Sweat, Less Blood. Department of the Army Pamphlet 20-132. Washington, D.C.: Department of the Army, February 1951.

The Officer's Guide. Harrisburg, Pa.: The Military Service Publishing Company, 1950.

Official Army Register, vol. 1, *United States Army Active and Retired Lists.* Washington, D.C.: Department of the Army, January 1, 1950.

Physical Training. Field Manual 21-20. Washington, D.C.: War Department, January 1946.

Physical Training. Training Circular Number 7. Washington, D.C.: War Department, July 10, 1946.

Qualification Scores. Training Circular Number 9. Washington, D.C.: Department of the Army, July 6, 1949.

Rifle Platoon, Rifle Company, TO&E 7-17N. Army Field Forces Training Test 7-2. Washington, D.C.: Department of the Army, September 27, 1948.

Rifle Squad, Rifle Company, TO&E 7-17N. Army Field Forces Training Test 7-1. Washington, D.C.: Department of the Army, September 27, 1948.

Selective Service System. *Physical Examination of Selective Service Registrants.* Special Monograph Number 15. Washington, D.C.: U.S. Government Printing Office, 1947.

Semiannual Report of the Secretary of the Army, January 1 to June 30, 1950. Washington, D.C.: Department of the Army, 1950.

The Soldier in Combat. Department of the Army Pamphlet 20-135. Washington, D.C.: Department of the Army, April 1951.

Special Problems in the Korean Conflict. Seoul, Korea: Headquarters, Eighth U.S. Army Korea, 1951.

Table of Organization and Equipment 7-17N, Infantry Rifle Company. Washington, D.C.: Department of the Army, December 9, 1947.

Weapons Familiarization Courses. Training Circular Number 10. Washington, D.C.: Department of the Army, July 20, 1949.

BIBLIOGRAPHY

Interviews and Surveys
Lt. Col. (Ret.) Joseph Bell, B Battery, 8th Field Artillery Battalion, December 10, 2001.
Sgt. 1st Class (Ret.) Joe Christopher, F Company, 8th Cavalry Regiment, January 30, 2002.
Daniel Cooper, G Company, 27th Infantry Regiment, February 8, 2002.
Brig. Gen. (Ret.) Uzal W. Ent, B Company, 27th Infantry Regiment, September 8, 2001.
Col. (Ret.) David H. Hackworth, G Company, 27th Infantry Regiment, April 6, 2001.
Col. (Ret.) Wilson Heefner, M.D., with author, December 1, 2001.
S.Sgt. (Ret.) J. A. Langone, B Company, 21st Infantry Regiment, February 2, 2002.
Gene Rohling, D Company, 27th Infantry Regiment, with Jim Malachowski, April 1998.
M.Sgt. (Ret.) Joseph E. Marlett, B Company, 27th Infantry Regiment, June 8, 2001.
Command Sgt. Maj. (Ret.) Robert Murphy, 8th Field Artillery Battalion, November 9, 2001.
Col. (Ret.) George A. Rasula, HQ, 3rd Battalion, 31st Infantry Regiment, March 12, 2002.
Col. (Ret.) John Stratis, C Troop, 72nd Constabulary Squadron, July 24, 2001.
William H. Trotter, Division Artillery, 6th Infantry Division, January 29, 2004.

Correspondence
E-mail, Lt. Col. (Ret.) Kincheon H. Bailey, 82nd Field Artillery Battalion, to author, November 9, 2001.
E-mails, Glenn Berry, G Company, 35th Infantry Regiment, to author, November 8 and 9, 2001.
E-mail, J. Jack Borden, D Company, 27th Infantry Regiment, to author, February 14, 2001.
E-mail, Robert H. Brothers, A Battery, 92nd Anti-Aircraft Artillery (Automatic Weapons) Battalion, to author, December 27, 2001.
E-mail, Daniel Cooper, G Company, 27th Infantry, to author, January 4, 2002.
E-mail, William R. Duffy, 62nd Signal Battalion, to author, December 19, 2001.
E-mails, Douglas C. Ellis, 142nd Ordnance Battalion, to author, November 11 and 12, 2001.
E-mails, Brig. Gen. (Ret.) Uzal W. Ent, B Company, 27th Infantry Regiment, to author, May 9 and 11, September 7, 2001.
Letter, Lt. Col. (Ret.) T. R. Fehrenbach, 72nd Tank Battalion, to author, January 29, 2002.
E-mail, Jack Goodwin, C Company, 21st Infantry Regiment, to author, November 29, 2001.
E-mail, Don Hansen, Heavy Mortar Company, 27th Infantry, to author, October 29, 2001.
Telephone conversation, Lee A. Hanson, 51st Signal Battalion, with author, January 1, 2002.
E-mail, Col. (Ret.) Robert W. Hill, C Company, 27th Infantry Regiment, to author, August 21, 2001.
E-mail, Louis E. Holmes, E Company, 31st Infantry Regiment, to author, November 3, 2001.
Letter, Col. (Ret.) Harvey C. Jones (USMA '45), February 25, 2004.
E-mail, Col. (Ret.) Karl H. Lowe to author, January 10, 2005.
Letter, M.Sgt. (Ret.) Joseph E. Marlett, B Company, 27th Infantry Regiment, to author, March 25, 2001.
E-mail, Ed Parmenter, B Troop, 8th Cavalry, and Headquarters Troop, 2d Cavalry Brigade, to author, March 18 and December 29, 2008.
Letters, Lloyd F. Pittman, F Company, 17th Infantry Regiment, to author, December 17 and 27, 2001.

Telephone conversation, Lloyd F. Pittman, F Company, 17th Infantry Regiment, with author, December 17, 2001.

Letter, George F. Rasula, Headquarters, 3rd Battalion, 31st Infantry Regiment, to author, February 19, 2005.

Letter, Frank S. Raynor, Headquarters and Headquarters Battery, 24th Division Artillery, February 14, 2002.

E-mail, Command Sgt. Maj. (Ret.) Paul S. Spescia, 7th Engineer Battalion, January 5, 2002.

Unpublished Documents

Carter, Donald A. "From G.I. to Atomic Soldier: The Development of U.S. Army Tactical Doctrine, 1945–1956." Ph.D. diss., The Ohio State University, 1987.

Davies, Col. William J. "Task Force Smith: A Leadership Failure?" Study project, U.S. Army War College, Carlisle Barracks, Pennsylvania, 1992.

Donnelly, William M. "Army Readiness in 1950." Paper, U.S. Army Center of Military History, 2002, copy in author's possession.

Jordan, Kelly C. "Three Armies in Korea: the Combat Effectiveness of the United States Eighth Army in Korea, July 1950–June 1952." Ph.D. diss., The Ohio State University, 1999.

Kerin, James R. "The Korean War and American Memory." Ph.D. diss., University of Pennsylvania, 1994.

Price, Joseph E. "The Wages of Unpreparedness: The United States Army in the Korean War, July 1950." M.A. thesis, East Texas State University, 1982.

Wiersema, Richard F. "No More Bad Force Myths: A Tactical Study of Regimental Combat in Korea, July 1950." Unpublished monograph, U.S. Army Command and General Staff College, Fort Leavenworth, Kansas, 1996.

Books and Articles

"AFF Makes Its Postwar Report," *Army Information Digest* 4, no. 12 (December 1949), 22–33.

Alexander, Bevin. *Korea: The First War We Lost*. New York: Hippocrene Books, 1986.

Appleman, Roy E. *South to the Naktong, North to the Yalu*. United States Army in the Korean War series. Washington, D.C.: U.S. Army Center of Military History, 1961.

Archibald, Sasha. "Million Dollar Point," *Cabinet Magazine Online* 10 (Spring 2003), 1, http://www.cabinetmagazine.org/issues/10/million_point.php.

Baldwin, Hanson W. "The Condition of the Army," *New York Times*, June 22, 1950.

The Bark of the Wolfhounds, 27th Infantry Regiment: Organization Day, 2 May 1950. Osaka[?]: 27th Infantry Regiment, 1950.

Barth, Brig. Gen. George Bittman. *Tropic Lightning and Taro Leaf in Korea*. Athens, Greece: U.S. Embassy, 1955.

Bateman, Robert L. "G.I. Life in Postwar Japan," *MHQ: The Quarterly Journal of Military History* 15, no. 1 (Autumn 2002).

Battleground Korea: The Story of the 25th Infantry Division. Tokyo[?]: 25th Infantry Division History Council, 1951.

Bell, William Gardner. *Commanding Generals and Chiefs of Staff of the Army 1775–1995*. Washington, D.C.: U.S. Army Center of Military History, 1997.

BIBLIOGRAPHY

Binder, L. James. "No More Task Force Smiths," *Army* 42, no. 1 (January 1992), 18–26.
———. "Dealing with Change in 'America's Army,'" *Army* 42, no. 1 (January 1992), 21.
Blair, Clay. *The Forgotten War: America in Korea, 1950–1953*. New York: Times Books, 1987.
Boal, Sam. "New Soldiers for New Tasks," *New York Times Magazine*, July 23, 1950, 7–9, 40–42.
Boatner, Capt. Mark M., III. "Martinets or Mollycoddlers," *Combat Forces Journal* 1, no. 5 (August 1950), 11.
Boettcher, Thomas D. *First Call: The Making of the Modern U.S. Military, 1945–1953*. Boston: Little, Brown, 1992.
Bowers, William T., William M. Hammond, and George L. McGarigle. *Black Soldier, White Army: The 24th Infantry Regiment in Korea*. Washington, D.C.: U.S. Army Center of Military History, 1996.
Bradley, General Omar N. "One Round Won't Win the Fight," *Army Information Digest* 4, no. 4 (April 1949), 31–35.
———, and Clay Blair. *A General's Life: An Autobiography by General of the Army Omar N. Bradley*. New York: Simon & Schuster, 1983.
A Brief History of the 19th Infantry Regiment. Tokyo[?]: Headquarters, 19th Infantry Regiment, 1954.
Burkhardt, Paul. *The Major Training Areas of Germany: Grafenwöhr/Vilseck, Hohenfels, Wildflecken*. 4th ed. Amberg, Germany: Druckhaus Oberpfalz, 1994.
Bussey, Charles M. *Firefight at Yechon: Courage and Racism in the Korean War*. Washington, D.C.: Brassey's, 1991.
Cameron, Robert. "There and Back Again: Constabulary Training and Organization 1946–1950." In *Armed Diplomacy: Two Centuries of American Campaigning*. Fort Leavenworth, Kan.: Combat Studies Institute, 2003.
"Canned Guns Inspected," *Infantry Journal* 44, no. 6 (June 1948), 55.
Cannon, Maj. Michael. "Task Force Smith: A Study in (Un)Preparedness and (Ir)Responsibility," *Military Review*, February 1988, 63–73.
Chaze, Edward. *Stainless Steel Kimono*. New York: Simon and Schuster, 1947.
Cishin, Ira H. "Officers' Attitudes Towards Their Careers," *Army Information Digest* 4, no. 9 (September 1949), 55–58.
Clark, Gen. Mark. "The Payoff in Training," *Army Information Digest* 5, no. 1 (January 1950), 3–8.
Cole, Hugh M. *Ardennes: The Battle of the Bulge*. United States Army in World War II: The European Theater of Operations series. Washington, D.C.: U.S. Army Center of Military History, 1961.
Coleman, Lt. Col. C. D. "Observing Personnel Management at Work," *Military Review* 28, no. 19 (January 1949), 56–62.
Collins, J. Lawton. *Lightning Joe: An Autobiography*. Baton Rouge: Louisiana State University Press, 1979.
———. *War in Peacetime: The History and Lessons of Korea*. Boston: Houghton-Mifflin, 1969.
Condit, Doris M. *History of the Office of the Secretary of Defense*, vol. 2, *The Test of War, 1950–1953*. Washington, D.C.: Historical Office, Office of the Secretary of Defense, 1988.

Condit, Kenneth W. *History of the Joint Chiefs of Staff*, vol. 2, *The Joint Chiefs of Staff and National Policy, 1947–1949*. Wilmington, Del.: Michael Glazier, 1979.

Connolly, Capt. Robert D. "Men and Machines in Occupied Japan," *Army Information Digest* 5, no. 6 (June 1950), 17–22.

Corley, Col. John T. "Lean and Hungry Soldiers," *Combat Forces Journal* 1, no. 12 (July 1951), 16–18.

Cumings, Bruce. *The Origins of the Korean War*, vol. 2, *The Roaring of the Cataract, 1947–1950*. Princeton: Princeton University Press, 1990.

Dannenmeier, William D. *We Were Innocents: An Infantryman in Korea*. Urbana: University of Illinois Press, 1999.

Davidson, Bill. "The New G.I. Joe: He Never Had It So Good," *Collier's* 126, no. 14 (September 30, 1950), 24–25, 71–75.

Dean, Maj. Gen. William F., and William L. Worden. *General Dean's Story*. New York: The Viking Press, 1954.

Devers, Gen. Jacob L. "Training the Army of Today," *Army Information Digest* 4, no. 4 (April 1949), 3–8.

Devine, Maj. Gen. John M. "What Is a Tough Soldier?" *Army Information Digest* 4, no. 9 (September 1949), 11–14.

Disposal of Surplus Property, 1 July 1946–30 June 1947. Occupation Forces in Europe Series. Karlsruhe, Germany: Historical Division, U.S. European Command, 1949.

Doughty, Robert A. *The Evolution of U.S. Army Tactical Doctrine, 1946–1976*. Leavenworth Paper Number 1. Fort Leavenworth, Kans.: Combat Studies Institute, U.S. Army Command and General Staff College, 1979.

Edwards, Paul M. *To Acknowledge a War*. Westport, Conn.: Greenwood Press, 2000.

———. *The Pusan Perimeter: An Annotated Bibliography*. Westport, Conn.: Greenwood Press, 1998.

Eichelberger, Robert, and Milton Mackaye. *Our Jungle Road to Tokyo*. New York: The Viking Press, 1950.

8th Cavalry Regiment: Honor and Courage. On-line journal of the 8th Cavalry Regiment Association. Cavalry Outpost Publications, http://www.firsteam.us/journals/8th_rgmt/.

Ent, Uzal W. *Fighting on the Brink: Defending the Pusan Perimeter*. Paducah, Ky.: Turner Publishing Company, 1996.

Epley, William. *America's First Cold War Army, 1945–1950*. Arlington, Va.: Association of the United States Army, 1999.

Fearey, Robert A. *The Occupation of Japan: Second Phase, 1948–1950*. New York: MacMillan, 1950.

Fehrenbach, T. R. *This Kind of War: A Study in Unpreparedness*. New York: MacMillan, 1963.

Fitzpatrick, Richard, ed. *Twenty-fifth Infantry Division: Tropic Lighting*. Paducah, Ky.: Turner Publishing, 1988.

Fleming, Thomas. "The Man Who Saved Korea," *Military History Quarterly* 5, no. 2 (Winter 1993), 54–61.

Flint, Roy K. "Task Force Smith and the 24th Infantry Division: Delay and Withdrawal, 5–19 July 1950." In *America's First Battles, 1776–1965*. Ed. Charles E. Heller and William A. Stoft. Lawrence: University Press of Kansas, 1986.

Fry, Col. James C. "Career Planning for Officers," *Army Information Digest* 2, no. 8 (August 1948), 7–12.

Gibney, Frank. "Advance Patrol Pushes Up through Enemy Fire," *Life* 29, no. 3 (July 17, 1950), 36–37.

Guernsey, Maj. Paul D. "New Army, New Soldiers," *Army Information Digest* 3, no. 5 (May 1948), 26–30.

Hackworth, David H., and Julie Sherman. *About Face: The Odyssey of An American Warrior.* New York: Simon and Schuster, 1989.

Hallahan, Robert F. *All Good Men: A Lieutenant's Memories of the Korean War.* New York: iUniverse, 2003.

Hammond, Paul Y. "Supercarriers and B-36 Bombers: Appropriations, Strategy, and Politics." In *American Civil-Military Decisions.* Ed. Harold Stein. Birmingham: University of Alabama Press, 1963.

Hati, Ikuhiko. "The Occupation of Japan, 1945–1952," *The American Military and the Far East,* Proceedings of the Ninth Military History Symposium, United States Air Force Academy, 1–3 October 1980. Ed. Joe Dixon. Washington, D.C.: U.S. Government Printing Office, 1980.

Herr, Maj. Gen. John K., and Edward S. Wallace. *The Story of the U.S. Cavalry, 1775–1942.* Boston: Little, Brown, 1953.

Hewes, James E., Jr. *From Root to McNamara: Army Organization and Administration, 1900–1963.* Washington, D.C.: U.S. Army Center of Military History, 1975.

Higgins, Marguerite. *War in Korea: Report of a Woman Combat Correspondent.* Garden City, N.Y.: Doubleday, 1951.

Hille, Lt. Col. H. L. "The Eighth Army's Role in the Military Government of Japan," *Military Review* 27, no. 11 (February 1948).

History of the Occupation of Japan. Osaka[?]: 25th Infantry Division, 1948.

Horchow, Col. Reuben. "Careers for Infantrymen," *Army Information Digest* 2, no. 9 (September 1947), 23–27.

House, Jonathan M. *Combined Arms Warfare in the Twentieth Century.* Lawrence: University Press of Kansas, 2001.

James, D. Clayton. *Refighting the Last War: Command and Crisis in Korea, 1950–1953.* New York: The Free Press, 1993.

Jeffcoat, George D. *United States Army Dental Service in World War II.* Washington, D.C.: Office of the Surgeon General, 1947.

Johnson, Cressie. *Korea, 1950–1951: A Wolfhound Story.* El Paso, Tex.: privately published, 2000.

Jordan, Donald A. *China's Trial By Fire: The Shanghai War of 1932.* Ann Arbor: University of Michigan Press, 2001.

Kinkead, Eugene. *In Every War but One.* New York: W. W. Norton and Company, 1959.

Knox, Donald. *The Korean War: Pusan to Chosin, an Oral History.* New York: Harcourt Brace Jovanovich, 1987.

Koons, Capt. William B. "A Soldier in Kyushu," *Army Information Digest* 2, no. 10 (October 1947), 16–22.

Lawrence, W. H. "A Day in the Life of a Platoon," *New York Times Magazine,* September 10, 1950, 13, 70.

Lee, Mabel. *A History of Physical Education and Sports in the U.S.A.* New York: John Wiley & Sons, 1983.

Levin, Harold. "Hell Country: Of Mud, Muck, and Human Excrement...," *Newsweek* 36, no. 6 (August 7, 1950), 20–21.

Lewis, Maj. Gen. John T. "Ground General School Training," *Army Information Digest* 4, no. 6 (June 1949), 19–24.

Love, Edmund G. *The 27th Infantry Division in World War II.* Washington, D.C.: The Infantry Journal Press, 1949.

Luery, S.Sgt. Rodney. *The Story of the Wolfhounds: 27th Infantry Regiment.* Tokyo: Japan News, 1953.

MacArthur, Douglas, General of the Army. *Reminiscences.* New York: McGraw Hill, 1964.

McCarthy, Col. Charles W. "Lessons for All Ranks," *Army* 14, no. 2 (September 1963), 82.

McFarland, Keith D. *The Korean War: An Annotated Bibliography.* New York: Garland Publishing, 1986.

———, and David L. Roll. *Louis Johnson and the Arming of America: The Roosevelt and Truman Years.* Bloomington: Indiana University Press, 2005.

Maddox, Robert J. *The Unknown War with Russia: Wilson's Siberian Intervention.* San Rafael, Calif.: Presidio Press, 1977.

Maihafer, Harry J. *From the Hudson to the Yalu: West Point '49 in the Korean War.* College Station: Texas A&M University Press, 1993.

Malina, Robert M., and G. Lawrence Rarick. "Growth, Physique, and Motor Performance." In *Physical Activity: Human Growth and Development.* Ed. G. Lawrence Rarick. New York: Academic Press, 1973.

Mansoor, Peter R. *The GI Offensive in Europe: The Triumph of American Infantry Divisions in World War II.* Lawrence: University Press of Kansas, 1999.

Marshall, S. L. A. *Bringing Up the Rear: A Memoir.* San Rafael, Calif.: Presidio Press, 1979.

———. "The Critics of the Army," *Combat Forces Journal* 1, no. 12 (July 1951), 22–23.

———. *Men Against Fire: The Problem of Command in Future War.* New York: William Morrow, 1947.

———. "Our Army in Korea: The Best Yet," *Harper's Magazine* 203, no. 1215 (August 1951), 21–27.

Martin, Harold H. "The Colonel Saved the Day," *Saturday Evening Post*, September 9, 1950, 32–33, 187–89.

"Men of Quality," *Combat Forces Journal* 1, no. 9 (April 1951), 9–10.

Metz, Leon C. *Fort Bliss: An Illustrated History.* El Paso, Tex.: Mangan Books, 1981.

Michaelis, Brig. Gen. "Mike," with Bill Davidson. "This We Learned in Korea," *Collier's* 128 (August 18, 1951), 38–45.

Millett, Allan R. *The Korean War.* The Essential Bibliography series. Dulles, Va.: Potomac Books, 2007.

———. *The War For Korea: A House Burning.* Lawrence: University Press of Kansas, 2005.

Millis, Walter, ed. *The Forrestal Diaries.* New York: The Viking Press, 1951.

"Motti Tactics," *Infantry Journal* 46, no. 1 (January 1950), 8–14.

Mydans, Carl. "It's One Ration. Save It, Boys," *Life* 29, no. 2 (July 17, 1950), 36–37.

"News and Comment," *Infantry Journal* 46, no. 3 (March 1950), 27.

Newton, Col. Henry C. "The Officer Problem," *Infantry Journal* 44, no. 12 (December 1948), 19–21.

The Nineteenth Infantry Regiment, 1861–1949. Organization Day brochure. Beppu, Japan: Headquarters, 19th Infantry Regiment, 1949.

"No Place for the Unfit," *Infantry Journal* 44, no. 2 (February 1948), 60.

Occupation Diary: First Cavalry Division, 1945–1950. Tokyo: Headquarters, 1st Cavalry Division, October 1950.

O'Neill, Lt. Col. Larry J., and Maj. Ernest E. Steck. "Preparation and Conduct of Field Exercises, Part I," *Military Review* 30, no. 6 (September 1950), 57–62.

———. "Preparation and Conduct of Field Exercises, Part II," *Military Review* 30, no. 7 (October 1950), 56–62.

Operation Roll-up: The History of Surplus Property Disposal in the Pacific Ocean. Washington, D.C.: Department of the Navy, 1948.

Osborne, John. "U.S. Counters Mass with Mobility," *Life* 29, no. 8 (August 21, 1950), 15.

"Our Military Requirements," *Army Information Digest* 3, no. 5 (May 1948), 61–63.

Pacific Stars and Stripes: The First 40 Years, 1945–1985. Novato, Calif.: Presidio Press, 1985.

Pakenham, Compton. "Green Men under Fire," *Newsweek* 36, no. 3 (July 17, 1950), 16–18.

Paul, Lt. Gen. Willard S. "Guiding Army Careers," *Army Information Digest* 2, no. 8 (August 1947), 2–9.

———. "Putting the Personal into Personnel," *Military Review* 29, no. 2 (May 1949), 25–32.

Pearson, Haydn S. "An Argument for Military Training," *New York Times Magazine*, August 27, 1944, 19.

"The Peripatetic 27th: It Is Exhibit 'A' of the U.S. Defense Effort in Korea," *Life* 29, no. 11 (September 11, 1950), 43–48.

"Plans for Army Troop Distribution," *Army Information Digest* 4, no. 5 (May 1949), 46–54.

Poole, Walter S. *History of the Joint Chiefs of Staff*, vol. 4, *The Joint Chiefs of Staff and National Policy, 1950–1952*. Washington, D.C.: Office of Joint History, Office of the Chairman of the Joint Chiefs of Staff, 1998.

Quinn, Bernard J. "Triple R Helps EUCOM Pay Its Way," *Army Information Digest* 4, no. 10 (October 1949), 20–24.

Quinn, Capt. Kevin A. "The Leaders and the Led," *Combat Forces Journal* 1, no. 8 (March 1951), 36–37.

Rearden, Steven L. *History of the Office of the Secretary of Defense*, vol. 1, *The Formative Years, 1947–1950*. Washington, D.C.: Historical Office, Office of the Secretary of Defense, 1984.

"Representative Army Divisions," *Army Information Digest* 4, no. 12 (December 1949), 33–42.

Rhodes, Col. Frank B., Jr. "A Practical Combat Firing Course," *Infantry Journal* 44, no. 8 (August 1948), 50–52.

Ridgway, Matthew B. *The Korean War*. New York: Doubleday, 1967.

———. Speech quotation page filler, *Military Review* 31, no. 10 (January 1951), 109.

———, and Harold H. Martin. *Soldier: The Memoirs of Matthew B. Ridgway*. New York: Curtis Publishing, 1956.

Rishell, Lyle. *With a Black Platoon in Combat: A Year in Korea.* College Station: Texas A&M University Press, 1993.

Rivette, Capt. Donald E. "Stop That Tank," *Infantry Journal* 46, no. 3 (March 1950), 7–11.

Robertson, William Glenn. *Counterattack on the Naktong, 1950.* Leavenworth Paper Number 13. Fort Leavenworth, Kans.: Combat Studies Institute, U.S. Army Command and General Staff College, 1985.

The Rock of Chickamauga, 1861–1972. Schofield Barracks, Hawaii: 25th Infantry Division, 1972.

Ross, Steven T. *American War Plans, 1945–1950.* London: Frank Cass, 1996.

Royall, Kenneth C. "Civil Functions of the Army in the Occupied Areas," *Military Review* 29, no. 5 (August 1949), 37–43.

Sawicki, James A. *Cavalry Regiments of the U.S. Army.* Dumfries, Va.: Wyvern Publications, 1985.

———. *Infantry Regiments of the U.S. Army.* Dumfries, Va.: Wyvern Publications, 1981.

Sayre, Maj. Gordon E. "A Division Trains Its Technicians," *Army Information Digest* 4, no. 6 (June 1949), 51–53.

Schnabel, James F. *Policy and Direction: The First Year.* United States Army in the Korean War series. Washington, D.C.: U.S. Army Center of Military History, 1977.

Sparrow, John C. *A History of Personnel Demobilization in the U.S. Army.* Washington, D.C.: Department of the Army, 1952; reprint, U.S. Army Center of Military History, 1994.

Stokesbury, James L. *A Short History of the Korean War.* New York: Quill/William Morrow, 1988.

Takemae, Eiji. *Inside GHQ: The Allied Occupation of Japan and Its Legacy.* Trans. Robert Ricketts and Sebastian Swann. New York: Continuum, 2002.

Terry, Addison. *The Battle for Pusan: A Korean War Memoir.* Novato, Calif.: Presidio Press, 2000.

31st Infantry Regiment: History, Lineage, Honors, Decorations, and Seventy-third Anniversary Yearbook. Fort Sill, Okla.: 4th Battalion (Mechanized), 31st Infantry Regiment, 1989.

Tomedi, Rudy. *No Bugles, No Drums: An Oral History of the Korean War.* New York: John Wiley and Sons, 1993.

Tropic Lighting in Korea. Atlanta, Ga.: Albert Love Enterprises, 1954.

Van Houten, Col. John G. "Keep That Doughboy Lightly Loaded," *Infantry Journal* 46, no. 3 (March 1950), 12–13.

Van Way, Col. C. W. "Career Guidance—A New Army Function," *Military Review* 27, no. 2 (December 1947), 9–17.

"Walker Creates Dual Deputies," *Stars and Stripes*, October 17, 1948, 3.

Weigley, Russell F. *A History of the United States Army.* New York: MacMillan, 1967.

White, John Albert. *The Siberian Intervention.* Princeton: Princeton University Press, 1950.

"Why Are We Taking a Beating," *Life* 29, no. 4 (July 24, 1950), 21.

Wiley, Lt. Col. Bell I. "The Building and Training of Infantry Divisions, Part 4: Effects of Overseas Requirements upon Training, 1944–1945," *Infantry Journal* 44, no. 5 (May 1948), 30–36.

Williams, F. D. G. *SLAM: The Influence of S. L. A. Marshall on the United States Army.* Washington, D.C.: U.S. Army Center of Military History, 1990.

Witsell, Maj. Gen. Edward F. "Administration and the New Army," *Army Information Digest* 4, no. 2 (February 1949), 3–7.

Young, Maj. Leilyn M. "Perfecting Ground Weapons," *Army Information Digest* 4, no. 6 (June 1949), 43–50.

INDEX

Note: page numbers referring to illustrations or captions are italicized.

Aebano Maneuver Area, 47, 50–52
air transportability, 70–71, 105–106, 131n27
Alexander, Lt. Col. Walden J., 84
Almond, Lt. Gen. Edward N., *gallery 2, 9*, 29–30, 62
American Legion, 5
amphibious assaults, 89
Andreasen, Lt. E. K., *gallery 19*
Anogahara Training Area, 46–47, 50, 52
Appleton, Roy E., 8–9
Army, U.S.: demobilization of, post-war, 23–25, 28, 38, 110–11; discipline of soldiers in, 21, 120n11; Japan Occupation role of, 14–20; Marine Corps' performance compared to that of, 7, 11; motives for enlistment in, 6, 119n8; tension between Regular and Reserve officers in, 29; weakening of, 109–10
Army Field Forces (AFF): Mobilization Training Plan 21-1, 31; Office of the Chief, 26–27; strength and readiness report, 33; Training Test 6-2, 68; Training Test 7-1, 63; Training Test 7-2, 65–66; Training Test 7-10, 67; Training Test 7-12, 103; Training Test 8-1, 73; Training Test 21-1, 80; Training Test 31-1, 73; Training Test 31-2, 73
Army Field Manual 21-20, 43–44
Army Ground Forces (AGF), 22–23
Army Reorganization Act (1950), 33
Army Service Forces (ASF), 22
athletic competitions, 64
Ayres, Lt. Col. Harold B "Red," 5, 50, 53

Bank of Japan, 96
Base Industrial Group 5, 114, 116
Bateman, Robert, 11
Battle of Baksan (1913), 91
Bazzano, Pfc. Matthew F., *gallery 8*
Berlin blockade, 16
Bernard, Col. Carl F., 40
Biggs, Capt. Lawrence W., 100
Bishop, 1st Lt. Bertram, 47–48, 50
Black Soldier, White Army: The 24th Infantry Regiment in Korea (Bowers et al.), 10
Blair, Clay, 8
Bollard, Lt. Col., 64
Bradley, Gen. Omar N., 6–7, 13–14, *gallery 3*, 111
Britt, Lt. Col. Henry C., 80
Brodie, Bernard, 42
Bull, Maj. Gen. Harold R., 29
Bussey, Charles M., 10

Caler, Pvt. Charles L., *gallery 13*
Camp Chickamauga, 76, 81, 83–85, 88–89
Camp Crawford, 57–59, 67, 69–70
Camp King, 92, 97, 107
Camp McGill, 89
Camp McNair, 30, 96–103, 106
Camp Sakai, 46–47, 54–55
Camp Zama, 106–108
Career Guidance Program, 34, 59
career management, 33–37
Chase, Brig. Gen. William, 92–93
Chazal, Col. E. A., 37, 127n24
Check, Lt. Col. Gilbert J., 50, 52–53
Cheney, Lt. Col. Wherlen F., 100
"Chicks" *See* 19th Infantry Regiment

153

INDEX

Childs, Col. John W., 46, 52
China, People's Republic of, 16
Chitose, 69
Civil War, U.S., 75
Clainos, Peter, 18–19
Clark, Gen. Mark, 26, 36
Cold War, 16
Collins, Gen. J. Lawton: assignment of blame for Korean War failures by, 7; basic training's expansion, 26; inspections by, 101; photos, *gallery 3, gallery 4*; training and readiness inspection, 51
Combat Effectiveness Reports, 52, 72
combined arms live fire exercises (CALFEX), 66–67
Command Post Exercises (CPXs), 17
conscription, 1, 23
Constant Flow Programs, 26, 46, 66, 77, 94
contingency planning, 17
Corley, Col. John T., 5
Craig, Maj. Gen. Louis A., 29, *gallery 6*
Cuba, 91
Cumings, Bruce, 9–10
Cutler, 1st Lt. Elliot, 87
Czechoslovakia, 16

Davies, Col. William J., 11
Dean, Maj. Gen. William F.: NCO shortage, 60; ROK ability to counter KPA, 55; testing, 89; training programs, 87; Wiersema on, 10
Defense, U.S. Department of, 13, 25, 28, 110
demobilization, 23–25, 28, 38, 110–11
Devers, Gen. Jacob, 26, 114
Dick, Lt. Gen. W. W., 4
Dilley, Lt. Col. John H., 94
Directorate of Organization (DOT), 31
Doolittle Board, 6, 120n11
Dusoblom, Pvt. Walter D., *gallery 15*

Edwards, Paul, 6
Eichelberger, Lt. Gen. Robert L., 19–20
Eighth Army: Air Transportability School, 70, 105–106; Character Guidance Program, 6; Command Post Exercises (CPXs), 17; conflicting views of, 3–4; Constant Flow Program, 26, 46, 66, 77, 94; discipline issues, 21; equipment shortages in, 49; Fehrenbach's portrayal of, 7–9; IG's report on readiness in, 29–30; Japan Occupation duties, 14–20; low-aptitude troops sent to, 20, 27; Naktong battle victories by, 10; Replacement Training Center, 25; seen as victorious against KPA, 9–10; training areas, limitations of, 115–16; Training Directive Number Four, 18–20, 30–32; Training Directive Number Five, 51; training programs' success, 109–10. *See also individual regiments*

8th Cavalry Regiment: 1st Battalion, 92, 100–102, 106–108; 2nd Battalion, 92, 100, 102, 106–107; discipline problems in, 95, 100–102; early history of, 91–92; Heavy Mortar Company, 99; Japan Occupation duties of, 92–93, 95–96, 116; Korea deployment of, 108; leadership shortage in, 94–95; MTP certification, 105; readiness ratings of, 96; recertification of squads and platoons, 106–107; remedial education, 103; small arms tournament, 106; training at Camp McNair, 30, 96–103, 106

82nd Airborne Division, 13
Eisenhower, Gen. Dwight D., 6, 23, *gallery 2*, 111
equipment shortages: in the 8th Army, 49; in the 8th Cavalry Regiment, 108; in the 19th Infantry Regiment, 86–87; in the 31st Infantry Regiment, 67; in Europe, 123n15; Operation Roll-Up and, 38–40, 116
Ethridge, Pvt. Hal, *gallery 15*

Far East Command (FECOM): contingency planning regarding Communist threat, 17; division of responsibilities under, 19; G-1 staff, 26, 62; personnel replacements shipped to, 77
Fehrenbach, T. R., 7–9, 11
Field, Lt. Col. Eugene J., 100–101
5th Cavalry Regiment, 106

57th Field Artillery Battalion, 71
Firefight at Yecheon: Courage and Racism in the Korean War (Bussey), 10
fire protective line, 131n26
1st Cavalry Division, 19, 92; 271st Field Artillery Battalion, 22; Armored Cavalry School, 99; demobilization, 24; leadership school, 94; organizational changes in, 94; small arms tournament, 106; training guidance for, 104; transfers to 27th Infantry Regiment from, 46. *See also* 8th Cavalry Regiment
Fort Riley, Kansas, 91
Frazier, Lt. Col. D. P., 98–99
Fuji-Susono Maneuver Area, 46, 49–54

G-1 staff, 34
Garcia, Calixto, 75
Gay, Maj. Gen. Hobart R., *gallery 4*, 104–105, 107
Gibney, Frank, 5
Graves, Maj. Gen William S., 56
Greene, 1st Lt. Byron D., 83
Grenelle, Lt. Col. Edward, 50
Ground General School, 9
Grunert, Lt. Col. William, 96–97
gunboggans, 69
Guomindang, 16
Hardaman, Lt. Col. Wayne, 22
Harris, Col. F. M., 27, 68, 83, 102
Hertel, Capt. Richard J., 69, *gallery 24*
Hijudai Maneuver Area, 81, 84, 88–89
Hill, Pvt. Frank B., *gallery 4*
Hodes, Brig. Gen. Henry I., 101
"hollow army," 22–25
Hoover, Herbert, 56

In Every War but One (Kinkead), 5
Infantry Journal, 35, 43, 49
Infantry Rifle Company, The (FM7-10), 82
intelligence and reconnaissance (I&R) platoons, 50–51, 68, 73, 84, 88
Ishigaki Maneuver Area, 82–83, 85, 88–89
Itami Air Force Base, 54
IX Corps, 59, 65

Jackson, Lt., *gallery 9*
Japan: Communist Party, 93; Korean expatriate groups in, 93; Occupation, 14–20, 45, 76, 92–93, 95–96, 116; Operation Roll-Up, 39–40; readiness phase in, 15–18; repatriation of soldiers from Soviets, 72; road system deficits, 67, 88; Soviet invasion of, possible, 17–18; stabilization phase in, 15–16; zones of responsibility for defense, 18, 19
Jensen, Lt. Col. Carl C., 88
Johnson, Louis A., 6, *gallery 2*
Joint Chiefs of Staff (JCS), 20, 41–42, 106
Joint Strategic Planning and Operations Group (JSPOG), 17
Jumomji Maneuver Area, 83–84, 88

Kean, Maj. Gen. William, 49, 51, 53
Kim Il-Sung, 111
King, Maj. Gen. Edward P., 57
Kinkead, Eugene, 5
Korean People's Army (KPA), 1, 4, 10, 90; 4th Division, 2, 74
Korean War: assigning blame for failure in, 4–7; economic impact of, 7; initial attack (25 June 1950), 1–3, 90, 108; Task Force Smith, 1–3, 10, 40, 74, 117
Kreidberg, Lt. Col., 77

Leighton, Lt. Col. Ralph E., 59
Lenin, V. I., 45
Lepski, Lt., 98
Life, 4
Lincoln, Abraham, 75
Lord, Maj. Edward B., 80
Louisiana Maneuvers (1941), 114
Lovless, Col. Jay B., 87–88
Lynch, Col. Charles P., 79–82

MacArthur, Gen. Douglas: amphibious assault, 89; on Appleton, 9; combat readiness, 78, 94; JCS conflict with, 20; Operation Roll-Up, 38; removal of, 2; Task Force Smith, 1
machine guns, 46, 82

Manus Island, 92
Marburg Replacement Depot, 27
Marine Corps, U.S., 7, 11
Maris, Brig. Gen. Ward, 89
Marlett, M. Sgt. Joseph E., 127n16
Marshall, Gen. George C., 22, 114
Marshall, S. L. A., 11, 50
Matranga, Pvt. Andrew R., *gallery 7*
Mayton, PFC Bobby L., *gallery 19*
McAuliffe, Maj. Gen. Anthony C., 62–63, 77–78, 87
McCarthy, Col. Charles W., 8
McCoy, Pvt. Sidney, *gallery 6*
McGrail, Lt. Col. Thomas M., 86
McNabb, Col. Alexander, 95–97
McNamara, Robert S., *gallery 2*
Meloy, Col. Guy S., 82, 84–85, 87
Mexico, 75–76, 89, 92
Michaelis, Lt. Col. John H., 88, 112
Military Review, 49
Miller, Col. John D., 60–61, 63–64, 66–67
Millett, Allan, 9–10
mobilization paradigm, 30–31, 113
Mobilization Training Plan (MTP), 59, 96, 98, 100, 105
Mori Maneuver Area, 81, 84
mortars, 46–48, 68–70
Mount Fuji, 30, 49, 97
Mydans, Carl, 5

Naktong battles, 10–11
National Security Council document: NSC13/2, 16
New Hebrides, 38
Newsweek, 4
Niblo, Gen. Urban, 39
19th Infantry Regiment: 1st Battalion, 76, 79–81, 83, 86, 88–89; 2nd Battalion, 76, 79, 81, 83, 86, 88–89; 3rd Battalion, 76; basic training program for, 80; Civil War role of, 75; combat effectiveness reports, 85–87; equipment shortages, 86–87; Heavy Mortar Company, 77, 80, 83–84, 86–87; Medical Company, 77; North Korean invasion, 90; personnel increases in, 79; platoon-level training, 83–84; squad and crew proficiency, 82–85; testing of, 79; weapons training, 81
99th Field Artillery Battalion, 103
noncommissioned officers (NCOs): Career Guidance Program's effect on, 34–35; lack of, 22, 25, 58–60, 66, 72, 87, 94; Potential NCO School, 77; training of, 98; "universal," 112–13. *See also* officers
North Atlantic Treaty Organization (NATO), 28
Nuclear weapons, 6, 110–13

Officer Personnel Act (1947), 35
officers: during the Occupation, 14, 21; Officer Personnel Act's effect on, 35–37; on physical training, 43; reductions in rank for, 112; shortage of, 73, 76, 79, 96; tensions between regulars and reserves, 29, 112; "universal," 112–13. *See also* noncommissioned officers (NCOs)
Oita Maneuver Area, 82
Olson, Maj. Lester K., 65, 135n59
Olweiler, Pvt. Frank, *gallery 7*
O'Neil, Lt. Col. Gilbert M., 84
Operation Roll-Up, 38–39, 116
Osan, 3, 74
Ovenshine, Col. Richard P., 70–71, 74, *gallery 13*
overhead inventory, 32

Pakenham, Compton, 4
Palmer, Col. Raymond D., 96, 98, 100–101, 103, 107
Patton, Gen. George S., *gallery 2*
Paulus, Lt. Col. Lawrence G., 87
Pershing, Gen. John J., 92
Philippines, 45, 56, 76, 91–92
physical education, 42
physical fitness, 41–44
Polar Bears. *See* 31st Infantry Regiment
preparedness, 7–9
procurement, 117
proficiency exams, 34
Puerto Rico, 76
Pyongtaek, 2

Queenin, Capt. Hugh, 96–97

racism, 10
readiness: deemphasis on, 6; during the Occupation, 93; equipment, 37–41; gap in, 13–14; need for, 16–18; reporting of, 32–33; testing for, 50–52
Regimental Leadership School, 60–61, 66–67, 71
Reilly, Lt. Col. William R., 73
remedial education, 103
Republican Party, 23
Ridgway, Lt. Gen. Matthew B., 5–7
Rishell, Lyle, 10
Rivette, Capt. Donald E., 49
Rocking Horse. *See* 8th Cavalry Regiment
Rock of Chickamauga, 75, *See also* 19th Infantry Regiment
Rowan, 1st Lt. Andrew S., 75
Royall, Kenneth C., 13
Rumsfeld, Donald, *gallery* 2

Schewe, Lt. Col. Marion W., 60
2nd Cavalry Brigade, 92–93
Selective Service Act (1940), 41
Selective Service reauthorization, 1, 24, 93, 111
7th Cavalry Regiment, 100
7th Infantry Division, 70, 72, 94, *See also* 31st Infantry Regiment
Sewell, Maj. Milton A., 85
Shanghai Incident, 56
Shiloh, 75
Shimamatsu Maneuver Area, 63, 67–69, 71
Shinodayama Training Area, 47–48, 50–52, 54
Siberian Expedition, U.S., 45, 56
Smith, Lt. Col. Charles B., 1–2
Smith, Lt. Col. David H., 87–88
Song-Hu Armistice (1932), 56
South to the Naktong, North to the Yalu (Appleman), 8–9
Soviet Union, 16–18
Spanish-American War, 75–76
spiritual weakness, 9

Staiger, Capt. Theodore S., 67
Starkey, Lt. Posey L., 53
Stephens, Col. R. W., 88
stockpiles, 113
Sugita Ordinance Plant, 39
Sullivan, Gen. Gordon R., 9, 11
Summers, Lt. Col. Robert R., 73, 135*n*59
Surplus Property Act (1944), 38

Table of Organization and Equipment, 57, 77
Tachikawa, 93
tanks: M24 Chaffee, 14; M26 Pershing, 14
Task Force Smith, 1–3, 10, 40, 74, 117
Taylor, Gen. Maxwell, 43
technology, 6, 11
10th Mountain Division, 116
testing: battalion-level, 67–68; for Expert Infantryman's Badge, 78; for physical fitness, 65; platoon-level, 65–66; RCT retest, 72; written exams, 59
Third Imperial Guard Barracks, 106
13th Field Artillery Battalion, 88–89
31st Field Artillery Batallion, 66–68, 71
31st Infantry Regiment: 1st Battalion, 57; 2nd Battalion, 57–58, 61, 67–69, 72–73; 3rd Battalion, 57–58, 61, 67–69, 73; cold-weather training, 58, 69–70; Combat Team, 71; competitions for team building in, 63–65, 70; equipment shortages in, 67; Heavy Mortar Company, 58, 68–69; Korea deployment of, 74; lack of NCOs in, 58–60, 66; Medical Company, 58, 68; in the Philippines, 56–57; reconstitution in Japan of, 57–60, 62; Regimental Combat Team, 71; repatriation of Japanese soldiers, 72; Shanghai incident, 56, 63; Siberian Expedition, 56
34th Infantry Regiment: 1st Battalion, 2, 5, 87; 3rd Battalion, 87–88
This Kind of War: A Study in Unpreparedness (Fehrenbach), 7–8, 11
Thompson, Lt. Paul K., 102
313th Engineer Battalion, 24
Tokyo Ordinance Center, 95
Tokyo Quartermaster Depot, 95

training: on air transportability, 70–71, 105–106, 131*n*27; in basic skills, 103; basic training's expansion, 26–27, 32, 46–49, 80; battalion-level, 50–54; for cold weather, 58, 69–70; on crew-served weapons, 82; deficiencies in, 20, 25; development in Japan of, 17–20, 25; DOT/AFF division of responsibilities for, 31; drills as, 78; equipment shortages, 49, 108, 117, 123*n*15; "Fehrenbach School" on, 7–9; IG's report on, 29–30; individual, 87; inspections for, 51, 83; limitations of areas for, 115; marksmanship, 47, 60, 71–72, 81, 89, 100; medical, 48, 68, 73; memoranda for, 26, 59–60, 78; new focus on, 21–22; physical, 42–44; platoon-level, 83–84; specialty, 27, 30; training center approach to, 23; unit-based, 31; youthfulness of trainees and, 20–21, 27
Training Directive Number Five, 51
Training Directive Number Four, 18–20, 30–32, 46, 51, 77–78, 94, 103
Training Memorandum 18, 104, 106
Treaty of Brest-Litovsk (1918), 45
Tribble, Pvt. Alfred T., *gallery 7*
Triple-R program, 39
Trudeau, Maj. Gen. Arthur, 40
Truman, Harry S.: defense spending, 13, 24; distrust of professional officers by, 28; ground troops authorized by, 1; national military policy, lack of, 110, 112; photo of, *gallery 2*; universal military training, 14
12th Cavalry Regiment, 94
25th Infantry Division, 46, 53, 114. *See also* 25th Infantry Regiment
21st Infantry Regiment: 1st Battalion, 1; 3rd Battalion, 88
24th Infantry Division: journalists' view of, 4; lack of NCOs in, 94; personnel increases, 79, 114; Potential Noncommissioned Officer School, 77–78; Training Memorandum No. 8, 78; Training Memorandum No. 10, 78; Training Memorandum No. 12, 78
27th Infantry Regiment: basic training in, 46–49; battalion field exercises, 50–51; 1st battalion, 50–54; Heavy Mortar Company, 46–48, 50–51, 54; Japanese Occupation duties, 45; Korea deployment of, 55; Medical Company, 48; in the Pacific War, 45; 2nd Battalion, 50–51, 53–54; U.S. Siberian Expedition, 45
Typhoon Della, 80

Uji Maneuver Area, 47, 52
universal military training (UMT), 14, 42

Van Houten, Col. John G., 50
venereal disease, 32, 64, 100

Wakayama Training Area, 47, 54
Walker, Sam, 89, 122*n*20
Walker, Lt. Charles P., 92
Walker, Gen. Walton H.: combat effectiveness reports ordered by, 33; combat readiness, 78; Constant Flow Program, 26; death of, 5; "overhead inventory" ordered by, 32; photo, *gallery 2*; "stand or die" order, 2; testing, 89; training program development, 17–20, 31, 74, 94, 103, 114, 116
War, U.S. Department of, 23–24, 33, 91–92. *See also* Defense, U.S. Department of
war criminals, 95
War Fitness Conference, 42
warrior ethos, 22
Weigley, Russell F., 8
Wiersema, Maj. Richard, 10
Willoughby, Maj. Gen. Charles, 9, 17
Winstead, Lt. Col. Otho T., 86
With a Black Platoon in Combat: A Year in Korea (Rishell), 10
Wolfhounds. *See* 27th Infantry Regiment

Yokota, 93
Yongdong, 108

CPSIA information can be obtained
at www.ICGtesting.com
Printed in the USA
LVOW12*1932220318
570873LV00005B/31/P

9 781603 441674